W9-ANN-100

THREE CHINESE ECONOMIES
China, Hong Kong and Taiwan

FLORIDA STATE
UNIVERSITY LIBRARIES

NOV 3 1997

TALLAHASSEE, FLORIDA

FLORIDA STATE
UNIVERSITY LIBRARIES

NOV 3 1997

TALLAHASSEE, FLORIDA

Three Chinese Economies
China, Hong Kong and Taiwan:
Challenges and Opportunities

Edited by
Linda Fung-Yee Ng
and
Chyau Tuan

The Chinese University Press

© The Chinese University of Hong Kong 1996

All Rights Reserved. No part of this publication may
be reproduced or transmitted in any form or by any
means, electronic or mechanical, including photocopying,
recording, or any information storage and retrieval
system, without permission in writing from
The Chinese University of Hong Kong.

ISBN 962–201–670–7

THE CHINESE UNIVERSITY PRESS
The Chinese University of Hong Kong
SHA TIN, N. T., HONG KONG

HC
421.92
T4873
1996

Printed in Hong Kong by Nam Fung Printing Co., Ltd.

Contents

List of Figures and Tables

Acknowledgments

The Department of Decision Sciences and Managerial Economics, The Chinese University of Hong Kong, has organized several international conferences in the past four years in collaboration with respectable academic organizations, professional institutions, and prominent business firms in North America and Hong Kong.

The International Conference on "Business Forecasting" was first conducted in December 1991, with the co-operation of the America Chinese Management Educators Association (ACME). The International Conference on "Opportunities and Challenges of the Three Chinese Economies in 1990s," held in June 1993, was listed as one of the University's 30th Anniversary celebration activities. The conference was successfully conducted with the co-sponsorship of the Chinese Economic Association in North America (CEANA). This book is the product of selected papers presented at the above two conferences.

The Department would like to extend its greatest appreciation to all institutions which supported our conferences. Special thanks also go to all colleagues, friends, authors, and reviewers, who helped to make the conferences possible and successful.

Department of Decision Sciences and Managerial Economics
The Chinese University of Hong Kong

Introduction

During the past four decades, all three Chinese economies, that is, China, Hong Kong and Taiwan, have achieved remarkable economic development and growth. The latter two, operating under a market economic system, were even included as part of the East Asian Miracle, according to a World Bank study in 1993.[1]

China, predominated by an ideology of socialism, began her economic modernization by adopting a planned economic system as its vehicle of growth from 1950 to 1960. Soon after the suffering of about ten years of socio-economic disorder, China quickly turned to a mixed type of economic system in the late 1970s so as to recover from the economic disaster left behind by the Cultural Revolution.

On the contrary, during the same period Hong Kong and Taiwan launched their export-led industrialization beginning in the early 1960s and demonstrated their success through a much distinct path. The relatively favourable global climate in international trade provided the two economies with golden opportunities to establish their market shares in major developed countries in the world market. A market-oriented economy and efforts in building up infrastructure and human capital, and the unfailing attempts to furnish foreign and domestic investors with a friendly business environment and effective administration have made both Hong Kong and Taiwan two of the four distinguished "Little Dragons" since the 1980s.

Beginning in the early 1980s China, and Guangdong Province in particular, entered the world market by following strategies in promoting direct foreign investment and export-led growth, as adopted by the other two

---

[1] The World Bank (1993), *East Asian Miracle: Economic Growth and Public Policy* (New York: Oxford University Press).

Chinese economies. Facilitated by the heavy inflow of direct foreign investment mainly from Hong Kong and Taiwan, China effectively materialized her comparative advantages in factor cost and resource supply, and recorded tremendous economic growth in the late 1980s. However, the continuing development of the three Chinese economies is, and still will be, critically influenced by the evolving external trade environment and their coming restructuring of political relationships. Specifically, Hong Kong will become part of China following the Sino-British Joint Declaration under the "One Country, Two Systems" principle and Taiwan is being approached by China for some kind of "reunification" in the near future.

If the future development in this regard is moving in the most ideal direction, the solid formation of the "Southeast China Growth Triangle" will be not too far away.[2] Integration of economic capacity will place the three Chinese economies as one of the major economic powers in the world — being top in net foreign exchange reserves and the top three in volume of international trade. Nevertheless, if things were to move to the other end, the four decades' of achievement in economic development in Hong Kong and Taiwan could be ruined. Such disaster could also drag their economic progress behind for years to come. Considering the uncertain future the economies would have to face and the possible impact it may have upon the global economy, the opportunities and challenges to be confronted by the three Chinese economies should be major issues of current interest and concern in economic and business studies.

In view of the above, this book addresses the subject through a collection of eleven articles selected from papers presented at two conferences organized by the Department of Decision Sciences and Managerial Economics at The Chinese University of Hong Kong in the past years.

The first article presents some reflections on the three Chinese economies, beginning with the ideology of China in turning to a "planned socialist commodity economy", Hong Kong's multifaceted roles in the three Chinese economies context, and Taiwan's Six-Year Plan for huge provision in infrastructural investment.

---

[2]   Lin Tsong-biau, Linda F. Y. Ng and Chyau Tuan (1995), "The South China Growth Triangle: Integration of the Economies of South China, Hong Kong, and Taiwan," *Project Report*, International Center for Economic Growth (U.S.A.).

The second article addresses specific challenges facing the three Chinese economies: becoming quasi-developed, becoming fully developed, and the consequences of having a large population. The economic consequences of ideology are contended to be the road to quasi-development and the economics of institutions and culture to be the road to full development.

The next article describes the extent to which the economies of Greater China have begun to develop their capabilities based on indigenous technological development and technological co-operation. The fourth article studies the problem of "Dutch Disease" with reference to Taiwan and relations with China. It further suggests that the three Chinese economies would be able to create a new Pacific era in the 21st century if their remaining ideological differences were to be overcome.

The next three articles study several issues in Hong Kong including forecasting practices and performance in Hong Kong business firms, an inter-industry comparison of business cycles and the choice of an "ideal" industry, and Hong Kong's exchange rate policies compared with Singapore's.

The remaining four articles investigate several issues of the Taiwan economy. In these articles, an econometric study of trade-oriented Taiwan is constructed to provide a policy simulation and forecast for the economy of Taiwan. The significance of Taiwan-United States trade is explored by the study of their complementary and competitive relations. While Taiwan develops into a maturing economy, her financial policies in the 1980s are critically examined. The last paper provides an evaluation of the effectiveness of government automation promotion schemes with specific reference to the electrical component industry in Taiwan.

Finally, the industrious efforts of the authors of the articles in revising the manuscripts upon reviewers' suggestions, resulting in this collection to be shared with interested readers, are again gratefully acknowledged.

Linda F. Y. Ng and Chyau Tuan
Department of Decision Sciences and Managerial Economics
The Chinese University of Hong Kong

CHAPTER 1

Some Reflections on the Three Chinese Economies

Anthony M. Tang
Vanderbilt University, U.S.A.

I. INTRODUCTION

Let me preface my remarks with the statement that I wish to refer to the Three Chinese Economies (TCEs) as co-extensive with, in order of size, mainland China, Taiwan, and Hong Kong. The neutral geographical appellations are preferred for obvious reasons. As I am offering a collection of thoughts, I will not append copious notes and references to these pages.

The full significance of the subject only became clear as I began to think about my assignment. Several thoughts have occurred to me in this regard. The 1990s is not only the *fin de siècle*, as the French best put such matters of epochal significance, but also the end of a millennium. The epoch bears witness to man's unprecedented triumph in all fields of human endeavour — science and technology, to be sure, but also the arts, letters, philosophy, economics, politics, and the humanities.

Turning to matters closer at hand, I see several events converging to make the subject truly significant. Deng Xiaoping, a giant among the twentieth century greats in my view, electrified the region where we are gathered today with his talk in January last year in Shenzhen. His talk had the effect of making mainland China's commitment to market economy irreversible. The Hong Kong stock-market took off and remains undaunted by the Governor's useful but controversial political reform plan. Meanwhile, the mainland produced a stunning growth rate of 12.8% in that year.

Deng's clarion call this last January in Shanghai to grasp the country's historic opportunity for rapid growth presumably at all costs, implying that the opportunity is both unique and fleeting, lent a renewed sense of urgency to the all-consuming task of nation-building. All the while he dismissed conservative concerns about too much capitalism. His consideration is utilitarian, based on what works for growth. One is reminded of his old "cat and mouse" metaphor. The only concession to ideology he has been willing to make is to insert the word "socialist" in front of his "market economy". As recently as two years ago, the system used to be called "planned socialist commodity economy". But the word "socialist" does not seem to matter much judging from his actions.

Against such a background, Hong Kong's future beyond 30 June 1997 would seem secure with respect to the terms of the 1984 Sino-British Joint Declaration (supposedly enshrined in the 1991 Basic Law). A "stable and prosperous" Hong Kong is indispensable to Beijing's plan for rapid catch-up growth for the 1990s and beyond. In the Three Chinese Economies context Hong Kong's multifaceted roles are all the more important. The problem is how to convince the territory's people that there will be correspondence between Beijing's (good) intentions and the actions of its appointed officials. In this connection, the Governor's proposed political reform for the Legislature, though annoying to Beijing, is best seen as an effort to add institutional assurance to the continuity of Hong Kong in a systemic sense after the transfer of sovereignty. Hong Kong's ambitious airport and related infrastructural projects, though progressing haltingly, are further preparations for the territory's larger role ahead.

Across the straits, big things are also stirring. The Six-Year Plan with its $300 billion provision for infrastructural investment — too large to be credible according to cynics — has attracted wide international attention among traders, bankers, contractors as well as in governmental circles. Taiwan's overriding goal to join the ranks of developed countries by the year 2000 seems within easy reach. In fact Taiwan, along with Hong Kong and Singapore, is already a "high-income" country by World Bank definition, being in the same category as Organization for Economic Cooperation and Development (OECD) countries, although the United Nations still considers these Asian entities (including Taiwan, were it a member) as developing areas. Cross-straits trade and investment (all supposedly indirect) continue their dramatic increases. Economic intercourse between the TCEs seems to be working wonders. In all three, growth rates in the foreseeable 1990s are forecasted to range between 6–10%, with the higher end likely to be occupied by the mainland. Against a background of economic malaise, particularly in the U.S., Japan, and the European Community (EC), in recent years and in looking ahead in near terms, what the TCEs are showing us is indeed stunning.

II. CHINESE ECONOMIC GROUPING

The heady feeling among Chinese observers and others is that the TCEs, seen as a grouping of some kind, may be the only large economic power to see the millennium out in grand style. The notion of the TCEs as a formal grouping would further solidify Hong Kong's status as a truly autonomous Special Administrative Region (SAR). In addition to the factors enumerated above, the excitement was heightened by the recent flurry of purchasing-power-parity-adjusted income and output statistics for the mainland. As I understand it, last year Beijing commissioned an international financial consulting service to conduct a Purchasing Power Parity (PPP) study of the mainland's income accounts. The resulting USD–RMB rate of conversion was 1.25 RMB to 1 USD (cf. the current official rate of 5.8 to 1 and swap rate of 11 to 1), placing the 1990 estimate of Gross National Product (GNP) at $1.4 trillion — or $1,220 per capita (as compared with the conventionally calculated figure of $350). If these adjustments are eye-catching, the recently released ones by the International Monetary Fund (IMF) and the World Bank border on the fanciful, as suggested by the critics. The World Bank PPP-results place the mainland China's GNP for 1990 at $2,000 per capita, or $2.3 trillion in total, which would put it ahead of Germany, making it the third-ranking economy behind the U.S. and Japan. The IMF results for 1992 are $1,600 per capita and $1.85 trillion in total. Beijing is privately elated while protesting publicly that these estimates are much too high. The flattering figures may be costly if the mainland loses the concessionary borrowing rates accorded low-income developing nations.

It is popular to play the numbers game. We may as well join the game. A simple compound interest calculation shows that if we take an annual rate of growth of 6% for the TCEs and 3% for the U.S. (1992 GNP at $6 trillion) and we adopt the IMF 1992 PPP-estimate of $1.85 trillion as the benchmark for the mainland, together with the conventional estimates for Hong Kong and Taiwan ($80 billion and $210 billion, respectively), the TCEs are seen to overtake the U.S. by the year 2028 in total GNP (at $17.43 and $17.39 trillion, respectively). Taking the mainland alone, the catch-up takes place five years later. The exercise is in 1992 constant dollars.

Lawrence Klein, in forecasting increasing difficulties (if not the end) for the traditional export-led growth strategy, suggested in passing the idea of an Asian grouping — in particular, a free trade bloc for the TCEs (*Journal of Asian Economics*, Spring 1990). The idea was to promote intra-trade within the bloc in order to reduce the impact of anticipated market loss in the EC and North American blocs. As Klein pointed out, it is difficult to praise theoretically trading blocs. Welfare-reducing trade diversions and the likelihood of trade wars between blocs readily come to mind. There is much concern (over job loss) in the U.S. about North American Free Trade Area (NAFTA) including Mexico, as the treaty awaits review by the Clinton Administration prior to submission to the Senate for ratification. With the TCEs, net job loss in Taiwan and Hong Kong has not materialized even as their low-wage industries shifted *en masse* to the mainland. In fact, full employment has been maintained while jobs have been restructured away from low-productivity, low-wage employment to high-productivity, high-wage activities, exactly as economic theory predicts. This points up the fact that trade theory assumes full employment, along with homogeneous labour, and instantaneous and costless adjustments. In Taiwan and Hong Kong, where such adjustments are called for and where because of full employment high growth, together with the other conditions being more nearly met than, say, in the U.S., the increasingly close relations of the TCEs (though shy of a free trade association) have brought faster growth and job upgrading for all three. This perspective should give the TCE grouping further impetus.

III. TAKING THE TCE GROUPING A STEP FURTHER

What are the prospects for a TCE free trade grouping? For EC-style monetary union, common economic policy, and a community-wide integrated labour market? And ultimately, for political union within some suitable framework? There are basically two requirements:

   (a) Dialogue and negotiation in an atmosphere of mutual respect, civility, and equality, where common grounds and interests are highlighted and differences given deferred consideration. This message is for the mainland and Taiwan. Discussions between the mainland and Hong Kong (London) are of a different sort, more in the nature of problem solving within the framework of a set of existing understandings.

(b) Time to elapse for certain preconditions to develop. The EC would be faring better, had it not the great disparities posed, on the one hand, by Portugal and Greece and, on the other, by Germany (with its own severe internal imbalance upon unification with its Eastern half). The mainland needs time to narrow the gap, economic and systemic, that separates it from Taiwan and Hong Kong before EC-type union becomes feasible. But formation of a free trading bloc need not wait for reasons already stated. But even for that, dialogue must first take place. For a "free trade" pact can run more than a thousand pages long as NAFTA shows.

With each Chinese side armed with a set of "no's" — every one of them said to be non-negotiable — substantive talks that might show some promise of results are not likely to take place. In fact, there is first of all a procedural deadlock that so far has appeared to be insuperable. Let me put this in the form of procedural questions. How is each side to be addressed by the other? And in what capacity does each side presume to speak? In today's coded phrases, Beijing insists on "one country, two systems" with its implied answers to the above questions; Taipei says it is "one country, two districts or two governments or two administrations", with its implied answers to the questions.

To remove the procedural barrier, I suggest the "don't ask, don't tell" format which has emerged as the likely resolution to an exceedingly delicate issue in the U.S. — an issue concerning some totally unrelated matter which need not concern us. Let neither Chinese side ask the other the two questions, then no one need answer or tell. In front of each side's chairman, there will be a sign reading "Mainland Authority" and "Taiwan Authority", respectively. Each refers to the other as "your side." And that is what the public will be told and shown. By comparison, using the façade of two "private bodies" (called an Association on the mainland and a Foundation on Taiwan) to conduct negotiations would seem disingenuous. Under our proposal official face-to-face talks need not wait. The format could also be helpful in the international forums. This perspective is important. For as James Lilley has aptly put it, the constant "bullying and humiliating of Taiwan" by the mainland in the international arena serves only to bolster the "Independent Taiwan" movement. Why insist on "Chinese Taipei" or "Taipei, China" when "Taiwan" is properly ambiguous under the proposed format? Nor is it inappropriate to recall — apropos Taiwan's current interest in "rejoin-ing" the United Nations — that the former U.S.S.R. used to hold three seats in the U. N. General Assembly. The two additional seats were occupied by Ukraine and Byelorussia.

Once mainland-Taiwan talks are institutionalized under the format, on-going discussions will as a matter of course lead to increasingly more advanced forms of economic integration and ultimately some form of political union, much as the EC has done over the years. Beyond the free trade grouping, the TCEs can look forward to monetary union, common economic policy, and an integrated labour market. On the political level, let me say that at an international conference which took place in Taipei in the first week of January 1988, I presented a paper to which a section had been appended addressing this very issue. The particular section, however, was not included in the presentation or subsequent publication as I thought better of it after consultation with wiser heads. The time was not ripe, I was advised, since cross-straits relations had just taken their first tentative steps. In that section I proposed a Confederation, called China, under whose umbrella the two sides would open up to each other, gradually at first but ultimately leading to an agreement between the two sides for a nationwide two-party electoral system where the Chinese Communist Party (CCP) and Kuomintang (KMT) (there was no other party then), each a party national in scope, would contend peacefully to govern China. Needless to say, the KMT–CCP reference is symbolic in our context; there could be other parties operating nation-wide under the Confederation. Following a national election, the Confederation would lose its *raison d'être*, and a unitary China would emerge. The Confederation proposed need not be all that different, initially, from what the EC has evolved into, with its European Parliament in Strasbourg (Taipei?) and its Executive Commission in Brussels (Beijing?). As a transitional forum, the Confederation would be flexible in allowing expansion of membership, all parties willing. In principle, there is no reason not to include (even if later) Hong Kong, Macau, and even Tibet and other minority-dominated areas, as well as certain "Special Economic Zones" designated by Beijing. There is no sovereignty issue here. China is sovereign over all these areas. The idea is to give all areas with sharply distinctive features a forum or framework within which to work out a better permanent arrangement together. In deference to the country's size, a Federal Republic may ultimately be a suitable form for a unitary China to assume.

IV. HOW TO CLOSE THE GAPS FASTER?

Given its Marxist past and its former Soviet-style development strategy and planning, mainland China's march towards an open, market-oriented economy has been remarkably successful. We only have to witness what has happened to the former Soviet Union, once a superpower with a more advanced economy and better technological underpinning. The mainland followed the right reform sequence — economic reform first, with political reform to follow either as a consequence or to be implemented later. This view may not be shared by everyone. However, I am constantly reminded by the rhetorical question: "What would have happened to Deng's economic reform and opening-up to the outside world, if he had had no more political capital than Gorbachev had left after his political liberalization?" — that Deng probably would have been eaten alive by his octogenarian adversaries, if I may be allowed a figure of speech. He also launched his economic reform, with agriculture with twin prices, and organizational reforms. This was exactly the place to begin for two reasons. First, it was readily doable. To address the so-called price scissors in agriculture was relatively easy, and that produced the right price signals for producers. To provide the incentive to respond to the new price signals, Deng returned to private family farming — something not feasible for large state industries which are not divisible. Secondly, a secure food supply for the population, to ensure at least subsistence living, is absolutely the first requirement of any reform. The electrifying production response in Chinese agriculture is history.

To be sure, the mainland had the singular asset of having Hong Kong as its doorstep, later reinforced by Taiwan beginning in 1988. Both territories are flush with capital, legendary entrepreneurs, modern management skills, and access to and knowledge about overseas markets (most particularly, the American market). Along the coastal strip of southeast China, we now witness another Asian miracle in the making. A fair question to ask is whether the former Soviet Union would have had the vision to open up to and call on such resources if they had been there. Even today, with all sorts of counter-examples before them, Russians close to official circles are still pathologically afraid of large-scale foreign investment. The motherland's dowry must be protected from foreigners.

But things are not perfect on the mainland. The legacies of 30 years of conditioning under a command, centrally planned system do not go away quickly. Chen Yun still issues periodical warnings against too much capitalism, chaos, profiteering, and base outside influences. The old discipline, dedication, cohesion, and frugality are gone, he says. Inflation once again is rearing its ugly head. Bottlenecks, especially in transportation, have further tightened their grip on the economy. Long-term neglect of agriculture by the centre has continued. There is a widespread feeling that Beijing may find the task particularly daunting this time. The centre's grip on the economy has slipped markedly so that its 1989 method of using command to clamp down on credit and other resource use may prove to be unavailing in 1993. Meanwhile, because of its incomplete reform, Beijing does not have the modern monetary institutions and control instruments at its disposal to address the problem. Its fiscal reach is circumscribed after much of the tax collection authority has been delegated to provincial and local governments. While agriculture has long been starved of state investment, and its incentive weakened by new price scissors, its real grievance stems from arbitrary actions by local authorities in the form of unauthorized *ad hoc* new taxes and fees, and issuance of IOUs in lieu of cash payment for state procurement of agricultural commodities.

Official corruption has reached a level probably not seen under the *ancien régime*. With 20% or more of the scarce basic materials still under direct government price control and allocation, rent-seeking opportunities abound. Local government land sales and widespread self-proclaimed development schemes and enterprise zones, unscreened by the market rate-of-return criterion, provide another bonanza for the well-connected. Deng's "get rich" call is being taken a little too literally. It is symbolic to see the first US$130,000 Ferrari on Beijing's streets while conservative leaders decry rapidly worsening income inequality in the nation. Nor is Beijing's leadership as thoughtful as it could be. The big black Mercedes limousines for top party and government officials are not exactly helpful image-builders. In contrast, Taiwan did not allow its cabinet officers to ride in anything bigger than the locally-assembled Yue Loong sedans equipped with 2,000 cc engines, until well after the island had entered the ranks of the affluent.

No doubt, the mainland would like to replicate the kind of growth experience enjoyed by Japan and the "Four Little Dragons" during their earlier miracle years: sustained 10% growth accompanied by relative price stability, improving or stable income distribution, social cohesion, and moderate official corruption. It is fair to suggest that for the mainland to achieve these results political and legal reforms are necessary to help push economic reform to its logical conclusion: an all market system where the remaining large-scale state enterprises (if not yet privatized) will have to stand on their own bottoms. A well-developed market system imposes economic discipline where chaos now rules. Such political and legal reforms, together with the implied rights and freedoms of the individual, need not be, initially, any more radical than what relatively authoritarian Taiwan and Singapore used to accept. Political reform makes local officials (now little "emperors" with virtually absolute powers over their domains) accountable. Legal reform introduces the rule of law, impersonal and impartial, in place of the arbitrary rule of man.

As an overseas Chinese scholar who left the mainland at the height of World War II with a heavy heart to serve his country as a young military officer in the U.S. and was later grateful to have been given an opportunity to complete his education in his adopted country, I humbly offer these thoughts, not in a spirit, critical for its own sake, against one of the TCEs that must assume the major task of reform and gap-closing, but in the hopes that they may all contribute to a process that is at the heart of this subject.

CHAPTER 2

Six Challenges Facing the Chinese Economies

Henry Wan, Jr.
Cornell University, U.S.A.

I. INTRODUCTION

At present, the three Chinese economies of Hong Kong, Taiwan and mainland China share two characteristics. In terms of growth rates, all these three enjoy respectable sustained performances which are impressive to Westerners. But in terms of per capita output, none of these three is "fully developed" in the sense of America, Japan or the Scandinavian states. Thus, continued growth is their common goal. To achieve their aspirations, these economies must identify and overcome the challenges facing them. This is not an easy task since these economies are all in transition, economically, sociologically and politically, heading toward unchartered waters. Their future cannot possibly be a simple extrapolation of their past. Moreover, the economic literature contains no well-developed theories for guidance.

It is important that we recognize at the outset that the best one can offer is educated speculation.

To make the discussion policy-relevant, one must draw insights from both economic theory and the historical record. History rarely repeats itself. To apply lessons from the past to issues facing the present, *mutatis mutandis*, one needs some theoretical framework. Theoretical analysis deduces sharp conclusions from simple, tractable scenarios, under a host of *ceteris paribus* assumptions. To make such results practically helpful, one also needs the historical perspective.

For illustration, let us consider the following important example. The industrialization of Hong Kong and Taiwan depended upon a labour force with high efficiency and low wage rates. Hourly wages in Hong Kong and Taiwan have never been low, compared to less developed lands like Bangladesh. Labour cost is low, only because the output per worker is quite high. The important question is then, how do these East Asian labour forces become so efficient, compared to those workers elsewhere, with comparable educational, social and perhaps ethno-cultural backgrounds? The issue is not just a matter of incentives. The labour forces in Hong Kong and Taiwan still perform better under similar reward systems. In many instances, an immediate answer is in on-the-job training programmes, which train the workers to produce outputs of high quality. Some economists therefore would attribute such human capital formation to "education", an interpretation which is certainly not wrong, yet for the sake of policy, it is also not entirely right. Unless there were an immediate payoff, no one would finance such highly job-specific programmes, certainly not as part of general, formal schooling.

Such labour skill may also be viewed as acquired through learning-by-doing. This interpretation is again quite correct descriptively, as such training is on an on-the-job basis, but as we shall see, unless such a conscious training programme is explicitly recognized, one omits the Danish prince from *Hamlet*. Such a programme is typically well-focused, training labour skills for outputs of a quality higher than is affordable on the local market, in view of the low local wage, and hence income. Thus, only in outward-oriented economies can such a training programme justify itself. This perhaps explains why in Hong Kong and Taiwan, labour is trained to produce high quality output, while in the insular market of India, the indigenous management of joint ventures often argues that the insistence of foreign partners for high product quality is rather pointless.

Again, on-the-job training programmes in Hong Kong and Taiwan are cost-effective, perhaps only because they are not reinvented on the spur of the moment. They often represent the tried-and-true systems transplanted by Japanese (or U.S.) multinationals (Watanabe 1980) which were forced by rising Japanese wages to relocate their factories. In this sense, the product cycle theory is highly relevant. On the other hand, the reason why Japanese firms invest in Hong Kong and Taiwan but not elsewhere may be related to a host of factors, from a hospitable policy of the host government to certain Sino-Japanese historical-cultural ties which economize the transaction cost (Kojima 1978).

The above example is important. It illustrates that, based upon simplistic interpretations of any current theory, one cannot formulate a policy to replicate the economic performance of Hong Kong and Taiwan.

The industrialization of Hong Kong and Taiwan bears some family resemblance to that of Japan, yet there are many differences. Much Japanese industrial competence was acquired either during the desperate and futile efforts in war during World War II, or because of the offshore procurement policies of the U.S. during the Korean conflict (for example, Morishima 1982). Foreign investment in pre-World War II days also helped, but perhaps to a lesser degree. The Japanese established their world-wide market channels and brand names on their own, but these were also utilized by them later to market goods made in Hong Kong and Taiwan, at least in the early phases (Levy 1990). In many ways, Hong Kong and Taiwan had an easier time than Japan in breaking into the world market, but they now also have a harder time becoming operationally independent, as well as establishing niches in the up-scale markets. Thus for policy purposes, reliance on historical analogy alone may again lead to misleading forecasts.

In many ways, the current development of mainland China resembles the earlier development of Taiwan and Hong Kong. Yet, in other aspects, it has its own rhythm and challenges. These will be discussed below, in due course.

II. PRELIMINARY CONSIDERATIONS

Broadly speaking, the developmental problems facing an economy depend upon both the "size" of its population and the "phase" of its development. The population of an economy can be "large", as for mainland China, "medium", as for Japan, and "small" as for Taiwan and Hong Kong. Economies can also be classified as "developing", like mainland China's, "quasi-developed", like Taiwan's and Hong Kong's and "developed" like Japan's. To proceed from a "developing" to a "quasi-developed" phase, an economy faces certain problems and needs certain policies. These are different from those of an economy proceeding from a "quasi-developed" to a "developed" phase.

It also matters whether an economy is a technology leader or follower, and whether an economy is culturally or geographically distant from the developed world.

India, Japan and the three Chinese economies are non-western societies. They all industrialize at a time when the West enjoys technological leadership. This is a fact one cannot ignore. It is a historical lesson that cross-fertilization is crucial to technological progress. Historically, Chinese culture stagnated after the Tang dynasty perhaps partly because of its geographical isolation from all the other centres of high culture, from Western Europe to the Indus-Ganges plain. The collapse of the Soviet economy has many causes. Its failure to interact with the non-communist world has certainly played a major role, causing its technical backwardness in the Electronic Age.

What confronts a backward and non-western economy is a two-fold problem, first, to develop its own economy by utilizing all that western technology can offer, and then, to continue to interact with the West so as to become a full partner. The former is a task which has been handled successfully by Hong Kong and Taiwan. Their record serves as a useful reference to mainland China. The latter is an area where Japan has risen up to the challenge. The Japanese experience is clearly relevant to both Hong Kong and Taiwan.

But neither Japan, Taiwan nor Hong Kong has a population so large that by the very act of becoming fully developed can it affect the world economy much. In this aspect mainland China belongs to a separate category. Whether and how mainland China will fully develop poses resource and environmental problems of a global scale. One cannot possibly dismiss them in any serious discussion.

The next three sections are devoted to the various specific challenges:

(a) in becoming quasi-developed, and
(b) in becoming (fully) developed, as well as
(c) the consequences of having a large population.

In each of these three challenges, we focus upon the two most important aspects, making six in total. Some concluding remarks follow, concerning the interactions among these three.

To summarize, we present Table 2.1.

Section III discusses how the mainland Chinese economy can become *quasi-developed*. The principal issue is ideological, and the main challenges are:

Table 2.1 Economies and Theories

Types of Economies	Population Sizes			Theories
	Small	Medium	Large	
Development Phases:				
Fully Developed	Switzerland Benelux The "Nordics" ↑	*Japan* Germany, France, Italy, U.K.	U.S. ↑	New Growth Theory
	—— (b) —— ↑	——————	—— (c) —— ↑	—————— New Trade Theory
Quasi-developed	*Hong Kong* *Taiwan*	——	↑ —— (a) —— ↑	
Less Developed	——	——	**Mainland China**	Ditto Institutional Economics Economic Demography Environmental Economics

Note: Italics for non-western societies; Bold for planned economy.

(a) to induce a "reversed brain drain" and

(b) to nurture private firms into well-established efficient enterprises.

Section IV discusses how Hong Kong and Taiwan can become (fully) developed. The issue is socio-cultural, and the main challenges are:

(a) the cultivation of professionally managed enterprises, and

(b) the acquisition of industrial niches, specifically, to market products of innovative design.

Section V discusses additional issues for the mainland Chinese economy to become (fully) developed. The issue is technological, and the challenges are:

(a) to achieve growth without being hampered by resource constraints, and

(b) to achieve growth without causing undue global environmental stress.

On these questions, the literature on economic theory offers much insight, but no concrete conclusions. It is for us to apply the available tools selectively and appropriately.

For the ideological issues facing mainland China today, one may refer to various writings in Institutional Economics, which are applicable to the current market transition of China. For the acquisition of market niches by Hong Kong and Taiwan, one may benefit from the extensive literature on the New Trade Theory, where product differentiation, innovation and product cycles are considered. Broadly speaking, goods with a high value-added ratio are often the fruits of the innovative process, produced under increasing returns and facing monopolistic competition. Such products typically are "skill intensive". The acquisition of such skill is a matter of human (or "knowledge") capital formation, as studied in the extensive literature on the New Growth Theory. The prospect of a fully developed China raises issues of both Resource Economics and Environmental Economics, as well as Economic Demography.

III. THE ROAD TO QUASI-DEVELOPMENT:
THE ECONOMIC CONSEQUENCES OF IDEOLOGY

Among the non-western World, economies in both East Asia and South Asia share a common characteristic: the scarcity of resources per capita. Contrary to the popular view, the saving/income ratios of these economies are not low relative to Great Britain and America, however their per capita real income is low in absolute terms. In such an economy, the improvement of real income per capita depends on the capacity for the formation and the utilization of human capital. The key is often not how to produce more of the same goods, but to attain a higher value of outputs with the same inputs. In the New Trade Theory, what distinguishes a developing economy from a developed economy is that whatever the former can produce, so can the latter, and whatever the latter alone can produce is demanded by all (for example, Krugman 1979). These factors decide whether one can afford imported resources and goods which are needed to support a high standard of living.

Nowadays, many such developing economies export manufactured goods to Europe and America. For example, apparel made in Bangladesh is widely marketed in the U.S. Typically, foreign direct investment and sub-contracting relationships are fruitful means of acquiring foreign technology at the early stage of industrialization. According to Uchida (1991) and Lall (1987), Japan in the late nineteenth century and India in the twentieth century have both experimented with import substitution as well as the limitation of foreign direct investment, both with unsatisfactory outcomes. As pointed out by Komiya (1972), in the first decades of the twentieth century, Japan welcomed foreign direct investment and this laid the foundations of both its automobile and its electric appliance industries. Significantly, once a sufficient level of industrial competence was acquired, Japan had no more need for the return of foreign direct investment after World War II.

What sets Hong Kong and Taiwan apart from the more recently industrialized economies (say, Cyprus and Mauritius) is their ability to shift their export mix from perfectly competitive commodities like shirts, to imperfectly competitive goods, like personal computers. For the former, all that is needed is a hardy, effective labour force. For the latter, one needs a labour force with creativity and expertise, and a well-established network of sub-supplier chains.

To be specific, according to Uchida (1991), a "reversed brain drain" occurred in Japan as early as in the late Meiji era, when people working in the West brought home technology on their return. This contributed to the acquisition of industrial competence. After World War II, with Japan already possessing the critical mass of technical manpower, firms like Sony refused to produce under foreign trademarks, but marketed products under their own brand name (Morita 1986).

A similar development has begun in Taiwan. Especially in the electronics industry, a sizeable number of experienced engineers and scientists have returned from America, helping to build up an information industry around the Hsinchu Science-based Industrial Park. More recently, firms like Acer have also begun to ship products of their own design and under their own brand name.

These need not be the only channels for acquiring foreign technology and competing in the world market, but history suggests that these are effective ones. Based upon tried-and-true acumen acquired inside the environment of industrially advanced societies, repatriate technical manpower can help firms to seize business opportunities as they see fit. It is a cost-effective option when compared to the alternative of competing for world market niches with purely domestically launched efforts. This is different from working under subcontracts, licensed production, or joint ventures, where the foreign partners have both the ability and the motive to keep local firms from becoming a rival in their favoured market. The mark of the genuine maturation of an industrial society is the growth of domestic private firms without government sheltering. Those firms who succeed under the baptism of competitive fire are more likely to be fitter than those which arise under state assistance. Significantly, according to Morishima (1982), Meiji Japan quickly privatized its state-owned heavy industry, when such firms piled up loss after loss. Recently, Taiwan was also forced to modify its protectionist policy on automobiles as the heavily protected Yueloon Motors failed to compete well, notwithstanding decades of government sheltering.

In fact, by such standards, the self-propelled rise of the Evergreen Marine Line is more indicative of the vigour of the Taiwanese economy than the growth of the government nurtured *chaebuls* are of the Korean economy's strength.

In assessing the long-term performance of the mainland Chinese economy, especially regarding its attempt to catch up with the Asian Newly Industrialized Economies (NIEs), these remain to be the only valid standards to apply.

Both in inducing a "reversed brain drain" and in cultivating private businesses, the current mainland Chinese economy suffers from ideological constraints of its own making.

Legally, private enterprises can operate either in rather limited spheres (like taxi operators), or in the guise of rural co-operatives, an arrangement which provides "political correctness". Yet, due to past history, from the "Anti-Rightist Campaign" to the more recent sporadic crack-downs in the aftermath of 1989, such local entrepreneurs perceive that they do not share the same *de facto* legitimacy enjoyed by their counterparts (and rivals!) in Hong Kong and Taiwan.

In contrast, firms in Taiwan operate under a stable but well understood *modus operandi*. According to Chu (1990), a great majority of firms under-report their taxes to a certain extent, with corrupt tax officials acquiescing. Those which "exceed certain limits" are prosecuted and punished. But by no stretch of imagination would any future government on that island suddenly condemn more than 90% of all private firms for tax evasion, by the full severity of the existing laws. *De jure*, that could be and perhaps should be done, but *de facto*, it will never be. The state continues to receive a diminished but largely adequate revenue, rarely running a budget deficit of a size comparable to that of OECD economies. Businessmen continue to operate in full legitimacy with a great sense of security. The working class enjoys a rapidly rising wage level under a continuing labour shortage. According to Chen *et al.* (1991), the state sector in Taiwan remains quite sizeable and inefficient, yet these industries are held in ridicule, not enshrined in the constitution as in mainland China. It is far from Utopia, but the complaints are far from serious.

Likewise, repatriate technical manpower is among those who lived for decades under western democracy where racism, crime and income inequality coexist with a high degree of personal and press freedom. Dissent may not always be effective, but it is tolerated in the society. Justice is not always done in the snarled courts with wrong-doers being defended by the best legal brains money can buy. When they return to Taiwan, repatriates find an environment less ideal in many ways, but not that strikingly unfamiliar. They can concentrate on their work, no longer under the incipient socio-cultural disadvantages of western societies. Their foreign-reared children may come back with rather radical views not deemed fully acceptable locally. Yet they would not get into immediate trouble.

In contrast, the environment in mainland China, even today, poses an entirely different set of problems. "Spiritual pollution" is still officially warned as dangerous. "Peaceful evolution" by any means is deemed an evil plot. Bourgeois democracy is the original sin in that land of Marxism-Leninism. Would-be repatriate engineers and scientists are largely apolitical. Yet, they perceive that in mainland China they may easily blunder into a political minefield, right and left, if they pull up their stakes in the West.

It is often argued in mainland China today that political ideology does not affect economic performance. Recent events make such a view dubious. It is in Taiwan and *not* in mainland China that the "reversed brain drain" has brought back many experienced former employees of foreign high-tech firms. It is in mainland China and *not* in Taiwan that entrepreneurs indulge in "short-term behaviour," rushing to emigrate after making a fast buck.

As a show case, the Rong family may enjoy political prominence, but do not head a lean-and-mean operation rivalling Acer or the Evergreen Marine Line, let alone Sony or Kyocera.

The future of the mainland Chinese economy is inseparable from the future of the mainland's political development. Various papers in Xu (1990) provide the institutional facts of this complex topic. The situation can best be understood by approaching it from the New Institutional

Economics — an emerging theory based upon the twin concepts of incomplete markets and incomplete contracts (for example, Kreps 1990). The essence of the theory is that the production process involves uninsurable risks, and no enforceable contract can encompass all those specific details crucial to the interpersonal relationships underpinning the modern economy. For production efficiency, the private ownership system assigns shares of profit stream to motivate decision-makers within the production system.

The insistence on the system of *ownership by the entire people* is enshrined in the current constitution of the People's Republic of China, along with the *leading role* of the Chinese Communist Party. The abandonment of the former is perceived as eroding the prestige of the latter. Yet, short of affirming the full political correctness of private ownership of Chinese firms by Chinese citizens, all expediencies devised so far appear to be problematical.

The "responsibility contract" system may motivate the manager to fulfil production quotas with apparent efficiency. Whether equipment and facilities are well maintained is not assured, in practice, let alone such issues like product development, brand reputation or institution-building.

The "profit-loss accountability" of state firms may promote efficient operations, but employees have no interest in reporting large taxable profit rather than spending the revenue on themselves and claiming that as a necessary expense.

The need for entrepreneurs to purchase "political correctness" in the guise of "local co-operatives" or "foreign-related joint ventures" makes their position vulnerable to extortion of every kind.

Attempts to control various irregularities have created a plethora of regulations, constraints, and opportunities for another host of civil servants to abuse their discretion for personal gain.

Even the increase in competitive pressure leads to difficulties. Many state firms fail to be competitive, not because of their inefficiency, but because they are saddled with responsibilities towards their retired employees. Those who survive may not be the fittest.

The above discussion does not argue that one should adopt one ideology or another on non-economic grounds. But ideologies, have their economic consequences. One can only ignore such facts at one's own peril.

IV. THE ROAD TO DEVELOPMENT:
THE ECONOMICS OF INSTITUTIONS AND CULTURE

The economic challenges facing Hong Kong and Taiwan are of a different sort. At present, the industrial competence of mainland China has been rising. Yet in dollar terms, the wage cost there has not. Paradoxically, the more desperate the state finance in mainland China is, the more likely the regime is to opt for inflation and hence devaluation. Hence, the more competitive its exports will be. To fend off competition and to take advantage of the difference in wage costs, many firms in both Hong Kong and Taiwan have moved their downstream production operations to mainland China. The reduction of wage cost allows the expansion of the downstream operations at the new site. The added demand for upstream inputs helps to absorb the reassigned labour force in Hong Kong and Taiwan, often into higher-paid jobs. What is retained is often a type of production process demanding more skill. But this process will end with the reallocation of the entire production process. This situation has been experienced by Japan before, when parts of its own industry were relocated to Hong Kong and Taiwan, a couple of decades ago. The countermeasure for Japan then was to produce goods with even higher quality and skill requirements, often by marketing commodities which had first been introduced to Japan, such as artificial fibre and electronic products. The threat facing both Hong Kong and Taiwan (as well as Singapore and South Korea) now is their inability, thus far, to market high quality, locally designed products, competing against Japan and other advanced economies.

Their inability to compete against Japan in upscale markets appears to be quite natural, since the latter is an economy with both a larger home market and a longer history of industrialization. But this is not so. In Europe, certain small economies like the four Scandinavian states, the three Benelux states, Austria and Switzerland, do not seem to share the same difficulties. They produce top-of-the-line products competing against firms in Italy, the U.K., France and Germany. Each of these small economies succeeds in capturing a set of niches on its own. By that token, Hong Kong and Taiwan today have not yet realized their true market potentials. The true nature of such shortcomings remains elusive. Our discussion below is necessarily speculative.

There is much similarity between firms in these small European states and firms in Hong Kong and Taiwan: they are flexible in identifying and seizing opportunities in the world market and they often enter into joint ventures and subcontracting arrangements with foreign firms. But the differences are also marked. These European firms usually enjoy a reputation for producing top-of-the-line specialty goods and services. In contrast, firms in Hong Kong and Taiwan are often regarded as imitators who can only compete on price. The vicious circle of low reputation, thus low quality, and thus low reputation is discussed in Chiang and Masson (1988).

To move upscale, the challenges facing firms in Hong Kong and Taiwan are many, but among these two seem to be the most important. First, the Chinese enterprises are overly "person-based": they rarely employ professional management teams, and they have difficulties in retaining their best employees. At the present stage of development, productivity and wages rise rapidly. As a consequence, output-mixes also change in quick succession. The present high rate of personnel turnover may actually facilitate the diffusion of technology. But this is not helpful in developing proprietary technology and brand reputation, which are essential for high quality products. In the European context, the excellence of an outfit does not depend upon continued management under the original founder. Second, the Chinese enterprises have not developed marketing skills comparable to that of their European counterparts. They can offer goods and services of a relatively simple nature, such as ocean transportation, but not complex products, involving intricate design, such as upscale cameras, watches, and cars. These goods are what the Japanese succeeded in producing and marketing decades ago. Paradoxically, as a people, the Chinese do have design talents (e.g. in architecture), marketing experience (e.g. in shipping), and global connections in science and technology (e.g. the network which has given rise to the Hsinchu Science-based Industrial Park), as well as the traditional high regard for established brand names (e.g. in traditional businesses such as restaurants, liquor, herbal medicine, etc.). Yet, they have not been able to "get their act together" in offering top-of-the-line goods and services on the world market.

It would be simple to attribute all this to political uncertainties, such as Beijing's political claims over both Hong Kong and Taiwan. Since the current regime in mainland China does not have a long pro-business record, the firms in Hong Kong and Taiwan may not take the long view. But the matter seems to be more complex. After all, Singapore also has a Chinese society. It enjoys a perceived political stability which Hong Kong and

Taiwan lack. Up to now, Singapore has not done any better than Hong Kong and Taiwan in introducing upscale products of its own in the world market.

It would also be simple to assert that Chinese firms, wherever they are, suffer daunting cultural barriers in carving out highly coveted product niches in the world market. However, similarly located in a non-western society, Japanese firms do not seem to find such handicaps insurmountable.

All one can say now is that the challenges exist. They are not insurmountable, but can be overcome with conscious effort and time.

V. THE PROBLEMS OF A POPULOUS COUNTRY

We must now face some most intractable facts of life, which work against mainland China's aspiration of becoming fully developed. Currently, mainland China has more than four times the population of America. Whatever could reasonably be done in population policy, the Chinese population would not fall for many decades. Given the fact that the United States has the lion's share in the worldwide consumption of several key commodities, like petroleum, the arrival of China as a fully developed economy would cause havoc in the world market for such goods.

Broadly speaking, the challenges confronting mainland China are of two types:

First, the living standard of a developed economy requires a very high level of resource usage. Some of these like water, arable land as well as residential land must be supplied locally, and an "adequate" supply may not be possible. Others, like petroleum and natural gas, can be imported, in principle. But given the need to satisfy a population exceeding a billion, world trade can only transform the shortage of one economy to the shortage for the entire world. Worsening terms of trade and an export gap may be in store.

Secondly, even if enough resources can be obtained for the economy, one must still contend with the possibility of environmental degradation through acid rain, global warming or waste disposal, for example.

The practical implications are three-fold. All avenues for conservation must be explored, and an aggressive policy for population control must be preserved. Furthermore, if it is at all necessary, per capita consumption must be kept in check, until the population size has been greatly reduced.

This also imposes some delicate requirements in political development.

Further economic development requires democratization as well as a firm, long-term policy on demography, resources and the environment. These two requirements may well not mix.

VI. SOME CONCLUDING OBSERVATIONS

So far, we have considered the separate development of the three Chinese economies. We must now shift to issues of their economic integration and, in particular, how that process would influence their future development.

Recently, both laymen and economists have been excited by the implications of the economic integration of Hong Kong, Taiwan and China. This topic has aroused so much interest simply because first, the mainland Chinese economy, despite its scale advantages, has been lagging far behind the economies of Hong Kong and Taiwan in per capita terms, and second, the process of economic integration is viewed as a means to revitalize its performance. In contrast, if the economies of Sri Lanka and India were to merge into one, that would create much less excitement, not just because the populations of India and Sri Lanka are respectively somewhat smaller than those of mainland China and Hong Kong/Taiwan, but principally because the Sri Lankan economy is not expected to affect the post-integration aggregate economy much. Thus, quantitatively speaking, the integrated economy would not be appreciably different from a pre-integration Indian economy.

The situation is expected to be quite different for the three Chinese economies, and such expectations are in fact anchored in recent events.

The current economic reform in mainland China and the increased trade-cum-investment flow among the three Chinese economies have had a pronounced impact. Productivity, output, trade and export surplus have all grown in mainland China while profits have also risen for firms in Hong Kong and Taiwan. In fact, these three economies have become an island of prosperity within a world in recession. Western observers extrapolate such trends and predict that these, in turn, will smoothly bring these three economies to further growth.

Neo-classic economic theory also provides optimistic predictions of economic integration. It concludes that when barriers to the movement of productive factors and goods are removed, productive efficiency should rise so that those who gain can afford to compensate for those who lose, and everyone can be better off. Such predictions are made on assumptions of perfect information and complete markets.

However, we know for a fact that the neo-classic analysis is largely beside the point. What matters to the development of mainland China, and in particular to Guangdong Province, is not so much the flow of physical capital, but the human capital which has come with direct foreign investment. Jacob Viner has shown that to benefit from the inflow of foreign physical capital, an economy must run an import surplus, but mainland China enjoys an export surplus instead. Likewise, the fact that no important segment of the economies of Hong Kong and Taiwan is suffering is due to the "backward linkage" of the South China boom, and not to any side payment. The situation fits the product cycle theory well, yet that theory has so far not been exhaustively studied. One must turn to recent economic history for insight.

Two scenarios may be sketched for reference:

(a) The East Asian model, where the prosperity of Japan spills over to the Asian NIEs and the next NIEs of Thailand, Malaysia and Indonesia. As long as the advanced member, Japan, continues its advance, all ends well.

(b) The Eastern Europe-Soviet Union model, where post-World War II economic integration under Council for Mutual Economic Assistance (CMEA) provided both a supply of high quality products to the Soviets without requiring any hard currency payment, and unopposed market expansion for East German, Czechoslovak and Hungarian industries. However, by concentrating on such easy conquests, the technically more advanced industries in Eastern Europe eventually lost their vitality. Their industries eventually ended in stagnation, backwardness and collapse. This is a case of "united we fail."

For Hong Kong and Taiwan, much may also be learnt from the post-World War II Finnish economy. The latter prospered on Soviet trade and then suffered with the Soviet collapse. Symbiosis with a large, inefficient and potentially unstable neighbour is always a calculated risk. But the choices facing Hong Kong and Taiwan may be even tougher than those for Finland. In certain export markets, the combination of mainland wages and the technology and market access of Hong Kong can outcompete Taiwan, left by itself, and the same holds for PRC-Taiwan coalition against Hong

Kong. Likewise, a PRC-South Korea combination can undercut Hong Kong as well as Taiwan, should both refrain from working with PRC. The challenges are not insurmountable. But it takes the public airing of issues and the goodwill of various interest groups to devise an optimal course of action, and to implement it by sharing possible sacrifices.

This perhaps supplies us with a cautionary note: for Hong Kong and Taiwan to prosper in the long run, and in fact to be of any long-term use to the mainland Chinese economy, they must continue to compete in the world market for product niches of higher and higher quality, just as the Japanese have been doing all along. This is not an "easy way out" at all. In fact, there is no true "easy way out" in the long run, within our world of continuous technological dynamism.

REFERENCES

Chen, Shih-Meng, *et al.* (1991). *Disintegrating KMT-State Capitalism, A Closer Look at Privatizing Taiwan's State-and-Party-Owned Enterprises* (Text in Chinese). Taipei: Taipei Society.

Chiang, Shih-Chen and Robert T. Masson (1988). "Domestic Industrial Structure and Export Quality." *International Economic Review*, 29, pp. 262–270.

Chu, Cyrus (1990). "A Model of Income Tax Evasion with Venal Tax Officials." *Public Finance*, 45, pp. 392–408.

Kojima, Kiyoshi (1978). *Direct Foreign Investment: A Japanese Model, Multinational Business Operations*. London: Croom Helm.

Komiya, Ryutaro (1972). "Direct Foreign Investment in Post War Japan." In *Foreign Investment in Asia and the Pacific*, edited by Peter Drysdale. Toronto: University of Toronto Press.

Kreps, David (1990). *A Course in Micro-economic Theory*. Princeton, New Jersy: Princeton University Press.

Krugman, Paul (1979). "A Model of Innovation, Technology Transfer, and the World Distribution of Income." *Journal of Political Economy*, 87, pp. 253–266.

Lall, Sanjaya (1987). *Learning to Industrialize: The Acquisition of Technological Capability by India*. Hampshire: Macmillan.

Levy, Brian (1990). "Transaction Costs, the Size of Firms and the Industrial Policy: Lessons from a Comparative Case Study of the Footwear Industry in Korea and Taiwan." *Journal of Development Economics*, 34, pp. 151–178.

Morishima, Michio (1982). *Why Has Japan "Succeeded"? Western Technology and Japanese Ethos*. Cambridge: Cambridge University Press.

Morita, Akio (1986). *Made in Japan: Morita, Akio and Sony*. New York: Dutton.

Uchida, Hoshimi (1991). "The Transfer of Electrical Technologies from the U.S. and Europe to Japan: 1869–1914." In *International Technology Transfer: Europe, Japan and the U.S.A., 1700–1914*, edited by David J. Jeremy. Aldershot: E. Elgar.

Watanabe, Susumu (1980). "Multinational Enterprises and Employment Oriented Appropriate Technologies in Developing Countries." *ILO Working Papers* (Multinational Enterprise Programme), No. 14.

Xu, Dianjing, *et al.*, eds. (1990). *China's Economic Reform: Analysis, Reflections and Prospects* (Text in Chinese). Hong Kong: The Chinese University Press.

CHAPTER 3

Greater China:
An Emerging Technological Giant?[1]

E. Yegin Chen
Arral & Partners (Asia) Limited, Hong Kong

I. INTRODUCTION

The economic success of Hong Kong, the People's Republic of China (China), and the Republic of China (Taiwan) has resulted in part from an upgrading of their knowledge base in management and technology. For Hong Kong and Taiwan, this technological upgrading has led to enhanced total factor productivity (Chen 1979, Young 1992, Ng and Tuan 1991), movement into higher value-added industries, and competitive advantage based on knowledge, rather than low labour costs. For China, though these processes are at an early stage, progress has been made in productivity enhancement and quality improvement, particularly through foreign joint ventures.

In the mid-1990s and beyond, the three economies — collectively called "Greater China" in this essay — will continue to undergo dramatic change, but of a different nature than they have previously. After decades of technology imitation and transfer, the three economies are now undergoing two key developments in technology and productivity. First, the

---

[1] The essay was written when the author was a faculty member with the Department of Decision Sciences and Managerial Economics, The Chinese University of Hong Kong.

individual economies are undertaking ambitious initiatives to develop technology indigenously. Second, there will be growth in technological co-operation among the three Chinese economies. The core conclusion is that the Chinese economies are no longer content to remain the low- technology, low-cost producers of yesteryear. Instead, they have all coupled future economic prosperity with the growth of knowledge-based industries and have invested considerable resources to develop them.

II. UPGRADING IN HONG KONG

The most dramatic example of the region's new thinking regarding technology development occurs in Hong Kong. Renowned as a commercial and financial centre, Hong Kong's traditional approach to technology development has mirrored its renowned *laissez-faire* approach to many other economic matters. It has traditionally featured "minimum intervention" in industrial progress combined with "maximum possible support" through the provision of basic infrastructure and services (as described in *Hong Kong 1993: A Review of 1992*, Chapter 7). However, at least in productivity and technology, it has recently shifted its emphasis away from minimum intervention towards maximum support. Briefly examining this shift towards a more pro-active approach favouring the development of knowledge-based industries will shed light on policy and business motivations in the other Greater China economies, as well as those in other parts of Asia.

A Tradition of Technology Imitation

In the post-war era, the territory of Hong Kong based its economic prosperity on being a low-cost producer of consumer-related items, including textiles, clothing, and electronics. Taking advantage of low labour costs, low taxes, and minimal government regulation, the territory's entrepreneurs employed technology developed elsewhere to manufacture using non-capital intensive techniques. As such, Hong Kong's development and research capabilities have traditionally been on a small scale. The Government does not even keep statistics on Research and Development (R&D) expenditure, although estimates place expenditure at just 0.04% of gross domestic product (*Asian Business*, January 1992), among the lowest in the world.

The Need to Upgrade

As Hong Kong has prospered by producing increasingly sophisticated goods (described in Young 1992) and by moving towards a service economy, its low cost advantage has been seriously eroded. Sustained unemployment rates of approximately 2% resulted in nominal manufacturing pay per worker increasing by 289% from 1981 to 1990, as indicated by the data in Table 3.1.[2]

Table 3.1   The Erosion of Hong Kong's Cost Advantage
(Payroll per Person Indices for Hong Kong Manufacturing Sector)

Year	Nominal Index	Real Index
1980 (June)	100.00	100.00
1981	138.40	114.00
1982	150.70	113.10
1983	171.90	116.30
1984	190.30	123.00
1985	212.20	133.60
1986	242.40	147.20
1987	263.40	148.80
1988	307.40	161.40
1989	355.00	170.00
1990	389.40	167.30

Source: Census and Statistics Department, Hong Kong Government (1991).

Increasing labour costs, combined with a market demand for higher quality and competition from other developing lower-cost Asian producers, nudged Hong Kong towards a more pro-active approach for sustained growth. As envisioned by some industrial, academic, and government leaders, this approach suggested that Hong Kong develop its ability to use

---

[2]   Data for years subsequent to 1990 are not directly comparable to pre-1990 data because of changes in the classification system, and thus have not been presented.

and exploit new technologies, particularly those that could further the territory's growing role as a service economy and financial centre (as described in Jao 1993). The areas of emphasis would be information technology/telecommunication for the service industries and productivity enhancement for the manufacturing sector. As a result, the territory started initiatives in several sectors to boost research capabilities, develop human capital, and to enhance interaction between the public and private sectors. Key developments include the following:

Establishment of a Government Council on Technology

In early 1992, the Government established the Industry and Technology Development Council (ITDC). The Council is charged with advising the Government on how Hong Kong's industry could respond to world-wide technology developments, and devising strategies to assist technology development and application. Its formation is noteworthy because it unifies previously disparate advisory bodies, and seems designed to give technology a formal voice in the policy process, possibly for the first time. However, it suffers from only being an advisory body with limited resources.

Opening of University Science and Engineering Institutions

Two major Hong Kong institutions promoting science and technology have recently opened their doors. Opened in 1991, The Hong Kong University of Science and Technology features faculty from around the world as well as state-of-the-art equipment. The University offers first and advanced degrees in the schools of science, engineering, and business and management. Also in 1991, The Chinese University of Hong Kong formally established its Faculty of Engineering, featuring four departments in computer science, electronic engineering, information engineering, and systems engineering.

Government Support for University Research

In addition to upgrading, expanding, and opening institutions of higher learning capable of conducting research, the Government dramatically increased research funding for Hong Kong's seven universities, polytechnics, and colleges. Table 3.2 shows that research funding from the

Table 3.2 Increased Research Support in Hong Kong

Year	Academic Research Funding from Government
1985–1986	HK$10 million
1986–1987	HK$15 million
1987–1988	HK$20 million
1988–1989	HK$30 million
1989–1990	HK$40 million
1990–1991	HK$50 million
1991–1992	HK$100 million
1992–1993	HK$122 million
1993–1994	HK$155 million

Source: Research Grants Council of Hong Kong (1994).

Government has steadily and dramatically increased over the last nine years.[3]

Government Seed Money for Industry Development Projects

Hong Kong also recently introduced programmes to promote private sector development projects that could result in new products. In 1993, the Government unveiled the Applied Research and Development Scheme which provides funding support to commercial-sector applied R&D projects. With HK$200 million allocated, the Scheme may fund up to half the cost of approved R&D projects. As of October 1994, the Scheme has approved approximately HK$32 million for nine projects primarily relating to computer software development and communications.

A second, more flexible programme has also been made available, called the Additional Funding for Industrial Support Scheme. With HK$200 million available for 1995–1996, this Scheme has attracted 134 applications across seven technology areas totalling HK$677 million. Industry-related organizations accounted for over one-quarter of applications, with the remainder coming from the universities.

---

[3] Nevertheless, the absolute amounts for Hong Kong's academic researchers are still quite small compared to international standards: in 1989, for example, the U.S. institution M.I.T. received US$39 million (approximately HK$300 million) in research funding from industry sources alone.

Support Network for Technology-based Companies

In addition to mere funding, Hong Kong has taken steps to provide value-added support services for emerging technology-related firms. The Hong Kong Industrial Technology Centre was established in 1991 to facilitate technological innovation and the application of new technologies. It serves as an incubator for technology-based ventures, as well as a provider of technology transfer and other services. The Centre's incubatees thus far include firms involved with telecommunications, pen-based computers, automation, and other areas. In time, the technology centre will house approximately 50 to 60 companies. It faces the challenge of becoming more than a simple industrial estate. Also, in 1992, the Government commissioned and received a consultant's feasibility report which advocated a science park in Hong Kong.

New Technology — Transfer Roles for Universities and Colleges

In addition to establishing new institutions of higher education, Hong Kong is witnessing new roles for existing ones. Hong Kong's universities and colleges are now encouraged to apply their expertise directly to private sector companies. Though data are not readily available, the territory's higher education institutions have witnessed substantial growth in sponsored research, faculty consulting, and industrial training. Organizations such as The Chinese University of Hong Kong Asia Pacific Institute of Business, City Polytechnic of Hong Kong Consultancy Company,[4] and Hong Kong University of Science and Technology Research and Development Corporation were established to promote industrial training and consultancy projects, some involving enterprises in China.[5]

In summary, Hong Kong is upgrading its ability to provide competitive products and services through strengthening its abilities in research, development, and technological networking. Though this technological upgrading cannot produce a technology leader, technological upgrading

---

[4] The City Polytechnic of Hong Kong Consultancy Company will likely be renamed. In late 1994, Hong Kong's two polytechnics were upgraded to university status as part of the upgrading and expansion of the educational sector, and are now known as City University of Hong Kong and The Hong Kong Polytechnic University.

[5] Chen (1994) describes these developments in more detail.

serves to complement Hong Kong's renowned business and financial infrastructure, and lays the groundwork for continued economic vitality, particularly in the light of economic and political integration with China.

III. TECHNOLOGY REFORMS IN CHINA

Since the late 1970s, the world's most populous country has embarked on a well-known series of reforms towards a market-oriented economy. However, China's prosperity in the long run also depends on less widely-publicized reforms, those towards an innovation-oriented technology system. As early as 1982, in the early days of economic reform, the Chinese government began implementing R&D programmes with the explicit recognition that "economic construction must rely on science and technology, while science and technology must serve the needs of economic construction" (State Science and Technology Commission, the People's Republic of China 1992).

Having harnessed technology to market-oriented economics, the country faces formidable challenges in rebuilding a technology system disrupted by the Cultural Revolution. As a result, it has committed significant resources to rebuilding and upgrading its technological capabilities, while officially recognizing the importance of science and technology in economic progress. This section highlights recent initiatives to strengthen capabilities in the science and technology realm.[6]

China's Potential in Research and Production

As a result of its rebuilding efforts, China now has a large contingent of highly-trained scientists performing basic and applied research. If sheer quantity alone could produce discovery and innovation, then China would be a technological powerhouse many times over. Though government statistics require careful interpretation, Table 3.3 provides an indication of the country's foundation in technology development: a force of technically-trained scientists, engineers, technicians, and R&D personnel numbering in the millions.

---

[6]   Conroy (1989) and Simon and Rehn (1988) provide more detailed descriptions of the challenges in technology development in China.

**Table 3.3 China's Research Potential (Scientific,
Engineering, Technical, and R&D Personnel in
Various Economic Sectors, 1992)**

Sector	Personnel
State-owned	17,500,000
Collectively-owned units	628,000
Institutions of higher learning	262,000
State-owned R&D institutes	1,028,000
Large and medium-sized industrial enterprises	372,000
Technical development institutions affiliated with large and medium-sized enterprises	179,000
Approximate total	19,969,000

Source: State Statistical Bureau of the People's Republic of China (1993).

Further, China's resources devoted to innovation are not only large in magnitude, but they generally have also been increasing as the country places greater linkage between sustained economic growth and technological development. The scattered figures presented in Table 3.4 suggest that resources devoted to science and technology have been increasing in both absolute and relative terms, although the growth has been known to be periodically interrupted.

Table 3.4 General Growth in China's Technology Resources

Year	Scientific and Technical Personnel in State-owned units	Number of S&T Research Institutions	Ratio of R&D Expenses to GNP
1987	8,894,000		
1988	9,661,000		
1989	10,351,000	17,400	0.70
1990	10,809,000	18,700	0.71
1991	17,168,000	22,500	0.72
1992	17,597,000	20,425	0.70

Source: State Statistical Bureau of the People's Republic of China (1993).

Some of China's researchers have achieved regional or even international renown, particularly in the hard sciences. In 1990, they accounted for 7,823 papers in the "Science Citation Index", ranking fifteenth in the world in quantity of output (Republic of China National Science Council, 1992). However, China's engineers and scientists have yet to establish a reputation in research commercialization, particularly of goods for export markets. The country's major efforts to improve the application of technology to market demands are described in the paragraphs that follow.

Climbing Programme

Launched in June 1992, the National Basic Research Priorities Programme, known as the Climbing Programme, seeks to boost basic research capabilities in areas such as agriculture, energy, and raw materials. The Climbing Programme provides basic research funding, trains researchers, and promotes international co-operation and exchange (State Science and Technology Commission, 1992).

"863" Programme

Officially known as the High-Tech Research & Development Programme, the "863" Programme represents a major effort to boost capabilities in seven technological areas. It monitors emerging international technologies, strives for breakthroughs in areas with potential commercial results in a medium-term timeframe, and trains a new generation high-level technical workforce. The Programme's resources are allocated at national level through a bidding process.

Torch Programme Venture Funding and Science Parks

Launched in 1988 by the Science and Technology State Commission, the Torch Programme accelerates the application of technology in various business enterprises. It seeks to commercialize new technologies and promote economic growth with high-tech products competitive on the local and world markets. The Programme features two key components: funding for promising projects combined with a national set of new/high-tech development zones.

In its first component, the Torch Programme provides venture funding to noteworthy research findings from other R&D programmes (including those from state-owned enterprises, universities, and research institutes).

Funding is allocated through an application process involving the evaluation by external experts of projects based on three criteria: technical level, usefulness, and economic potential in both domestic and overseas markets.

The second main component of the Torch Programme is the group of 52 new/high-technology industrial development zones. These zones are home to over 2,500 high-technology enterprises having income of seven billion RMB in 1990 (Torch Programme China, The State Science and Technology Commission, People's Republic of China, 1991). Enterprises located in the zones enjoy assorted tax incentives, favourable accounting practices, priority for capital construction projects, and other benefits. Noteworthy zones include the Beijing "Electronics Street" and the Zhongshan zone, which have attracted substantial investment.

Though established with good intentions, many of the programmes have yet to show significant commercial results.[7] Nevertheless, current developments are steps in the right direction and promise to nudge China towards technological competitiveness. The nature of fundamental technological change as a long-term process suggests that China's overall technological ascent will require patience and sustained commitment. It has linked long-term economic reforms with technological reforms, particularly those with distinctly commercial goals. However, for the next few years, the country's main strength in terms of innovation will lie in its research capability.

IV. TAIWAN'S TECHNOLOGY COMMITMENT

In contrast to Hong Kong and the People's Republic of China, Taiwan has taken a pro-active, sustained science and technology approach over the last four decades. Such an approach has produced dramatic structural change, industrialization, and technological progress (described in Chiang 1993, and other sources). Taiwan has emerged among the world leaders in producing and designing quality consumer electronics, computers, computer accessories, memory chips, and micro-processors. Some Taiwanese

---

[7]   Evaluating the success of the various programmes is made difficult by official output measures still based on sheer numbers of "achievements" or "breakthroughs". However, the Torch Programme, in conjunction with the "863" Programme, claims success in commercializing various Chinese character information processing projects (Qiu 1994).

companies have developed successful international brand names such as Acer and are seeking a leadership role in developing software niches, particularly in Chinese language software.

Sustained Commitment

Significant sustained efforts in research and development, combined with technological networking, have been key to the Island's economic success and technological competitiveness. Table 3.5 displays data demonstrating its increasing commitment over the last decade in both absolute and relative terms.

Table 3.5 Growing Technology Emphasis in Taiwan

Year	R&D Expenditures (NT$100 million)	R&D as % of GDP	Number of Researchers
1982	168.00	0.89	18,300
1983	192.00	0.91	18,500
1984	224.00	0.95	22,300
1985	253.00	1.01	24,600
1986	287.00	0.98	27,700
1987	367.00	1.12	32,800
1988	438.00	1.22	35,400
1989	548.00	1.38	39,700
1990	715.00	1.65	46,000
1991	824.00	1.70	46,000

Sources: Republic of China, National Science Council (1992) and Republic of China, Government Information Office (1994).

The efforts in R&D have also been leveraged through Taiwan's cultivating extensive linkages with technology leaders, particularly the U.S., so as to have a source of technology to transfer. These technical linkages, combined with the experts and institutions supporting them, are similar to what Rosenberg (1990) calls an "information network", allowing the rapid acquisition and dissemination of technical knowledge by an economy.

Strong Technical Network

Taiwan benefits from assiduously cultivated technical networks which allow it to rapidly monitor, source, transfer, and absorb technology. The networks have both external and internal components.

In its external linkages, Taiwan not only sponsors and participates in numerous technical conferences and exchanges, but also actively seeks technical expertise on an international basis. Most of these efforts focus on people of Chinese heritage, either in the U.S. or in mainland China. Attracted by the increasing prosperity of the island, these professionals bring with them a wealth of professional expertise in technical areas, business experience, and contacts. The annual number of technically trained Taiwanese alone returning to the island has steadily increased from approximately 400 in 1985 to approximately 1,000 in 1991 (*Business Week International*, 30 November 1992). Several organizations assist the return of overseas Chinese scholars for short and long-term service in Taiwan; these organizations include the likes of the Chinese Institute of Engineers, USA.[8]

Taiwan's internal technical networks start from the top echelons of government, pervades all parts of society, and extends to the larger international Chinese community. Science and technology comprise a pervasive part of the entire policy process, with several entities providing input into government decisions. At the highest level, the President receives Science and Technology (S&T) policy counsel from the Committee for Guidance on Science Development. A National Science Council formulates policy, co-ordinates projects, and promotes strategy for S&T development, while the Academia Sinica is responsible for basic research.

More significant than the mere presence of governmental bodies is the integration of S&T functions throughout the government. Technology seems to be regarded not as a function separate from other aspects of society, but rather as an integral part of policy-making. The government's stated aim is to mesh economic development policies with science and technology policies. Various ministries, commissions, and administrations are responsible for applied research and development relevant to their needs. For example, the Department of Health oversees medical treatment and hygiene technologies. The technological network within Taiwan

---

[8] Lin (1992) describes these organizations in more detail.

appears to be co-ordinated and broad. Nowhere is this more apparent than in the Hsinchu Science-based Industrial Park.

Hsinchu Science-based Industrial Park

Established in 1980, the Hsinchu Science-based Industrial Park (HSIP) represents a broad-based effort by Taiwan to attract high-technology industries and experts, to spur R&D, and boost economic growth. Occupying approximately 2,100 hectares, the Park features industrial, research, and residential zones, resembling a small city. Over 140 private companies are located in the Park, in industries including semi-conductors, computers, telecommunications, and biotechnology. Their 1992 revenues totalled almost US$3.2 billion in technology-intensive goods (Republic of China Government Information Office 1994).

The Park serves as more than just an industrial estate for its companies. Successful applicants to the Park must invest a minimum proportion of sales on R&D, and also have a certain workforce percentage of scientists and engineers (*Asian Business*, March 1993). Once located in the Park, the firms become part of a technical network anchored by two research-oriented universities (the National Chiao Tung University and the National Tsing Hua University) and the Industrial Technology Research Institute (ITRI). ITRI serves as a bridge between academic institutions and industry, and also performs R&D in industrial technologies. It includes over 4,000 people in six research departments. As a result, the Park's enterprises are heavily committed to S&T development. The average R&D expenditure of Park companies is 6%, compared with about 1% for non-Park companies. R&D personnel comprise approximately 30% of the Park's workforce, including numerous overseas professionals.

In summary, Taiwan's technical networks have become well-developed, based significantly on connections with the U.S. and among the sectors of Taiwan's domestic economy. A recent development has been the potential for technological linkages with China and Hong Kong, which harbingers technological co-operation in Greater China.

V. TECHNOLOGICAL CO-OPERATION IN GREATER CHINA?

Given their individual efforts toward indigenous technological development, China, Taiwan, and Hong Kong have begun to deepen their extensive trade and investment relationships to include co-operation in technology development efforts. These efforts represent more than the well-documented technology transfer processes that basically involve equipment sales and direct investment (as described in Nyaw 1993, and other sources). Rather, the emerging technological co-operation described in this section represents a potentially more significant process, similar to the "international collaborative ventures" described by Mowery (1992). The technological co-operation referred to in this chapter involves active transborder efforts within Greater China to develop new knowledge and potential products in which each party contributes know-how and expertise. It thus excludes arms-length transactions such as licensing or equipment sales.

Technological Complementarity

In the foreseeable future, no single Chinese economy is likely to become a broad-based technology leader, particularly in commercial technologies. However, the three Chinese economies have the tantalizing potential to form a "technology bloc" that could result in a more competitive, technology-oriented Greater China.[9] The fundamental driving forces of technological co-operation in Greater China would be of economic self-interest in exploiting complementary technological abilities, geographic proximity, and cultural affinity. The Greater China economies have already established significant connections in trade, travel, and direct investment. As political obstacles are slowly resolved and as trade, travel, and investment links deepen, the three economies will likely begin large-scale technological co-operation.

Just as gains from trade result from differing economic production capabilities, so do gains from technology co-operation stem from differences in innovation capabilities. If China, Taiwan, and Hong Kong are relatively strong in different elements of the innovation process, then they could benefit by pooling their complementary capabilities. They could thus form strategic partnerships that leverage strengths, mitigate shortcomings, and access scarce technological resources. Such partnerships already occur in Greater China on a wide scale in production and marketing; the

---

[9] Several observers (such as Woo 1993, and Poon 1994) have envisioned co-operation, including technological co-operation, among the Chinese economies. However, they have generally focused on only China and Hong Kong.

fundamental drivers of co-operation are also present in technology development.[10]

The previous sections of this chapter have sketched the different capabilities of the three Chinese economies. Hong Kong is renowned as a financial centre and as a place attuned to the world markets. China has large numbers of skilled researchers and production workers, while Taiwan seems to be networked into the technical community and has proven itself in product design and development. From the many possible permutations of such co-operation, the most likely contribution of each party is summarized in Table 3.6.

Table 3.6   Roles in Technological Co-operation in Greater China

Access to technological networks	Taiwan
Basic research	China
Product development and design	Taiwan, China
Production	China
Market access	Hong Kong
Access to financial networks	Hong Kong

On a theoretical macro-scale, the case for technological co-operation among the three Chinese economies looks promising. In practice, such co-operation does not occur at the macro-economic level, but rather at the level of the firm, the institution, or industry. Also, it does not occur in some generic area called "technology", but rather in specific areas such as information systems, chemicals, and aerospace. Thus, at a more macro-level, the complementarities driving co-operation may not be as strong, or may be blocked by barriers that include the political. Therefore, the next section examines some of the initial cases of technological co-operation in Greater China to discern the areas of greatest complementarity.

---

[10] Sakikabara and Westney (1992) describe similar motivations for the transborder technical collaborations of Japanese firms. They note that Japanese firms established R&D bases outside of Japan partly because of a growing shortage of engineers and scientists in Japan. The Japanese firms also sought to become true multinationals, sourcing technology from the world over.

VI. INITIAL CASES OF CO-OPERATION

Co-operation among the three Chinese economies to enhance productivity and technological ability has already begun on a small scale. This section outlines some recent harbingers of greater co-operation, keeping in mind that developments occur rapidly and often unexpectedly. In this non-comprehensive sample, the harbingers fall primarily into two categories: those between Hong Kong and China, and those between Taiwan and China. Technology co-operation among all three Chinese economies is still uncommon.

Co-operation between China and Hong Kong

Even before the formal political unification of Hong Kong and China, Hong Kong and Chinese scientists and engineers have established technology-based linkages. These linkages are in addition to pervasive trade, travel, and investment connections between the two economies. They occur in the academic, governmental, and commercial realms:

Growing Academic Linkages

Academic exchanges between Hong Kong and China are becoming increasingly commonplace. Hong Kong government funding for academic technical exchange between China and Hong Kong has increased from $1.2 million in 1988–1989 to $1.7 million in 1990–1991 (Hong Kong University and Polytechnic Grants Committee 1991). In addition, technology and management-related conferences for both Hong Kong and Chinese scholars have become more common. For example, in late 1992, The Chinese University of Hong Kong held a conference on technology transfer with a large percentage of participants from China. In 1993, the same university hosted numerous Chinese and Taiwanese management scholars during a conference on management education in China. Also, an increasing number of Hong Kong faculty members are mainland Chinese who received their post-graduate education in the U.S.

Productivity Enhancement Programmes

The Hong Kong and Chinese governments have begun co-operating in the area of productivity improvement, particularly through training programmes. In November 1993, the Hong Kong Productivity Centre

(HKPC), a government entity, opened an office in Guangzhou, China, to foster closer ties between the two economies. A month later, senior officers from 16 productivity centres in China attended a training course at the HKPC. The HKPC has also organized training courses in China for workers in the plastics industry. These official efforts supplement the numerous training programmes held by Hong Kong companies to upgrade technical and management standards of their China operations (Hong Kong Productivity Council 1993).

Product Development in China

In the commercial realm, Hong Kong firms have begun to establish technology-related product development ventures in China. These ventures take advantage of an ample supply of skilled Chinese technicians. For example, Silicon Graphics Ltd. Hong Kong is working with Beijing's Qinghua University to develop an application based on imaging technology that can identify fingerprints (*South China Morning Post*, Technology Post, 11 May 1993). Another example is a developer and manufacturer of personal communications equipment that employs four full-time design engineers in southern China. Finally, several Hong Kong-based companies have begun employing mainland Chinese experts to help develop software. Typical is the case of one Chinese-language desktop publishing firm which employs only three developers in Hong Kong, but ten in China.

A related development is that of several Hong Kong firms' taking advantage of low costs of technically trained personnel in China. They are considering or have begun relocating technology-intensive backroom operations to southern China. For example, Cathay Pacific Airlines has moved some information-system functions to Shenzhen to reduce costs.

Sourcing Capital and Equipment

A subsidiary of one of China's leading technology firms, Stone Electronic Technology Ltd., has sourced both capital and technology from Hong Kong. With Japanese co-operation, Stone Electronic Technology Ltd. was the first Chinese company to develop, manufacture, and sell an integrated word processor. It sells the product under the "Stone" brand name. With over 200 technicians, the Stone Group has also developed four subsequent models of the product. Hong Kong serves as one site of the Group's R&D

activity due to the availability of advanced equipment and a ready supply of components (Stone Electronic Technology Ltd. 1993). Most importantly, Stone was listed on the Hong Kong Stock Exchange in 1993, thereby securing capital for further growth.

Co-operative Venture

In January 1992, a co-operative venture was announced between Chinese and Hong Kong parties to make state-of-the-art laser systems (*China Trade Report*, April 1992). A US$10 million collaborative venture located in Fuzhou, the venture members include the Chinese Academy of Science, Fujian Enterprise, Hongkong Phoenix Laser System, and China Resources (Holdings) in Hong Kong. Hongkong Phoenix Laser System already develops and manufactures laser systems for medical purposes.

Co-operation between China and Taiwan

Of greater significance and potential impact are the embryonic technology ties between Chinese and Taiwanese scientists and technical experts. Some of the harbingers of more widespread China-Taiwan technological co-operation include the following developments:

Encouragement of Technical Visits to Taiwan

In 1992, Taiwan's National Science Council lifted restrictions on visits by Chinese technology specialists. New guidelines govern the recruiting and hiring of Chinese technologists, residing both in China and overseas, to work in Taiwan and participate in scientific research. Chinese professionals in science, engineering, medicine, agriculture, and other areas can be recruited for a one-year contract to stay in Taiwan, with possibilities for extension (*Science Bulletin*, September 1992).

Exchange Visits to China

In the opposite direction, the Taiwanese National Science Council also plans to support its scholars and experts on short exchange visits to China for technology research (*Science Bulletin*, September 1992). These plans would be limited to 30 people per year.

Joint Design Venture

In early 1993, it was announced that China and Taiwan were planning to jointly design and build a telecommunications satellite through a Hong Kong partnership. Parties to the US$100 million project are to include the Kuomintang-controlled China Development Corporation, while Beijing's Great Wall Industrial Corporation, and possibly Japanese and Singaporean interests, may also participate (*Far Eastern Economic Review*, 25 March 1993).

Promotion of Chinese Industrial Areas

Taiwanese firms appear to be providing the impetus toward the development of technology areas in China. A Taiwanese venture capital firm, Taiwanvest, is sponsoring the development of an industrial park in China. Located in Kunshan, not far from Shanghai, the park is to be patterned after the Hsinchu science park, and involves 15 to 20 Taiwanese firms (*Asian Business*, March 1993). In a second case, Taiwanese computer firms began construction of the "Taiwan Electronics Street" in Shanghai in late 1992. Though initially a marketing-oriented venture to house 60 computer firms selling to the Chinese market, the "Taiwan Electronics Street" represents growing contact between Taiwan and China in the computer area (*Free China Journal*, 2 October 1992).

Co-operative Software Development

Taiwanese firms are interested in tapping not only the Chinese market for computers, but also China's expertise in the high-potential area of Chinese language software. Many Taiwanese (and Hong Kong) software firms are contracting software development functions to Chinese organizations, particularly those tied to universities (as noted in *Free China Review*, August 1992, p. 44, and other sources). Drivers of this cross-straits co-operation are similar to those involving Hong Kong and China: a growing demand for technical personnel by Taiwanese firms, and a growing supply of trained and motivated Chinese experts.

Evaluation

Overall, the extent of knowledge-oriented interaction among the three Chinese economies is small compared to the extent of trade, investment, and travel interactions among them. The technology-oriented interactions also tend to be bilateral, rather than trilateral. Further, the current links primarily involve scientific/academic exchanges, while commercial ventures appear limited to the area of information technology/computers.

If technological co-operation in Greater China offers such significant benefits, why are the case examples so few in number and in such a preliminary state? There are two main reasons.

First, given that a firm in one of the three Chinese economies seeks a strategic technology-related alliance, it is not obvious why the partner should be in another Chinese economy. There are numerous American, European, or Japanese firms that may make more attractive and prestigious partners for collaboration. However, as research and development initiatives in Greater China progress, it is possible that Greater China's firms and research institutions will be at the world's cutting edge in selected technological niches.

A second key obstacle to more transborder collaboration is the remaining political rivalry between mainland China and Taiwan. The current ban on direct transportation links, restrictions on many forms of scientific and personnel exchange, limitations on the trade of sensitive items, and Taiwanese concern over certain direct investments in China all dampen the potential for achieving potentially sizable gains. For example, in late 1992, the Taiwan Government initially opposed a US$6 billion investment by Taiwan's largest private conglomerate, Formosa Plastics, because it would transfer too much capital and technology to China. The ambiguity over Taiwan's technological relationship with China is made more complicated by both parties' continued emphasis on acquiring and developing sophisticated weapons technology. It is thus very possible that the technology relationship between the Chinese and Taiwanese governments will be schizophrenic: the two may co-operate in technologies related to consumer goods, but compete in technologies related to security.

VII. CONCLUSION

The three Chinese economies have entered a new era of technology development. Rather than relying upon imitation and transfer, they are investing substantial resources toward technology development with commercial objectives. Further, on a limited scale, they have begun technological co-operation amongst themselves, with the possibility of eventually creating an internationally competitive Greater China. Greater

China's emerging knowledge-based linkages are driven by complementarities in the capabilities of its individual economies. China seems suited to being the source of research expertise and production labour, while Taiwan is strong in development and design, and in accessing international technical knowledge. Finally, Hong Kong helps source capital through its myriad banks and venture capital/direct investment firms, while helping to bring products onto world markets.

However, a review of some preliminary cases of co-operation thus far suggests that technology co-operation is still bilateral, rather than trilateral. Furthermore, the co-operation has occurred mostly in the areas of scientific/academic exchange and information technology/computers. Nevertheless, the trend is clear: ideological differences are gradually being replaced by shared commercial interests, leading to links in trade, investment, and technology. Such links point towards the gradual emergence of an innovative and prosperous "Greater China" with many opportunities and challenges for business executives, policy makers, and scholars.

REFERENCES

Asian Business (1992). "Greenhouses for Ideas," January.

Asian Business (1993). "Cultivating Cooperation," March.

Chen, Edward K. Y. (1979). *Hyper-growth in Asian Economies*. London: Macmillan.

Chen, E. Yegin (1994). "The Evolution of University-Industry Technology Transfer in Hong Kong." *Technovation*, Vol. 14, No. 7, pp. 449–459.

Chiang, Jong-Tsong (1993). "Development of Technology Management in Taiwan." In *Developing Technology Managers: Comparative Pacific Rim Strategies*, edited by Karen Minden and Wong Poh Kam (manuscript in preparation).

China Trade Report, April 1992, p. 12.

Conroy, Richard (1989). "China's Science and Technology Policy." In *China: Modernization in the 1980s*, edited by Joseph Cheng. Hong Kong: The Chinese University Press.

———— (1990). "Domestic and Foreign Technology Factors Influencing Assimilation and Diffusion Capabilities." In *From Technology Transfer to Technology Management in China*, edited by Theodor Leuenberger, pp. 14–71. Berlin: Springer-Verlag.

Far Eastern Economic Review, 25 March 1993.

Free China Journal. Taiwan: various issues.

Free China Review. Taiwan: various issues.

Hong Kong Census and Statistics Department (1991). "Annual Digest of Statistics."

Hong Kong Government Information Services (1993). *Hong Kong 1993: A Review of 1992*.

Hong Kong Productivity Council (1993). *Productivity News*, December.

Hong Kong University and Polytechnic Grants Committee (1991). "Report for the 1988–91 Triennium: June 1988 to June 1991."

Jao, Y. C (1993). "Hong Kong as an International Financial Centre: Evolution and Prospects." In *The Asian NIEs: Success and Challenge*, edited by Tzong-biau Lin and Chyau Tuan, pp. 39–82. Hong Kong: Lo Fung Learned Society.

Lin, Wuu-Long (1992). "A Note on Channels of External Cooperation in Science and Technology Development." *Industry of Free China*, September, pp. 47–56.

Ng, Linda Fung-Yee and Chyau Tuan (1991). "A Comparative Study of Productivity in the Textiles and Electronics Industries in Hong Kong and Taiwan." *Journal of International Economic Studies*, Vol. 5, pp. 31–55.

Mowery, David (1992). "International Collaborative Ventures." In *Technology and the Wealth of Nations*, edited by Nathan Rosenberg, Ralph Landau, and David C. Mowery, Chapter 13. California: Stanford University Press.

Nyaw, Mee Kau (1993). "Direct Foreign Investment in China: Trends, Performance, Policies and Prospects." In *China Review: 1993*, edited by Joseph Cheng Yu-sek and Maurice Brosseau, Chapter 16. Hong Kong: The Chinese University Press.

Poon, Chung Kwong (1994). "Technological Cooperation with Greater China: Past, Present and Future Potentialities." In *Technology Transfer in the Globally Networked Pacific Basin*, edited by W. W. Liang, D. F. Simon, and W. M. Denny, pp. 173–178. Hong Kong: Pacific Economic Co-operation Council Science and Technology Task Force.

Qiu, Xiaoling (1994). "The Meaning of Technological Self-reliance in an Increasingly Interdependent World Economy." In *Technology Transfer in the Globally Networked Pacific Basin*, edited by W. W. Liang, D. F. Simon, and W. M., pp. 92–87. Denny. Hong Kong: Pacific Economic Co-operation Council Science and Technology Task Force.

Republic of China Government Information Office (1994). *Republic of China Yearbook 1994*.

Republic of China National Science Council (1992). *Indicators of Science and Technology: Republic of China*.

Rosenberg, Nathan (1990). "Why Do Firms Do Basic Research (with Their Own Money)?" *Research Policy*, pp. 165–174.

Sakakibara, Kiyonori and D. Eleanor Westney (1992). "Japan's Management of

Global Innovation: Technology Management Crossing Borders." In *Technology and the Wealth of Nations*, edited by Nathan Rosenberg, Ralph Landau, and David C. Mowery, Chapter 12. California: Stanford University Press.

Science Bulletin. Taiwan: National Science Council, various issues.

Simon, Denis and Detlef Rehn (1988). *Technological Innovation in China*. Cambridge, Massachusetts: Ballinger Publishing Company.

South China Morning Post. Hong Kong: various issues.

State Science and Technology Commission (1992). *The Main Programmes of Science and Technology*.

State Statistical Bureau of the People's Republic of China (1993). *China Statistical Yearbook*.

Stone Electronic Technology Ltd. (1993). "New Issue Prospectus." Hong Kong: Peregrine Ltd. and China Development Finance Ltd.

Torch Programme China, The State Science and Technology Commission of the People's Republic of China (1991). *Background Information on China's New and High Technology Industries Parks*.

Woo, Chia-Wei (1993). "China: A Major Hi-Tech Player in the 21st Century?" Paper presented at the "High Technology and Profitability for the 21st Century" Conference, Hong Kong, May.

Young, Alwyn (1992). "A Tale of Two Cities: Factor Accumulation and Technical Change in Hong Kong and Singapore." In *NBER Macroeconomics Annual*.

Zhu, Lilan (1993). "Hi-Tech Development and Its Outlook in China." Paper presented at the "High Technology and Profitability for the 21st Century" Conference, Hong Kong, May.

CHAPTER 4

Dutch Disease, Taiwan's Success and "The China Boom"

Justin Yifu Lin
Peking University, PRC, and University of California, Los Angeles, U.S.A.
Chen Chien-Liang
University of California, Los Angeles, U.S.A.

I. INTRODUCTION

The major challenge for the three Chinese economies in the 1990s is how to sustain their miraculous GDP growth rates achieved during the 1980s. The main opportunity for sustaining such high rates of GDP growth in the 1990s rests in the prospect of closer integration of the three economies, whose comparative advantages complement one another. Our prediction for the 1990s is based on the three economies' experiences in the 1980s, especially the experiences of Taiwan and China.

Before the 1960s, it would have been ridiculous for any economist to predict that an economy, whatever its size, could realize a sustained GDP growth rate of around 10% for over a decade or more. However, the experiences of the "four small dragons" — Taiwan, Hong Kong, Singapore, and South Korea — from the 1960s to the 1980s changed economists' views. Taiwan's annual growth rate of real GDP reached 9.2% in the period 1965–1981 (Scitovsky 1990), and Hong Kong's reached 10% in the years 1960–1970 and 9.3% in the period 1970–1980 (World Bank 1982, p. 113). These economies became "Newly Industrialized Economies" (NIEs) in only two decades. Taiwan's success in the 1960s and 1970s is a classic example of the model of export-led growth. The competitiveness of Taiwan's exports relies heavily on its abundance of cheap and disciplined labour. However, in the mid-1980s, the Taiwanese economy encountered a phenomenon similar to "Dutch Disease". The exchange rate, which had formerly been pegged to the U.S. dollar, appreciated dramatically from 39.85 NT$/US$ in 1985 to 28.55 NT$/US$ in 1987, a 28% appreciation within two years. The rapid appreciation weakened the competitiveness of Taiwan's traditional export sectors. Standard economic theory predicted that Taiwan's economy would trudge through a painstaking and prolonged structural adjustment, experiencing a recession with a high unemployment rate, before recovering its dynamism.[1] However, the average annual growth rate of real GDP increased from 7.2% in the years 1980–1984 to 8.1% in the period 1985–1990 (Asian Development Bank 1991, p. 21). The ease of shifting Taiwan's labour-intensive manufacturing industries across the Taiwan Strait to the coastal provinces of the mainland contributed much to the miracle.

The Chinese economy had been adherent to the Stalinist model of economic development before the reforms started in 1979. The essence of the Stalin model is an import-substitution, capital-intensive, industry-oriented development strategy. Characterized by rich labour endowments but scarce capital and arable land, the Chinese economy has comparative advantages similar to those of the four small dragons. Growth in the Chinese economy under the Stalinist model was thus sluggish, especially compared with the four small dragons. Major reforms began with the rural sector in 1979. The most important change was the replacement of the collective farming system with a household-based system — the household responsibility system. The institutional reforms greatly improved farmers' incentives and resulted in rapid output growth. The annual growth rate in Chinese agriculture reached 7.7% in the years 1978–1984, contrasting sharply with only 2.9% in the period 1952–1978. However, China did not join the East Asian club of export-led growth until 1985. The annual rate of export growth, measured in U.S. dollars, increased from 12.3% in the period 1979–1985 to 17.5% in the period 1985–1991. The reforms in the trading sector in 1985 and the shift in development strategy thereafter might explain much of the export boom. The rapid inflow of capital and technology from Taiwan's labour-intensive industries, together with related export

---

[1] Fry (1990) was the first economist to term the Taiwan phenomenon a "Dutch Disease."

market opportunities, to the coastal provinces, contributed much to this boom.

The organization of this essay is as follows. Section II introduces the stylized facts of the "Dutch Disease" and outlines the effects of "Dutch Disease" on the structural adjustments between booming and lagging sectors in an economy. We will then compare the standard "Dutch Disease" in the Netherlands with its variant in Taiwan. Section III provides a model for analysing a firm's reaction to "Dutch Disease", and discusses the response of Taiwan's firms to the exchange rate shock in the 1980s. Section IV examines Taiwan's and China's economic development in the 1980s and shows the interdependence of the two economies. The role of Hong Kong in the economic integration of China and Hong Kong is also analysed. Some concluding remarks are presented in Section V.

II. THE STYLIZED FACTS OF DUTCH DISEASE

The term "Dutch Disease", first appearing in *The Economist* in 1977, is used to describe the mixed blessing of a sudden boom in the trading sector of an open economy. The booming sector could be North Sea oil for Britain in the 1970s, Schlockteren natural gas in the 1960s for the Netherlands, or minerals for Australia in the 1950s.[2] The key issue of Dutch Disease is that rapid expansion in some specific export sectors will bring about two important effects: namely, the resource movement effect, and the spending effect (Corden and Neary 1982). Both effects have implications for structural changes. The mechanism in a classic Dutch Disease model is straightforward. In a three-sector economy, including a non-tradable sector (service) and two traded-goods sectors (manufacturing and energy, respectively), the boom, taking the form of a rapid and unanticipated expansion in the energy sector, typically follows the discovery and exploitation of natural resources. Energy becomes one of the major exported goods. Expansion in the energy sector brings in considerable increases in foreign reserves and, therefore, in national income. The income increases result in a demand shift. Part of the revenue is spent on both traded and non-traded goods. Since the prices of traded goods are

---

[2]   "Dutch Disease" appears not only in the extractive kind of resource boom but also in agricultural export booms, for example, the effect of the movement in world coffee prices on the Columbian economy (Edwards 1986).

fixed by world prices, the effect of an expansion in expenditure is to raise the relative prices of non-traded goods to those of traded goods, thus leading to a real appreciation. This is an income effect. On the other hand, the rising marginal product in the expanded sector attracts mobile factors out of the other sectors into its own and pushes up the wage rate. This is a resource reallocation effect. Suffering from the dual pressures of real appreciation and resource outflows, the traditional (non-expanding) manufacturing sectors will decline. This is the so-called de-industrialization effect of Dutch Disease. However, if the booming sector attracts relatively few resources out of the other sectors of the economy, the resource reallocation effect will be minor and only the income effect will be dominant. Therefore, expansion may appear in the booming sector only or in both the booming and the non-tradable sectors.

Traditionally, the comparative advantages of the Dutch economy have been in the agricultural sectors, which rely on relatively high-skilled labour

Table 4.1 Gas Exports and Total Exports in the Netherlands, 1969–1988

Year	Gas exports	Total exports	Ratio (%)
1969	400	36,139	1.1
1970	602	42,166	1.4
1971	867	47,832	1.8
1972	1,142	52,622	2.2
1973	1,512	65,323	2.3
1974	2,576	87,794	2.9
1975	4,074	88,464	4.6
1976	5,417	105,517	5.1
1977	6,464	107,195	6.0
1978	6,324	108,189	5.8
1979	7,575	127,689	5.9
1980	10,631	146,973	7.2
1981	14,634	170,772	8.6
1982	13,788	176,761	7.8
1983	14,376	184,307	7.8
1984	15,900	210,095	7.6
1985	16,702	224,845	7.4
1986	9,874	196,880	5.0
1987	5,134	187,530	2.7
1988	4,065	203,937	2.0

Source: *IFS Yearbook* (1990).

and abundant natural resources. The Netherlands discovered a huge gas reserve in the late 1950s. In the early 1970s, soaring international oil prices made the natural gas a valuable endowment. As Table 4.1 shows, natural gas became a major export of the Netherlands in the 1970s. The resource boom caused a real appreciation, raised the real wage rate, and resulted in a high inflation rate as well as a high unemployment rate (see Table 4.2). The boom also deteriorated the competitiveness of the agricultural sector (Fardmanesh 1991). These are the stylized features of the "Dutch Disease".

A major characteristic of the Dutch economy is its openness. As indicated in Table 4.3, the sum of exports and imports amounted to more

Table 4.2 Real Exchange Rate, Inflation Rate, Wage Inflation Rate, and Unemployment Rate in the Netherlands, 1967–1988

Year	Real exchange rate		Inflation rate (CPI) (%)	Wage inflation (hourly) (%)	Unemployment rate (%)
	Gud/SDR	Gud/US			
1966	3.60	3.60	5.7	10.3	1.0
1967	3.62	3.62	3.6	6.4	2.0
1968	3.62	3.62	3.7	7.6	1.9
1969	3.62	3.62	7.5	9.7	1.4
1970	3.62	3.61	3.6	10.8	1.1
1971	3.51	3.49	7.5	11.6	1.6
1972	3.48	3.20	7.9	12.6	2.8
1973	3.33	2.79	7.9	13.4	2.8
1974	3.23	2.68	9.5	16.9	3.5
1975	3.07	2.52	10.3	13.6	5.0
1976	3.05	2.64	9.1	8.9	5.3
1977	2.86	2.45	6.3	7.0	5.1
1978	2.70	2.16	4.1	5.8	5.0
1979	2.59	2.00	4.2	4.6	5.1
1980	2.58	1.98	6.5	4.4	5.9
1981	2.94	2.49	6.8	3.2	9.1
1982	2.94	2.67	5.9	6.7	12.6
1983	3.05	2.85	2.8	2.6	17.1
1984	3.28	3.20	3.3	1.2	17.2
1985	3.37	3.32	2.3	4.9	15.9
1986	2.87	2.45	0.1	1.6	N.A.
1987	2.61	2.20	−0.7	1.4	N.A.
1988	2.65	1.97	N.A.	N.A.	N.A.

Sources: *IFS Yearbook* (1990); *Statistical Yearbook*, United Nations, various issues.

Table 4.3 GDP, Exports, Imports, and the Openness of the Netherlands in the Period of Dutch Disease, 1967–1988 (Unit = Billions of Guilders)

Year (1)	GDP (2)	Export (goods + services) (3)	Import (goods + services) (4)	Openness (5) = [(3) + (4)]/ (2)
1966	73.83	32.63	33.72	0.90
1967	81.00	34.78	35.55	0.87
1968	89.81	39.02	39.03	0.86
1969	107.99	45.90	49.16	0.85
1970	121.18	54.30	56.41	0.91
1971	136.53	62.02	62.43	0.91
1972	154.26	69.40	65.15	0.87
1973	176.04	83.41	77.76	0.91
1974	199.78	107.78	102.31	1.05
1975	219.96	109.72	102.34	0.96
1976	251.93	128.47	119.93	0.99
1977	274.93	130.74	127.40	1.03
1978	297.01	133.34	133.23	0.89
1979	315.96	155.06	156.69	0.99
1980	336.74	176.81	178.62	1.05
1981	352.85	204.62	192.24	1.12
1982	368.86	212.60	196.83	1.10
1983	381.02	219.77	205.21	1.12
1984	400.25	248.56	227.75	1.19
1985	418.18	265.54	245.50	1.22
1986	428.61	232.52	213.01	1.04
1987	431.22	226.41	213.21	1.02
1988	451.23	246.07	227.80	1.05

Source: *IFS Yearbook* (1990).

than 100% of GDP in most years after 1973. Taiwan is a small, open economy, too. The degree of its openness is comparable to that of the Netherlands (see Table 4.4). However, Taiwan is a resource-poor economy. Its comparative advantages come from its abundant and well-educated labour force. The exports that led the Taiwanese economy to a take-off in the early 1960s were mainly the commodities of labour-intensive industries produced with low and medium technologies.

**Table 4.4 GDP, Exports, Imports, and the Openness of Taiwan in
the Period of Dutch Disease, 1980–1989 (Unit = Billion of US$)**

Year (1)	GDP (2)	Exports (goods + services) (3)	Imports (goods + services) (4)	Openness (5) = [(3) + (4)]/ (2)
1980	41.42	22.63	23.45	1.11
1981	48.22	26.08	25.47	1.07
1982	48.57	25.69	23.31	1.01
1983	52.42	28.83	24.38	1.02
1984	59.14	34.74	27.59	1.04
1985	62.06	35.43	25.98	0.99
1986	75.43	46.29	29.72	1.01
1987	101.13	61.48	42.78	1.03
1988	122.23	71.56	61.46	1.07
1989	146.86	79.56	66.32	0.99
1990	157.01	81.07	69.56	0.96

Source: *Taiwan Statistical Yearbook 1991.*

The effects of Dutch Disease shown above are closely linked to the real appreciation of the domestic currency. As argued by Edwards (1986), the change in the real exchange rate is the main transmission mechanism that causes a commodity export boom to lead to a structural adjustment in the economy. In the mid-1980s, Taiwan experienced a rapid appreciation of its currency. Compared with the case of the Netherlands, the appreciation happened in a shorter period and was larger in magnitude (see Figure 4.1).[3] Unfortunately, the real appreciation in Taiwan was caused by exogenous political pressure instead of a resource boom. This means that Taiwan had Dutch Disease but without an oil boom. Surprisingly, contrary to the experiences of other economies encountering Dutch Disease, Taiwan did not suffer the symptoms of the disease but performed as well as before. The remaining parts of this essay will try to provide an explanation for this puzzle.

---

[3]   Japan encountered a similar experience in the second half of the 1980s.

Figure 4.1 Exchange Rate in the Period of Dutch Disease

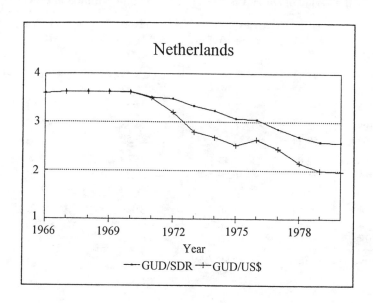

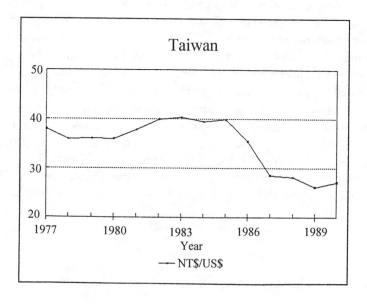

III. STRUCTURAL ADJUSTMENTS AND THE IMPACT
OF DUTCH DISEASE IN TAIWAN

Background

Taiwan is one of the most rapidly growing economies in the world. The average annual growth rate of real GDP from 1965 to 1990 was more than 9%. From the early 1960s, economic planners in Taiwan perceived the constraints of its lack of natural resources and chose a policy of promoting the export of labour-intensive commodities. As a result, Taiwan's exports expanded at a phenomenal rate, from US$449.7 million in 1965 to US$22,611.2 million in 1981 to US$52,248.5 million in 1989. The value of exports grew to more than 50% of GDP in the 1980s (see Table 4.4). The growth in Taiwan is a typical case of an export-led growth. The relationship between real export growth and real GNP growth clearly explains the story (Lau 1990, p. 188).

The success of export-led growth brought about two consequences:

(a) Rapid economic growth caused considerable purchasing power to accumulate in the private sectors, and boosted domestic demand for non-tradable services and consumer goods.[4] Since surplus labour in the agricultural sector was soon absorbed, the increased demand for non-tradable services and goods attracted the labour force out of the tradable sectors to the non-tradable sectors, and pushed the wage rate up.[5] Starting in the late 1970s, the wage rate in Taiwan kept increasing annually by a considerable rate (see Table 4.5).

(b) Beginning in the early 1980s, the current account surplus grew steadily alongside the expansion of trade.[6]

The currency of Taiwan had been closely pegged to the U.S dollar since the 1960s. Due to a conservative financial policy and strong central bank intervention, the official exchange rate remained undervalued by the

---

[4]   Chow (1990) found that domestic output growth has had a more significant impact on labour demand than export growth in the last three decades.

[5]   Taiwan has experienced a labour shortage in recent years. In 1992, 70,000 firms applied to import foreign labour.

[6]   By the end of 1991, Taiwan's central bank had accumulated a foreign reserve of nearly US$80 billion, ranked highest in the world.

Table 4.5 Real Exchange Rate, Inflation Rate, Wage Inflation Rate, and Unemployment Rate in Taiwan, 1980–1992

Year	Real rate (NT$/US$)[a]	Inflation rate (CPI) (%)	Wage inflation (manufacturing) (%)	Unemployment rate (%)
1980	36.93	19.01	0.19	1.23
1981	38.88	16.34	6.92	1.36
1982	40.09	−7.53	0.70	2.14
1983	40.27	12.85	7.59	2.71
1984	39.48	−0.02	−0.36	2.44
1985	39.85	−0.17	2.15	2.91
1986	35.50	0.71	7.12	2.66
1987	28.55	0.52	7.93	1.97
1988	28.17	1.28	7.46	1.69
1989	26.17	4.41	10.55	1.57
1990	27.11	4.13	13.50	1.67

Note: [a] spot rate = (buying + selling rate)/2
Source: *Taiwan Statistical Yearbook 1991*.

late 1970s. The persistence of a large trade surplus prompted the U.S., the main source of Taiwan's trade surplus, to press for the appreciation of the New Taiwan dollar (N.T. dollar). The Taiwan Government finally yielded to the pressure and allowed the N.T. dollar to appreciate against the U.S. dollar in the mid-1980s. From 1985 to 1990, the N.T. dollar appreciated by more than 35% (see Figure 4.1). This rapid appreciation is similar to what occurs with Dutch Disease.

Suffering from both the appreciation of the N.T. dollar and rising labour costs, Taiwan's firms have lost the competitive edge which they previously held. Many traditional labour-intensive exporting industries — such as textiles, clothing, umbrellas, and shoes, in which Taiwan held a significant share in the world market — became non-competitive. Agriculture and domestic consumption industries have also been threatened by potential import competition. An analysis based on international economics indicates that both the export and import substitution tradable sectors would have been hurt by the deterioration of terms of trade. Furthermore, Taiwan basically did not have a booming sector when sharp appreciation occurred. It would seem that the radical exchange rate shock should inevitably have hindered economic growth to a considerable extent. On the contrary, none of the miserable consequences of Dutch Disease were observed in this period. Taiwan remains one of the most dynamic economies in the world, its per capita GNP reach US$10,000 in 1992. Exports and imports expand steadily, and the inflation rate and unemployment rate have stayed at a long-lasting low level (see Table 4.5). If the rapid economic growth of the 1960s and the 1970s was the first economic miracle that Taiwan created, the continuous dynamism in the second half of the 1980s is Taiwan's second economic miracle. The key to understanding the second miracle is in the adaptability of Taiwan's industries and the possibility of Taiwan's labour-intensive industries migrating to China.

An Inter-industrial Structural Adjustment Model[7]

Structural adjustment in a prosperous economy is usually induced by technological innovation and/or economic growth. Expanding firms and industries rapidly absorb available resources from the lagging sectors. The withdrawal of resources from stagnant or declining firms and industries takes place more or less smoothly and is facilitated by the existence of ample employment opportunities in the growing firms and industries.

The structural adjustments in Taiwan in the mid-1980s were not led by technological innovation or economic growth, but instead were triggered by the exogenous exchange rate shock. The traditional labour-intensive industries lost their competitiveness in the world markets because of the appreciation of the exchange rate and the rapid increase in the wage rate. The production of low-tech commodities, which uses labour as the major input, was no longer profitable. Because of the lack of an expanding sector's absorbing capacity and because of the sudden loss of its original international markets, Taiwan's structural adjustments under such an exogenous shock were expected to be sluggish and prolonged, and to result in a considerably long and extended recession. Nevertheless, as noted, economic growth in Taiwan has not been hampered by the sudden currency

---

[7]   The model focuses on the effect of currency appreciation on a firm's choice of production technology. For other aspects of Dutch Disease, see Corden (1985). See Corden and Neary (1982) for resource movement and spending effect, Yokoyama (1989) for labour market adjustments, Wijinbergen (1984) for the learning effect, Enders and Herberg (1983) for foreign investment, and Fardmanesh (1991) for the long-run effect.

appreciation. The economy keeps booming. De-industrialization did occur in the labour-intensive export industries, but, simultaneously, pro-industrialization followed in the relatively high-tech, capital-intensive export industries.

Due to a shortage of natural resources and capital in the incipient stage of its development, a large part of Taiwan's exports were products of simple processing or assembly. Key parts and high-tech components, as well as sophisticated production machines, were imported.[8] The major input cost of labour-intensive low-tech production is labour wages. When firms switch to relatively capital-intensive, high-tech production, labour costs become smaller, and intermediate inputs become increasingly important in the cost structure. If the exchange rate appreciates, foreign technical knowledge and intermediate capital inputs become relatively cheap. The costs of shifting to high-tech and higher value-added products are reduced.

We will use simplified Leontif Production Functions to illustrate how exporting firms choose different factor intensities and technology levels under different exchange rates.[9]

The basic model is as follows: assuming labour and capital are inputs for production, firms could choose from two kinds of input intensities — labour-intensive or capital-intensive — to produce different outputs.

$$Q = A * min (bK, L)$$
$$Q'= A'* min (K, aL)$$

A and A' are technology coefficients. K and L are capital inputs and labour inputs respectively. Capital is assumed to be an imported intermediate input, and labour is the domestic labour force. Terms a and b are input ratio coefficients with the assumption that $1/b > a$, which means that the first production function is relatively more labour-intensive than the

---

[8]   An export processing zone is an extreme case of this. Firms in the zone assemble imported components from abroad and then export them. Labour is the only domestically produced input in the production process.

[9]   For the purpose of minimizing production costs in the case of a change in relative input prices, firms can either rely on input substitution in the same production function or choose a different production function that uses more of the relatively cheaper input. If the change in relative input prices is substantial, the adjustment within a production function may not be as relevant as choosing a different kind of production.

second one. A higher capital intensity represents a higher technical level and higher value-added production.[10]

Assume the world market is perfectly competitive. A small, open economy faces the world price as given, and no excess profits exist for a firm's export. If a firm minimizes costs in production,[11] the objective function is:

$$min\ erK + wL$$
$$s.t.\ Q = Q'$$

where e is the exchange rate, r is the foreign capital input price, w is the domestic labour wage rate. Because we assume capital to be an imported intermediate input, the price of capital depends on both the exchange rate and the foreign capital input price. The relative price of these two inputs is w/er. As shown in Figure 4.2, the factor price ratio determines the choice of technology.

Suppose the initial equilibrium is at point E, then, relatively cheap labour combined with a high exchange rate determines the adoption of labour-intensive production techniques. Given a fixed world price, when the exchange rate declines, the prices of imported intermediate capital inputs decrease. When the relative input price reaches a threshold, $er/w = b(a - 1)/a(b - 1)$, firms are indifferent to both technical levels. If the exchange rate continues to decline, the optimal response of the firm is to switch to the higher technical production function, which uses relatively less labour and more imported capital inputs. The new equilibrium is at E'. Similarly, the increase in labour wages has the same effect as appreciation. The movement from the initial equilibrium, E, to the new equilibrium, E', is expected to take a certain period of time and to result in a moderate recession and unemployment rate along the path toward the new equilibrium.

In an open economy like Taiwan's, industrial structure and international competitiveness are interrelated. To regain competitiveness, the industrial structure of the economy needs to adjust according to changing comparative advantages. However, the speed and the ease of adjustment

---

[10] For simplicity, we may assume both A and A' are equal to 1.

[11] According to duality theory, minimizing cost can be converted to maximizing profit.

**Figure 4.2 Optimal Production Strategy under
the Leontif Production Function**

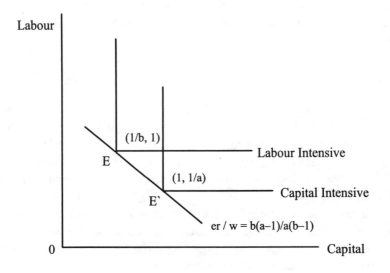

from one structure to another depend on other features of the economy, such as factor intensities and sizes of firms, the labour force's human capital, the economies of scale of industries, R&D, the condition of capital markets, and so on. Furthermore, the actual outcome of the restructuring also depends on how the Government intervenes in the adjustment process.

A marked change in the industrial structure within the manufacturing sector did take place after rapid appreciation. The Government practises a policy of promoting technical upgrading. The capital markets also function rather efficiently. Moreover, a predominant feature of Taiwan's economy is that there are a large number of small- and medium-sized enterprises;[12] they account for more than 95% of the total number of enterprises in Taiwan. The advantage of this firm size is its mobility and flexibility. Small firms also enhance the economy's adaptability for innovation and the vitality to dampen competition from abroad. The above factors may have contributed

---

[12] Small- and medium-sized enterprises hire less than 50 employees.

to the swift recovery of the competitiveness of enterprises in Taiwan. But these factors are not sufficient to cause a rapid restructuring without incurring a high unemployment rate. It takes time to re-train workers. Most equipment is industry-specific. Machines, tools, and other equipment used in labour-intensive industries become obsolete in capital-intensive industries. One essential factor in explaining Taiwan's swift industrial restructuring without a recession is that China provided cheap land and labour for the migration of Taiwan's labour- intensive industries.

Evidence for Industrial Restructuring and Out-migration in Taiwan

In this subsection, we will analyse the changes in the industrial structure in Taiwan in response to the exchange rate shock. By examining the changes in production and trade patterns, we may trace the route of the adjustment process.

Between 1986 and 1989, textiles, apparel, leather, and furniture declined 2.5%, 16%, 6.5% and 13%, respectively; whereas machinery grew 37.5%, and electrical machinery, appliances and precision instruments grew approximately 45% (*Taiwan Statistical Yearbook 1991*). These trends demonstrate de-industrialization and pro-industrialization in industries with different factor intensities. The changes in the trade patterns are represented by three prominent exporting sections in Taiwan: textiles,[13] footwear and umbrellas,[14] and machinery.[15] Between 1984 and 1989, the weight of textiles and textile articles in total exports decreased from 19.37% to 15.62%, whereas the weight of their import decreased from 5.04% to 3.74%. A similar trend occurred in the export of footwear and umbrellas. Their weight decreased from 9.03% to 6.75%. The above commodities are relatively labour-intensive, low-tech, light industrial products. However, if one looks at relatively capital-intensive, high-tech, manufacturing sectors —

---

[13] This section includes textiles and textile articles.

[14] Section 12 includes footwear, headgear, umbrellas, sun umbrellas, shades, walking-sticks, seat-sticks, whips, riding-crops and parts thereof, prepared feathers and articles made therewith, artificial flowers, articles of human hair.

[15] Section 16 includes machinery and mechanical appliances: electrical equipment, sound recorders and reproducers, televisions, image and sound recorders, and reproducers, and parts and accessories of such articles.

including machinery and mechanical appliances, televisions, sound systems and electrical equipment — one sees that their weight in total exports
and imports was increasing. Their weight in imports increased from
23.44% in 1984 to 28.58% in 1989, and their weight in exports from
24.71% to 33.95%. The changes in production structure and trade patterns
provide direct evidence of the economy's adjustment to higher technology
industries in response to currency appreciation.

Both Southeast Asia and China have Taiwan's previous comparative
advantage — relatively cheap labour. In the early 1980s, more firms chose
to move to Southeast Asia than to China because of the Taiwanese
government's prohibition of direct investment in China. However, as Bhagwati (1985, p. 131) noted, "Shifting production abroad is not particularly
meaningful since foreign firms are likely to have Hymer-like advantages,
and immigrant firms have instead such disadvantages in operating abroad."
However, Taiwan's industries do not have such disadvantages in China.
People in Taiwan and mainland China share the same culture, have the
same customs and speak the same language. The island of Taiwan is
separated from the mainland by the narrow Taiwan straits.[16] A considerable
number of Taiwanese still have relatives, or even immediate family members, in China. Ethnic, cultural, social, and language similarities, and especially the very evident complementary nature of the two economies,
outweigh the political disagreements between the two political entities.
After the exchange rate shock, most firms in traditional labour-intensive
industries chose first to migrate to the southeastern provinces of China and
then, gradually, to the rest of China. The possibility and ease of shifting the
production of labour-intensive industries to China helped Taiwan eschew a
recession that was expected to be the concomitant of appreciation.

IV. THE INTERDEPENDENCE OF MAINLAND CHINA AND TAIWAN

Since 1978, China has been engaged in far-reaching reforms of its traditional Soviet-type planning system. The reforms started with the replacement of the collective farming system with a household-based system —

---

[16] The average distance between the two coasts is less than 100 miles.

the household responsibility system. This institutional change in farming resulted in remarkable growth in agriculture between 1978 and 1984. The annual growth rate in grain production doubled from 2.4% in the years 1952–1978 to 4.8% in the years 1978–1984, and the growth rate of the whole agricultural sector almost tripled from 2.9% per year in the period 1952–1978 to 7.7% per year in the period 1978–1984 (Lin 1992). Prompted by the success of rural reform, in 1985 the Chinese government set in motion a series of industrial, commercial, fiscal, financial, and other reforms that gave greater scope to market forces. Consistent with the reforms of the domestic economy, China has also attempted an "open-door" policy toward international trade and the world economy.

The open-door policy was actively pursued with the establishment of the Special Economic Zones (SEZs) and the designation of specific cities as "open cities" to attract foreign investors. In the early 1980s, China established four SEZs. The policy was then extended to 14 coastal cities and several coastal economic development zones. By the early 1990s, 28 coastal cities, eight areas along the Yangtze River, and 13 border cities had been added to the list. According to official statistics, the GDP in five coastal provinces in east and southeast China registered an annual growth rate of 13.3% in the period 1985–1990 in contrast to 6.9% in the rest of the nation. The rapid growth in the coastal provinces has been fuelled by capital and, especially, technical knowledge from Hong Kong, Macau, and Taiwan. These overseas Chinese communities provide China with access to foreign markets, technology, and human as well as physical capital. Direct investment from overseas Chinese is widely regarded as an important factor behind the phenomenal growth of the coastal region (Wang and Mody 1993).

In the early 1980s, investments from Taiwan were mostly carried out indirectly through proxies in Hong Kong because of the Taiwanese Government's restrictions on direct investment in China. Therefore, the official statistics on Taiwanese investments in China has serious underestimations. As the Taiwanese Government's restrictions have relaxed,[17] more and more Taiwanese enterprises have invested directly in China. Taiwan was listed as the fourth largest foreign and overseas direct investor

---

[17] Taiwanese enterprises still have to report to and file with the authorities before directly investing in China (as of early 1993).

in China in 1990 and 1991. In 1992, Taiwan became the second largest overseas direct investor, second only to Hong Kong and Macau.

Taiwan's investment in China tends to concentrate on small-scale, medium-technology, labour-intensive manufacturing firms. For example, an average overseas investment in Guangdong Province in 1989 was US$168,000 for a Japanese investment, US$127,000 for a United States investment, and US$43,000 for investments from Hong Kong and Macau, whereas it was only US$28,000 for an investment from Taiwan (*Guangdong Statistical Yearbook 1949–1989*). The small size of Taiwanese investments is consistent with the dominant pattern of Taiwan's small and medium firm sizes.

The composition of China's exports shifted markedly from primitive goods (50.6% in 1985 to 28.5% in 1990) to manufactured goods (49.4% in 1985 to 74.4% in 1990) after 1985 (*China Statistical Yearbook 1991*). Meanwhile, China's share of world markets in textile fibres, travel goods, handbags, clothing, and accessories, which used to be the main exports of Taiwan, also jumped dramatically in the period. The influx of Taiwanese investors is consistent with the massive increase in China's export of miscellaneous light-industry products.[18] The reform of China's industrial and trade policies in 1985 coincided with the sudden appreciation of Taiwan's currency. This coincidence of events and the complementary nature of their economic structures naturally facilitated a close integration of these two economies. Taiwan is short of land and resources. After the exchange rate shock, Taiwan even lost its comparative advantage in labour-intensive industries. However, after decades of rapid economic growth, Taiwan has accumulated a huge stock of human and physical capital. The SEZs and coastal areas in China have proven to be a convenient location for the marriage between the abundant land, raw materials and manual labour of China and the capital, technology, and entrepreneurial skill of Taiwan.

The integration of the two economies constitutes a specific two-level co-operative mode. First, because of the currency appreciation and the wage rate escalation, Taiwan's enterprises shifted their uncompetitive low and medium technical production to China, using the cheap labour and inputs there to maintain their international competitiveness. Most of the

---

[18] The export of miscellaneous light-industry products increased from US$207 million in 1980 to US$11,625 million in 1990.

revenue created in China flows back to Taiwan. The industries remaining in Taiwan use the continuous profit stream from production in China to augment their funds to upgrade their production toward better techniques and higher value-added export goods. The investments flow out from Taiwan to China and then revenue flows in from China to Taiwan. The two-way flow consists of a closed-loop capital flow. Second, Taiwan imports part of its raw materials from China and combines them with higher production techniques and skilled labour to produce more competitive, higher value-added export commodities. China uses the imported capital and technology from Taiwan and combines them with her own cheap labour to produce labour-intensive commodities for export. Specialization in accordance with the different comparative advantages of the two economies reinforces the international competitiveness of both economies. The closed loop of capital flow combined with the two reversed open loops of raw materials and technical knowledge represent a model of vertical integration between the two economies. Successful integration has contributed to the rapid growth and smooth but speedy reform of both economies in the second half of the 1980s.

In the integration of the two ideologically different economies, Hong Kong has played a crucial role. Statistics show that Hong Kong is the most rapidly growing trading partner of Taiwan since 1985 (*Taiwan Statistical Yearbook 1991*).[19] Table 4.6 shows the crucial role that Hong Kong plays in international trade involving China. Hong Kong contributed to more than a quarter of China's total imports and exports in 1989 and 1990. Hong Kong owns the largest and deepest port, and most modern port facilities along the China coast. By the end of the 1980s, Hong Kong had become the transfer port for trade between China and Taiwan.[20] Hong Kong also provides a convenient centre for trade and financial negotiations between China and Taiwan. Indirect trade between Taiwan and China accelerated in the second half of the 1980s, at an average growth rate of 30–40% per year. It reached US$5.8 billion and US$7.3 billion in 1991 and 1992 respectively. Taiwan

---

[19] Total imports to Taiwan (c. i. f.) from Hong Kong increased from US$0.32 billion in 1985 to US$1.45 billion in 1990 and exports to Hong Kong (f. o. b.) from US$2.54 billion to US$8.56 billion, respectively.

[20] Almost all of the trade between Taiwan and China is still made through a third place, mostly through Hong Kong.

Table 4.6 Total Exports and Imports of China by Regions, Countries, and Areas (Unit = Billions of U.S. Dollars)

Year	Total		Export		Import	
	1989	1990	1989	1990	1989	1990
Total	111.67	115.43	52.53	62.09	59.14	53.34
Asia	67.86	73.55	37.17	44.55	30.69	29.00
Hong Kong	34.45	40.90	21.91	26.65	12.54	14.25

Source: *China Statistical Yearbook 1991.*

was the seventh largest trading partner of China in 1991, and the fifth in 1992. Meanwhile, Taiwan was China's fifth largest importer in 1990, and the fourth in 1991 and 1992, just following the United States, Japan, and Hong Kong.

In 1992, the volume of China's and Taiwan's international trade was, respectively, the world's eleventh and twelfth largest.[21] The combined trade volumes of China, Taiwan, and Hong Kong ranked as the world's fourth largest. In recent years, there have emerged numerous proposals for the construction of a regional organization for co-operation among the three economies. Hong Kong and Taiwan have become the major overseas investors in China since the early 1980s. Because of the diverse but complementary nature of China's, Taiwan's and Hong Kong's endowments with human capital, physical capital, knowledge of the international market, raw materials, and the labour force, the integration of these three economies will become a driving force for economic growth not only in the three economies but also in the neighbouring regions. The economic co-operation of a "giant dragon" and two "little dragons" will signal the

---

[21] According to the *United Nations Monthly Bulletin* of January 1993, trade volumes by country/area from January to September in 1992 were as follows: The United States, US$735.229 billion; Germany, US$617.978 billion; Japan, US$424.556 billion; China, US$109.867 billion; Hong Kong, US$167.154 billion; Asia, US$447.310 billion. The total trade volume of China, Taiwan, and Hong Kong constituted more than 65% of Asian trade and added up to be the fourth largest in the world. Note that a considerable amount of trade by the three economies is mutual trade among them.

coming of a new Pacific era. If the twenty-first century is to be the Chinese century, integration and co-operation among the three economies must be the corner-stone.

V. CONCLUSION

In this essay, we have examined economic development in China and Taiwan in the 1980s. The impact of Taiwan's sudden currency appreciation in 1985, under political pressure from the U.S., resembled that of "Dutch Disease" but without a resource boom. The currency appreciation made labour-intensive products, traditionally Taiwan's major exports, uncompetitive in international markets. To maintain Taiwan's international competitiveness, it has been necessary to upgrade Taiwan's economy to more capital-intensive, high-technology industries. This industrial restructuring was expected to cause a recession and a high unemployment rate for a period of time. However, such a slump did not occur in Taiwan. The adaptability of small- and medium-sized Taiwanese enterprises, well-functioning domestic capital markets, and the Government's policy of technical upgrading contributed much to the successful regaining of Taiwan's competitiveness. However, the low transaction cost of migrating labour-intensive industries to the coastal provinces of China is also one of the major explanations for Taiwan's averting a recession and a high unemployment rate along the path of industrial restructuring after the sudden shock of currency appreciation. The exodus of labour-intensive industries from Taiwan to China, however, also contributed much to China's success in reforming its economy from one with a structure moulded by an import-substitution, capital-intensive, industry-oriented development strategy to one with a structure based on the principle of comparative advantages. China, Taiwan, and Hong Kong are in different stages of economic development. The comparative advantages of the three economies are different and complementary to one another. From their experiences in the 1980s, we conclude that, if it is possible to overcome remaining ideological differences and continue the process of economic integration of the three economies, in the 1990s the three economies will continue to enjoy the high GDP rates of the 1980s. Moreover, by the end of the 1990s, the three economies will be ready to create a new Pacific era in the twenty-first century.

REFERENCES

Alvin, Rabushka (1987). *The New China: Comparative Economics Development in Mainland China, Taiwan, and Hong Kong.* Boulder, Colorado: Westview Press.

Ansari, I. Mohammed (1991). "An Econometric Model of Structural Change: A Case Study of Canada." *Applied Economics*, Vol. 24 (April), pp. 791–797.

Asian Development Bank (1991). *Key Indicators of Developing Asian and Pacific Countries.* Manila: Asian Development Bank.

Bhagwati, Jagdish N. (1985) "Structural Adjustment and International Factor Mobility: Some Issues." In *Structural Adjustment in Developed Open Economies*, edited by Karl Juhgenfelt and Douglas Hague, pp. 127–149. New York: St. Martin's Press.

Carlsson, Jerker, and Timothy M. Shaw, eds. (1988). *Newly Industrializing Countries and the Political Economy of South-South Relations.* New York: St. Martin's Press.

Chow, C. Y. Peter (1990). "Output Effect, Technology Change and Labour Absorption in Taiwan, 1952–1986." *Economic Development and Cultural Change*, Vol. 39(1) (October), pp. 77–88.

Corden, W. Max (1985). *Protection, Growth and Trade: Essays in International Economics.* New York: Blackwell.

Corden, W. M. and J. P. Neary (1982). "Booming Sector and De-industrialization in a Small Open Economy." *Economic Journal*, Vol. 92, pp. 825–848.

Council for Economic Planning and Development (1991). *Taiwan Statistical Yearbook 1991.* Taipei: Council for Economic Planning and Development.

Edwards, Sebastian (1986). "A Commodity Export Boom and the Real Exchange Rate: The Money-inflation Link." In *Natural Resources and the Macroeconomy*, edited by J. Peter Neary and Sweder van-Wijnbergen. Massachusetts: MIT Press.

Enders, Klaus and Horst Herberg (1983). "The Dutch Disease: Causes, Consequences, Cures and Calmatives." *Weltwirtschaftliches-Archiv.*, Vol. 119(3), pp. 473–497.

Fardmanesh, Mohsen (1991). "Dutch Disease Economics and the Oil Syndrome: An Empirical Study." *World Development*, Vol. 19 (June), pp. 711–717.

Findly, Ronald (1987). "Factor Proportions and Comparative Advantage in the Long Run." In *International Trade*, edited by J. Bhagwati. Massachusetts: MIT Press.

Frijns, M. Jean (1986). "The Dutch Disease in the Netherlands: Comment." In *Natural Resources and the Macroeconomy*, edited by J. Peter Neary and Sweder van-Wijnbergen. Massachusetts: MIT Press.

Fry, J. Maxwell (1990). "Taiwan's Current Account Surplus: Incipient Dutch Disease?" *International Economic Journal*, Vol. 4 (Autumn), pp. 93–112.

Jungenfelt, Karl, and Douglas Hague, eds. (1985). *Structural Adjustment in Developed Open Economies*. New York: St. Martin's Press, 1985.

Kremers, M. Jeroen (1986). "The Dutch Disease in the Netherlands." In *Natural Resources and the Macroeconomy*, edited by J. Peter Neary and Sweder van-Wijnbergen. Massachusetts: MIT Press.

Lau, J. Lawrence, ed. (1990). *Models of Development: A Comparative Study of Economic Growth in South Korea and Taiwan* (Revised and expanded edition). San Francisco: ICS Press.

Lin, J. Y. (1992). "Rural Reforms and Agricultural Growth in China." *American Economic Review*, Vol. 82 (March), pp. 34–51.

Rivera-Batiz, A. Luis, and Paul M. Romer (1991). "Economic Integration and Endogenous Growth." *The Quarterly Journal of Economics*, Vol. 106 (May), pp. 531–555.

Sato, Ryuzo, and Takashi Negishi, eds. (1989). *Development in Japanese Economics*. New York: Academic Press.

Scitovsky, Tibor (1990). "Economic Development in Taiwan and South Korea, 1965–1981." In *Models of Development: A Comparative Study of Economic Growth in South Korea and Taiwan*, edited by J. Lawrence Lau (Revised and expanded edition). San Francisco: ICS Press.

State Statistical Bureau (1990). *Guangdong Statistical Yearbook 1949–1989*. Beijing: China Statistical Press.

———— (1991). *China Statistical Yearbook 1991*. Beijing: China Statistical Press.

Van-Wijnbergen, J. Sweder (1984). "The 'Dutch Disease': A Disease after All?" *Economic Journal*, Vol. 94 (March), pp. 41–55.

Wang, Fang-Yi, and Ashoka Mody (1993). "Explaining Rapid Growth in Chinese Coastal Provinces: Evidence from Industry Level Data, 1985–89." Working Paper, World Bank, February.

World Bank (1982). *World Development Report, 1982*. Oxford: Oxford University Press.

Yokoyama, Hisashi (1989). "Export-led Industrialization and the Dutch Disease." *Developing Economics*, Vol. 27 (December), pp. 427–445.

CHAPTER 5

Forecasting Practices and Performance in Hong Kong Business Firms

Chou Win-lin
The Chinese University of Hong Kong, Hong Kong

I. INTRODUCTION

The purpose of this essay is to examine how business firms in Hong Kong prepare their forecasts, what methods they prefer, and the accuracy of their predictions. The essay consists of two parts. The first part of the essay reports the results of a survey, which was conducted in April 1990, to determine how a forecast is prepared and used for business planning and decision-making in Hong Kong; which forecasting techniques have been most commonly used by firms in Hong Kong; how these methods are utilized in preparing a forecast; and whether the forecasters in Hong Kong keep records of forecasting performance.

Many economists believe that people make the best economic forecasts they can, given the available information. This is the rational expectations hypothesis. In the second part of the essay we test whether survey forecasts for Hong Kong's gross domestic product and its components, and for inflation, by two of the most experienced forecasters in Hong Kong, are rational.

A number of surveys on forecasting practices have been carried out in the United States to determine forecasting technique usage and practice in business, and the results can be found in Dalrymple (1987), Huss (1987), Mentzer and Cox (1984), and others. But this is the first time this kind of survey has been done in Hong Kong. Though it would be desirable to compare our results with those surveys conducted in neighbouring countries such as Singapore, Taiwan, or South Korea, unfortunately no similar survey results were available. Our survey results will be compared with those summarized in Dalrymple's study on sales forecasting practices in the United States. For ease of comparison between our findings and those in Dalrymple (1987), we have included in our questionnaire such issues as forecasting needs, techniques used, forecast performance and uses, as addressed in Dalrymple's survey. The remainder of this essay discusses the results of this survey and assesses the current state of economic forecasting in Hong Kong.

II. METHODOLOGY

The survey was carried out by mail questionnaire.[1] Forty-nine copies of the three-page questionnaire were sent to large private enterprises, academic and research institutions, and government officials who are engaged in forecasting the course of the Hong Kong economy. The private enterprises comprised 33 companies listed on the Hang Seng Index of share prices, and 10 large foreign companies operating in Hong Kong. The selection of the sample companies was biased towards large companies in view of the fact that large-size firms are better capable of forecasting than smaller ones.

There were 16 usable questionnaires returned, a response rate of 33%. The respondents were in various parts of the economy, including banking and finance, television and broadcasting, and public utilities (e.g. gas, electricity, telecommunications, etc.). Responses were also received from the Government and academic sectors.

III. RESULTS

The survey participants were asked questions in the following areas:

(a) the importance of forecasting;
(b) the techniques used to forecast;
(c) the usage of computer software in forecasting;
(d) the criteria used to evaluate forecasts; and
(e) forecast uses.

---

[1] Copies of the questionnaire can be obtained from the author.

The remainder of this section discusses the participants' responses to these questions.

Importance of Forecasting

One of the important purposes of forecasting is to enable decision-makers and policy-makers to understand the uncertainties of the future. All respondents were asked about the importance of forecasting in three typical forecasting situations, namely, business strategies, macroeconomic environments, and product demand. The respondent firms felt forecasts for macroeconomic environments and product demand (56.3% and 56.3% respectively) were "very important". Of the 16 firms which responded, all of them indicated that forecasts for macroeconomic environments were "important or very important," and forecasts for product demand were considered "important or very important" by 75%.

A related question was how firms obtain their forecasts. We found that most companies used an internal study approach to make forecasts for assessing business strategies and product demand. A high percentage of respondents obtained their forecasts for macroeconomic environments through mass media. The results also show that 31.3% of the firms purchased their forecasts from outside consultants. And 75% of respondents reported that they used more than one source to obtain forecasts.

Respondents were asked how frequently they prepared their forecasts. The results show that forecasts were most often prepared annually. And most of these forecasts concentrated on assessing the macroeconomic environment.

Respondent firms were asked whether their forecasting needs were satisfied and if so to what extent they were satisfied. We found that, on average, more than 75% of their overall needs were satisfied. The degree of satisfaction with forecasts for product demand was the highest (81%), followed by forecasts for assessing business strategies (78.8%), and macroeconomic environments (76.3%). We also found that the internal study approach did very well in satisfying forecasting needs; there is a positive effect of internal study on the degree of satisfaction.

Forecasting Techniques

One of the most interesting survey areas may be that of forecasting methods used in Hong Kong. Business firms were asked to indicate the usage of 13 forecasting techniques. They were also asked to state the number of key variables used often in forecasting. The forecasting methods considered in our survey are similar to those included in Dalrymple (1987).

The jury of executive opinion approach was the most frequently used subjective forecasting procedure in our survey. About 63% of firms reported that they used this approach in forecasting. These results agree with findings reported by Dalrymple (1987).

The most popular extrapolation technique in Hong Kong was the percentage rate of change approach, with a usage rate of 56.3%. But this technique, together with the unit rate of change and line extension methods, ranked fourth in usage of all the techniques in Dalrymple's survey.

The moving average and leading indicators were the second most frequently used extrapolation procedures in this survey, each with a usage rate of 50%. But in the U.S. survey, the preference for leading indicators was greater than for the moving average.

Exponential smoothing, line extension, and unit rate of change were less popular extrapolation procedures in Hong Kong. Their relative rankings were similar to those found in the U.S. survey. Despite the fact that the exponential smoothing approach generally produces more accurate forecasts than the moving average technique, twice as many respondents reported the use of moving average (50%) than reported the use of exponential smoothing (25%). The results suggested that the popularity of the moving average approach may be based on familiarity rather than on ability to perform. The situations are the same as those reported in Dalrymple's study.

While the naïve approach was found to be the most popular extrapolation forecasting technique by the U.S. survey, with a usage rate of 50.7%, it was hardly used by the Hong Kong business firms. Only one respondent reported that it used the naïve method in preparing its quarterly forecasts. One possible reason for its low usage rate is that forecasters with private enterprises in Hong Kong are not familiar or are unimpressed with the naïve method.

Quantitative forecasting methods have historically required access to a mainframe computer and the use of software that requires subscription and maintenance. The constraints of mainframe requirements have prevented the wide use of quantitative techniques by private enterprises, especially smaller businesses. But with the rapid development of microcomputer technology, business firms can now engage in forecasting without having to purchase a mainframe computer. In recent decades, considerable progress has been made in the application of quantitative forecasting methods in both the academic and practical fields in Hong Kong.

Our survey results showed that multiple regression analysis was the most popular quantitative technique, with a 56.3% usage rate. This result agrees with that reported in Dalrymple's study, which claimed that multiple regression analysis was more widely used by U.S. firms than any other quantitative method.

The Box-Jenkins technique and simple regression analysis, each with a usage rate of 37.5%, were equally preferred by firms in Hong Kong. In contrast, the Dalrymple study found the use of the Box-Jenkins time series analysis by U.S. companies to be the lowest (8.9%) of all the techniques mentioned.

Econometric models were used by about 44% of responding firms, a figure which exceeded that for the use of Box-Jenkins and simple regression. Firms using econometric models were asked about the number of key variables used often in their forecasting, and the nature of their econometric models. Six (or 37.5%) firms responded to the question. The number of key variables frequently used was found to range from 2 to 20. All econometric models were basically of a Keynesian type; and none incorporated the supply side.

The areas of combining forecasts, and the seasonal adjustment of economic time series have received a lot of attention in recent years (see Clemen 1989; Bell and Hillmer 1984). For the combination of forecasts, our survey shows that 37.5% of the respondents usually or frequently used this method. Fifty per cent of the firms did not respond to this question. One reason for the low response rate may be that the combining technique was relatively new to business forecasters in Hong Kong; most of them were unfamiliar with the method.

On the other hand, the use of the seasonal adjustment technique was more popular in Hong Kong, compared with the combined forecasts approach. Eight (or 50%) firms reported that they usually or frequently used seasonally adjusted forecasts.

Computer Usage

Firms were asked to provide information on the use of computer software in economic forecasting. The results of our survey show that in Hong Kong, the use of computer programmes was quite different from that in the United States. More than 50% of the Hong Kong forecasters purchased a software package to do the forecast. The proportion of firms that had developed their own computer programmes for use in forecasting was slightly more than 40%. In contrast, a majority of the U.S. companies (71%) had developed computer programmes for use in sales forecasting internally. No respondent in Hong Kong bought computer forecasting programmes from outside, but 8% of the U.S. survey firms reported that their computer forecasting software was provided by outside consultants.

As in Dalrymple's findings, no single computer software package dominates the Hong Kong forecasting software market. Eight software packages suitable for forecasting, plus several general purpose software packages such as Lotus 123, Symphony, and dBASE were mentioned in our survey responses, with the SAS (Statistical Analysis System) package being mentioned seven times.

Forecasting Accuracy

Since accuracy analysis plays an important role in selecting and testing forecasting techniques, we expected that forecasters in Hong Kong would be interested in evaluating how accurate their historical forecasts have been. However, to our surprise, very few firms in Hong Kong did accuracy analysis for their historical forecasts. Only two of the respondents said they evaluated forecast performance in terms of mean absolute percentage error.

Further, business firms were asked to consider improving their forecast performance; they were provided with three alternatives, including the use of more sophisticated techniques, improving personnel ability, and the use of a more powerful software package. They were also encouraged to give other suggestions. Twelve firms responded to this question. The results show that improving personnel ability to forecast was considered the most important approach in improving forecast performance.

Forecast Uses

A major role of forecasting is to help managers in assessing various future alternatives. Thus, it is interesting to find out how forecasting relates to business planning and decision-making in Hong Kong. Firms were asked to rank the importance of forecasting in the decision-making process. Fourteen company analysts and managers responded to this question. The average score was 3.6 on a 5-point scale, suggesting that forecasting is very useful for evaluating various planning and decision-making problems.

IV. PERFORMANCE OF ECONOMETRIC FORECASTS FOR HONG KONG

In Hong Kong, the main organizations that use econometric models to forecast the behaviour of the economy include the Hong Kong Government, the Department of Economics of The Chinese University of Hong Kong (CUHK), the Hang Seng Bank Ltd. (HSB), and the Hongkong and Shanghai Banking Corporation. This survey collected forecast series, for a number of economic variables, made by three of these forecasters to see how they have performed. The three forecasters were the Hong Kong Government (HKG), the Department of Economics of The Chinese University of Hong Kong, and the Hang Seng Bank Ltd. These organizations reflect different backgrounds: CUHK is an academic economic modeller, while HSB is a business forecaster, and HKG provides a government perspective.

Evaluation of Forecasts

In Table 5.1 we use the mean absolute deviation between the actual growth and forecast growth[2] of six variables for the period 1984–1990 to appraise the forecasters' performance. The actual changes used to compute the errors are based on preliminary[3] estimates published in the annual budget speech. Results in Table 5.1 show that the Government model, on average, produced the best forecasts for the inflation rate (PC) and total investment (CF) over the last seven years. The model of the Department of Economics at The Chinese University of Hong Kong performed best in

---

2   The growth rates are based on one-year-ahead forecasts which were made late in the year *t–1* or very early in the target year *t*. The Hong Kong Government's forecasts were released in late February/early March each year.

3   As suggested in Keane and Runkle (1990), forecasts should be compared with initial rather than revised data.

Table 5.1 Performance of Econometric Forecasts for Hong Kong

Variables Predicted	CUHK[a]	HKG[a]	HSB[a]
	Mean absolute error[b]		
Gross Domestic Product (GDP)	3.87	4.01	4.04
Private Consumption Expenditure (CP)	2.03	2.46	2.51
Gross Fixed Investment (CF)	5.17	4.41	5.06
Total Exports of Goods (EC)	11.26	11.51	11.40
Total Imports of Goods (MC)	12.03	11.96	11.76
Consumer Prices (PC)	2.08	1.53	1.73

Notes: [a] CUHK = The Chinese University of Hong Kong; HKG = Hong Kong
           Government; HSB = Hang Seng Bank.
           [b] 7-year mean absolute error between the actual and predicted percentage
           changes for the period 1984–1990.

Sources: Department of Economics, The Chinese University of Hong Kong, *Outlook
          for the Hong Kong Economy* (mimeo), various issues; Hang Seng Bank
          Limited, *Economic Quarterly*, and *Economic Monthly*, various issues; Hong
          Kong Government, *Economic Prospects*, various issues.

predicting private consumption expenditure (CP), total exports of goods
(EC), and the gross domestic product (GDP). And the Hang Seng Bank
did best in forecasting the total imports of goods (MC). All models
seemed unable to predict the sharp increases in exports and imports in
1986 and 1987.

As the forecasters' errors have different degrees of variability, it may
be inappropriate to use average errors to evaluate forecasts. The approach
proposed in Stekler (1987), which examines score statistics, is therefore
used to determine whether some forecasters, on average, are better than
others. For each year and each variable, the three forecasters are ranked
according to their accuracy in predicting that variable. For each variable, a
score corresponding to their place in the ranking is then assigned, with the
top forecaster receiving a score of one; the last is assigned a score of three.
The process of ranking the forecasters is repeated for each of the seven
years under consideration. For each variable, the forecaster's seven scores
are summed. If all forecasters had equal forecasting ability, their scores
over the years would have the same expected value. The chi-square (χ^2)
goodness-of-fit test statistic may be used to test the hypothesis that all
forecasters have equal mean scores. Our test results show that for all six
variables, the calculated values of χ^2 are smaller than the critical 1% value.

Consequently, the hypothesis that all forecasters have equal (mean) ability is accepted, suggesting the differences in forecasting ability are insignificant. We conclude that, among the three forecasters, no single forecaster always outperforms other forecasters. Some forecasters that were good in one year may not have performed well in other years.

Tests of Rationality

From the results presented in Table 5.1, it is clear that some variables are easier to forecast than others. The trade variables are regarded as being more difficult to forecast than a variable such as private consumption expenditure which changes relatively slowly. It is necessary to take an alternative approach in defining a forecast as the best forecast that can be made in the circumstances. This is often referred to as the rational expectations forecast. It is defined as a prediction from economic theory using all the relevant information that is available at the time the forecast is made.

Of the three forecasters, the Hong Kong Government and The Chinese University of Hong Kong are the more experienced, and have longer forecast records, which began in 1978, enabling us to examine whether their *ex ante* forecasts were rational. The tests of rationality have been broken down into two basic types: the first is a test of unbiasedness, and the second is an efficiency test.

Because of the lack of a quarterly series on GDP,[4] forecasters in Hong Kong make their predictions with annual data. Unlike most research which uses quarterly forecasts in testing for rationality, this essay uses individual data on annual forecasts to test the rational expectations hypothesis. The two forecasters' one-year-ahead forecasts of variables GDP, CP, CF, EC, MC, and PC were tested.

Let A and P represent realized and predicted values of a given variable, respectively. Denotes $_tP_{i,t+k}$ a k-step ahead prediction made at time t by forecaster i; A_{t+k} represents the realized value[5] of the variable at time $t+k$. To test for unbiasedness, we run the regression:

---

[4] Quarterly GDP series were not available at the time the research was done. Their first release was made in August 1991 by the Hong Kong Government Census and Statistics Department.

[5] We use unrevised data to test the rationality of forecasts.

$$A_{t+k} = \alpha_0 + \alpha_1 \, _tP_{i,t+k} + u_{it,k} \cdots\cdots\cdots\cdots\cdots\cdots\cdots\cdots\cdots\cdots\cdots\cdots\cdots \quad (1)$$

where $u_{it,k} = A_{t+k} - {}_tP_{i,t+k}$. Unbiasedness requires that the coefficients in equation (1) may be restricted to $\alpha_0 = 0$, and $\alpha_1 = 1$.

Table 5.2 presents the estimation results of Equation (1) by using the technique of ordinary least squares (OLS). The joint null hypothesis that $\alpha_0 = 0$ and $\alpha_1 = 1$ is accepted for all regressions except the forecasts of trade variables, EC and MC. For EC and MC, as the values of α_0 deviate

Table 5.2 Tests for Unbiasedness

HKG Forecasts				CUHK Forecasts			
α_0	α_1	F^a	DW^b	α_0	α_1	F^a	DW^b
Gross Domestic Product (GDP)							
6.5388	0.1669	0.9517	1.96^o	7.7183	−0.0095	1.7824	1.871^o
(5.1588)	(0.7535)	(0.4184)		(4.1064)	(0.5459)	(0.2177)	
Private Consumption (CP)							
4.0661	0.5215	0.5695	2.147^o	1.3654	0.8057	0.1536	2.509^o
(4.0966)	(0.5634)	(0.5831)		(3.0651)	(0.3696)	(0.8596)	
Gross Domestic Fixed Capital Formation (CF)							
0.1644	0.8336	0.1644	1.172^x	1.7213	0.7616	0.0767	1.019^x
(5.3284)	(0.5591)	(0.8507)		(5.0625)	(0.6086)	(0.9267)	
Total Exports of Goods (EC)							
25.2646	−0.9313	5.8271	1.676^o	22.0010	−0.5487	5.7139	1.410^o
(7.8949)	(0.7310)	(0.0210)		(6.5424)	(0.5262)	(0.0221)	
Total Imports of Goods (MC)							
24.9953	−0.9311	3.7188	1.409^o	17.1809	−0.2067	3.0735	1.219^x
(9.4550)	(0.8203)	(0.0623)		(6.9310)	(0.5270)	(0.0911)	
Consumer Prices (PC)							
−2.8695	1.4393	2.0586	1.240^x	−1.0193	1.1194	0.1335	1.513^o
(2.1967)	(0.2591)	(0.1783)		(2.1557)	(0.2320)	(0.8766)	

Notes: Sample period: 1978 to 1989. The standard errors are shown in parentheses.

   [a] F ratios for H_0: $\alpha_0 = 0$, $\alpha_1 = 1$. Significance levels are given under F values.

   [b] o, means null hypothesis of no first-order auto-correlation in the u's is accepted at the 5% significance level; and x, result indeterminate. The 5% significance points of d_l and d_u for $n = 12$ and $k = 1$ are 0.971 and 1.331, respectively.

significantly from 0 and the values of α_1 from unity. The incidence of bias seems to be systematically related to the relative accuracy of the forecasts.

For EC and MC, the forecasts appear to be highly biased and are also relatively less accurate. Thus bias implies particularly large errors.

The Durbin-Watson (*DW*) statistics listed in Table 5.2 suggest that the residuals from the regressions of actual on predicted values for the six variables are essentially free of first-order auto correlations when 5% significance levels are used.

For GDP, CP, CF, and PC, we cannot reject unbiasedness, and we have to test the further implication of rational expectations: that the forecasts are efficient. A test of efficiency can be performed for these variables by including some additional variable $X_{i,t}$ in Equation (1) and running the regression:

$$A_{t+k} = \alpha_0 + \alpha_1 \, _tP_{i,t+k} + \alpha_2 X_{i,t} + u_{it,k} \quad \ldots\ldots\ldots\ldots\ldots\ldots\ldots\ldots \quad (2)$$

where $X_{i,t}$ is any variable in forecaster i's information at time t. Efficiency requires that any variable known at time t or before be orthogonal to $u_{it,k}$; that is, that $\alpha_0 = 0$, $\alpha_1 = 1$, and $\alpha_2 = 0$. Table 5.3 gives the results of our efficiency tests. For GDP, CP, CF, and PC, the variables that are shown not to improve the forecasts are: the lagged actual values and the lagged values of the forecaster's error.

Two variables that presumably had a large impact on Hong Kong's GDP, its major components, and the price level during the sample period, are the foreign demand and the competitiveness of Hong Kong's exports in the world market. Table 5.4 examines whether forecasters fully adjusted their predictions to changes in foreign demand and competitiveness. Table 5.4 also presents regressions that include the previous lagged values of the USGNP (USGNP$_{-1}$, USGNP$_{-2}$) and the trade-weighted effective exchange rate index (EX$_{-1}$, EX$_{-2}$) as regressors. The test of efficiency is not rejected in most of the regressions except in the case of total exports of goods. That is, individual forecasts for GDP, private consumption, private investment, total imports of goods, and inflation could not be improved by using the known past values of the USGNP or exchange rates in a more efficient manner.

In addition, a set of joint tests of forecast rationality using the variables from Tables 5.2, 5.3, and 5.4 is also performed. For example, in a joint test for GDP forecasts, the regressors include a constant, the one-step-ahead forecast, the lagged GDP level, the lagged forecast errors, and the lagged

Table 5.3 Tests for Efficiency

Forecaster	α_0	a_1	α_2	F^a	Regressor of α_2
	Gross Domestic Product (GDP)				
HKG	8.1868	−0.1333	0.0695	0.6041	lagged forecast errors
	(6.7019)	(1.0589)	(0.3742)	(0.6305)	
	7.6243	0.0095	−0.0307	0.5917	lagged GDP
	(6.1721)	(1.1822)	(0.4860)	(0.6377)	
CUHK	13.5929	−0.9570	0.2359	1.3995	lagged forecast errors
	(6.7200)	(1.0114)	(0.3317)	(0.3120)	
	11.7003	−0.8837	0.2031	1.2469	lagged GDP
	(6.0851)	(1.1257)	(0.4703)	(0.3553)	
	Private Consumption (CP)				
HKG	6.8927	0.0427	−0.1101	1.3940	lagged forecast errors
	(4.2898)	(0.6853)	(0.3897)	(0.3135)	
	7.2785	0.1907	−0.1962	1.4797	lagged CP
	(3.7214)	(0.7547)	(0.3920)	(0.2918)	
CUHK	5.6152	0.2112	−0.1942	0.9137	lagged forecast errors
	(4.8745)	(0.6771)	(0.3608)	(0.4764)	
	6.2121	0.3502	−0.2196	0.9680	lagged CP
	(4.5513)	(0.7600)	(0.3407)	(0.4538)	
	Gross Domestic Fixed Capital Formation (CF)				
HKG	6.1238	0.1499	0.6602	1.4790	lagged forecast errors
	(5.6835)	(0.6288)	(0.3433)	(0.2919)	
	3.2950	−0.2707	0.6586	1.3065	lagged CF
	(5.2876)	(0.7830)	(0.3676)	(0.3376)	
CUHK	8.6007	−0.3251	0.8669	2.6246	lagged forecast errors
	(4.6915)	(0.6248)	(0.3233)	(0.1224)	
	2.9056	−0.2290	0.6322	1.3853	lagged CF
	(4.6891)	(0.7351)	(0.3317)	(0.3158)	
	Total Exports of Goods (EC)				
HKG	32.7030	−1.9094	0.5249	6.2394	lagged forecast errors
	(8.0595)	(0.7900)	(0.2574)	(0.0172)	
	26.9497	−1.7723	0.4765	4.6450	lagged EC
	(8.5443)	(0.8883)	(0.3384)	(0.0366)	
CUHK	24.4946	−1.0114	0.4745	4.8023	lagged forecast errors
	(6.5984)	(0.5933)	(0.3029)	(0.0338)	
	20.0764	−1.2303	0.6037	4.6749	lagged EC
	(6.6188)	(0.6884)	(0.4003)	(0.0360)	

Table 5.3 Tests for Efficiency (Cont'd)

Forecaster	α_0	a_1	α_2	F^a	Regressor of α_2
	Total Imports of Goods (MC)				
HKG	30.7448	−1.7349	0.6067	4.6487	lagged forecast errors
	(8.7799)	(0.7968)	(0.2544)	(0.0365)	
	22.2077	−1.4149	0.5088	2.9705	lagged MC
	(9.3880)	(0.8783)	(0.3189)	(0.0970)	
CUHK	22.5756	−0.9926	0.6921	4.7217	lagged forecast errors
	(6.2587)	(0.5480)	(0.3097)	(0.0352)	
	16.8099	−1.4177	0.9088	5.0471	lagged MC
	(5.7321)	(0.6477)	(0.3851)	(0.0299)	
	Consumer Prices (PC)				
HKG	−1.4165	1.2247	0.3379	1.4428	lagged forecast errors
	(5.4016)	(0.6815)	(0.6805)	(0.3009)	
	−5.9384	2.2594	−0.4559	2.1849	lagged PC
	(2.9137)	(0.6190)	(0.3460)	(0.1676)	
CUHK	−0.6727	1.1185	0.0478	0.2192	lagged forecast errors
	(2.9289)	(0.3178)	(0.4551)	(0.8804)	
	−2.1301	1.9213	−0.6392	1.4300	lagged PC
	(1.8823)	(0.4647)	(0.3481)	(0.3041)	

Notes: Sample period: 1978 to 1989. The standard errors are shown in parentheses.
 [a] F ratios for H_0: $\alpha_0 = 0$, $\alpha_1 = 1$, $\alpha_2 = 0$. Significance levels are given under F values.

USGNP. The tests are rejected for the forecasts of total exports and total imports of goods.

Taking the results of the tests together, the forecasts for gross domestic product, consumer expenditure, gross domestic fixed capital formation, and inflation satisfy the requirements of unbiasedness and efficiency, whereas the forecasts for exports and imports of goods fail all tests.

V. CONCLUSIONS AND RECOMMENDATIONS

The survey results described in this essay support a number of conclusions.

(a) The respondents felt forecasting is important for assessing various planning and decision-making situations. This survey showed that a large number of firms prepare one-year forecasts. And for one-year forecasts, there is a strong preference for a subjective

Table 5.4 Further Tests for Efficiency

Forecaster	α_0	α_1	α_2	F^a	Regressor of α_2
	Gross Domestic Product (GDP)				
HKG	22.2672	−0.2241	−0.0045	0.8588	USGNP$_{-1}$
	(19.1961)	(0.8914)	(0.0053)	(0.4967)	
	22.9850	−0.2812	−0.0048	0.8102	USGNP$_{-2}$
	(21.8270)	(0.9614)	(0.0061)	(0.5195)	
CUHK	23.9649	−0.2846	−0.0049	1.4916	USGNP$_{-1}$
	(17.3119)	(0.6173)	(0.0051)	(0.2817)	
	11.7003	−0.3051	−0.0051	1.4301	USGNP$_{-2}$
	(18.8922)	(0.6432)	(0.0057)	(0.2971)	
HKG	3.4378	−0.4194	9.0049	0.8054	EX$_{-1}$
	(6.6356)	(1.0835)	(11.7172)	(0.5219)	
	0.2827	−0.6403	14.1047	1.6978	EX$_{-2}$
	(6.0216)	(0.8420)	(8.3698)	(0.2364)	
CUHK	3.1322	−0.4027	9.5301	1.4439	EX$_{-1}$
	(6.5234)	(0.6999)	(10.4722)	(0.2936)	
	−0.3600	−0.5942	14.8961	2.6433	EX$_{-2}$
	(5.6798)	(0.5805)	(7.9843)	(0.1130)	
	Private Consumption (CP)				
HKG	20.3052	0.2858	−0.0050	0.8400	USGNP$_{-1}$
	(14.5854)	(0.5902)	(0.0043)	(0.5054)	
	19.9855	0.2262	−0.0049	0.6906	USGNP$_{-2}$
	(16.9281)	(0.6420)	(0.0050)	(0.5804)	
CUHK	9.6644	0.6754	−0.0025	0.2120	USGNP$_{-1}$
	(14.4068)	(0.4413)	(0.0042)	(0.8856)	
	6.3849	0.7210	−0.0015	0.1269	USGNP$_{-2}$
	(16.1095)	(0.4702)	(0.0048)	(0.9418)	
HKG	−1.9175	0.0646	11.8033	1.0785	EX$_{-1}$
	(5.7724)	(0.6278)	(8.3788)	(0.4062)	
	−2.7481	0.0192	12.5283	1.4499	EX$_{-2}$
	(5.4369)	(0.5911)	(7.2516)	(0.2921)	
CUHK	−0.9173	0.6130	4.8872	0.1885	EX$_{-1}$
	(5.3575)	(0.5288)	(9.2284)	(0.9016)	
	−2.1584	0.5020	7.1769	0.3573	EX$_{-2}$
	(5.0698)	(0.5092)	(8.1694)	(0.7853)	

Table 5.4 **Further Tests for Efficiency** (Cont'd)

Forecaster	α_0	α_1	α_2	F^a	Regressor of α_2
	Gross Domestic Fixed Capital Formation (CF)				
HKG	7.1379	0.7602	−0.0022	0.1102	USGNP$_{-1}$
	(38.5010)	(0.7118)	(0.0119)	(0.9520)	
	19.4930	0.6457	−0.0063	0.1867	USGNP$_{-2}$
	(38.6239)	(0.6898)	(0.0124)	(0.9028)	
CUHK	19.7812	0.6327	−0.0059	0.1496	USGNP$_{-1}$
	(33.0710)	(0.6726)	(0.0106)	(0.9274)	
	28.3411	0.5629	−0.0089	0.2528	USGNP$_{-2}$
	(34.4487)	(0.6709)	(0.0114)	(0.8575)	
HKG	−11.3129	0.3600	19.8546	0.3095	EX$_{-1}$
	(15.6292)	(0.8316)	(25.3720)	(0.8182)	
	−17.8560	0.1744	28.5694	0.8391	EX$_{-2}$
	(13.2840)	(0.6946)	(19.4817)	(0.5059)	
CUHK	−13.0155	0.3748	22.4992	0.4780	EX$_{-1}$
	(13.9685)	(0.6912)	(19.9168)	(0.7055)	
	−18.2150	0.2597	28.5290	1.0353	EX$_{-2}$
	(12.5488)	(0.6300)	(16.6869)	(0.4225)	
	Total Exports of Goods (EC)				
HKG	−11.4147	−1.3279	0.0140	4.9819	USGNP$_{-1}$
	(26.6459)	(6.7481)	(0.0097)	(0.0263)	
	−10.2380	−1.2115	0.0135	4.7434	USGNP$_{-2}$
	(28.0647)	(0.7373)	(0.0103)	(0.0300)	
CUHK	−30.0488	−1.1870	0.0203	6.0419	USGNP$_{-1}$
	(27.8248)	(0.5745)	(0.0106)	(0.0154)	
	−27.6990	−1.0611	0.0196	5.6461	USGNP$_{-2}$
	(28.8255)	(0.5598)	(0.0111)	(0.0187)	
HKG	53.8624	−1.3863	−30.7861	5.9736	EX$_{-1}$
	(16.9831)	(0.7001)	(16.6178)	(0.0159)	
	51.3182	−1.5360	−24.1032	4.7330	EX$_{-2}$
	(21.3156)	(0.8440)	(18.4141)	(0.0301)	
CUHK	48.7721	−0.8661	−29.7665	5.5073	EX$_{-1}$
	(16.7978)	(0.5168)	(17.4475)	(0.0200)	
	39.3822	−0.8106	−17.4616	4.0608	EX$_{-2}$
	(19.6082)	(0.5980)	(18.5566)	(0.0443)	

Table 5.4 Further Tests for Efficiency (Cont'd)

Forecaster	α_0	α_1	α_2	F^a	Regressor of α_2
			Total Imports of Goods (MC)		
HKG	−0.9210	−1.1438	0.0097	2.7485	USGNP$_{-1}$
	(28.9558)	(0.8546)	(0.0102)	(0.1047)	
	3.4902	−1.0303	0.0080	2.5358	USGNP$_{-2}$
	(31.0441)	(0.8512)	(0.0109)	(0.1222)	
CUHK	−9.1060	−0.4355	0.0100	2.2292	USGNP$_{-1}$
	(31.8626)	(0.5992)	(0.0118)	(0.1541)	
	−5.9156	−0.3675	0.0088	2.1198	USGNP$_{-2}$
	(33.0478)	(0.5852)	(0.0124)	(0.1679)	
HKG	35.7404	−1.0206	−12.5394	2.4896	EX$_{-1}$
	(18.7102)	(0.8542)	(18.6533)	(0.1265)	
	32.4984	−1.0663	−7.2848	2.3167	EX$_{-2}$
	(21.5066)	(0.9239)	(18.5457)	(0.1441)	
CUHK	26.3239	−0.2642	−10.8628	2.0037	EX$_{-1}$
	(18.2667)	(0.5567)	(19.9515)	(0.1841)	
	18.2959	−0.2165	−1.2094	1.8463	EX$_{-2}$
	(18.9631)	(0.5762)	(18.9824)	(0.2091)	
			Consumer Prices (PC)		
HKG	1.0732	1.3946	−0.0012	1.3421	USGNP$_{-1}$
	(8.5787)	(0.2856)	(0.0026)	(0.3209)	
	0.7139	1.4128	−0.0012	1.3279	USGNP$_{-2}$
	(8.3894)	(0.2767)	(0.0027)	(0.3249)	
CUHK	−17.7530	1.4050	0.0049	0.8681	USGNP$_{-1}$
	(11.2124)	(0.2882)	(0.0032)	(0.4925)	
	−18.3626	1.3751	0.0053	1.0864	USGNP$_{-2}$
	(10.3046)	(0.2594)	(0.0031)	(0.4033)	
HKG	−5.7763	1.3840	4.3143	1.6955	EX$_{-1}$
	(3.6705)	(0.2653)	(4.3619)	(0.2369)	
	−5.9098	1.3792	4.2797	1.7805	EX$_{-2}$
	(3.5672)	(0.2630)	(3.9753)	(0.2207)	
CUHK	2.7672	1.3371	−7.3285	0.6367	EX$_{-1}$
	(3.6315)	(0.2825)	(5.7463)	(0.6100)	
	0.8976	1.2139	−3.3327	0.2165	EX$_{-2}$
	(3.7633)	(0.2823)	(5.2785)	(0.8825)	

Notes: Sample period: 1978 to 1989. The standard errors are shown in parentheses.
  [a] F ratios for H_0: $\alpha_0 = 0$, $\alpha_1 = 1$, $\alpha_2 = 0$. Significance levels are given under F values.

approach despite the increasing availability of microcomputers and forecasting software that make possible the efficient use of quantitative forecasting methods.

(b) Although accuracy analysis plays an important role in selecting a given forecasting technique, we found that very few respondent firms perform accuracy analysis for their forecasts. Firms tend to select forecasting methods on the basis of familiarity rather than ability to perform. The lack of records of forecasting accuracy suggests that they are likely to continue to use a method that fails to perform.

(c) Forecasting for Hong Kong's time series on exports and imports of goods is difficult in view of Hong Kong's exposure to the global and regional environment. This is confirmed by the accuracy analysis of the historical forecasts as well as the tests for rationality. The tests presented in Section IV show that the annual forecasts of gross domestic product, private consumption, gross domestic fixed capital formation, and inflation by two of the most experienced forecasters in Hong Kong are both unbiased and efficient — and therefore rational, suggesting that forecasters use the information they have when they make their forecasts. Two variables that fail all tests are total exports and total imports of goods. Of course, due to a lack of information we do not have evidence of whether or not the expectations of other forecasters are rational.

(d) The area of combining forecasts has received a lot of attention in recent years. Considerable literature has accumulated over the years concerning the combination of forecasts. Dalrymple (1987) presented evidence that firms in the United States are gradually beginning to combine forecasts; in his survey, about 40% of the firms frequently or usually combined forecasts. However, in many cases the combination methods used were an informal combination of judgemental estimates.

With the advent of inexpensive forecasting software for personal computers, virtually any decision-maker can generate multiple forecasts of a time series. Decision-makers are encouraged to use such software to create composite forecasts and to use these forecasts in making their decisions.

REFERENCES

Bell, William R. and Steven C. Hillmer (1984). "Issues Involved with the Seasonal Adjustment of Economic Time Series." *Journal of Business and Economic Statistics*, October, Vol. 2, pp. 291–320.

Chou, W. L. and J. Zhang (1990). "Economic Forecasting Practices in Hong Kong: A Survey." Working Paper, No. 11, Department of Economics, The Chinese University of Hong Kong, June.

Clemen, Robert T. (1989). "Combining Forecasts: A Review and Annotated Bibliography." *International Journal of Forecasting*, Vol. 5, pp. 559–583.

Dalrymple, Douglas J. (1987). "Sales Forecasting Practices: Results from a United States Survey." *International Journal of Forecasting*, Vol. 3, pp. 379–391.

Department of Economics, The Chinese University of Hong Kong. *Outlook of the Hong Kong Economy* (mimeo), various issues.

Hang Seng Bank Limited. *Hang Seng Economic Monthly*, various issues.

Hanke, John (1984). "Forecasting in Business Schools: A Survey." *International Journal of Forecasting*, Vol. 3, pp. 229–234.

Holden, K. and D. A. Peel (1985). "An Evaluation of Quarterly National Institute Forecasts." *International Journal of Forecasting*, Vol. 4, pp. 227–234.

Hong Kong Government. *Economic Prospects*. Hong Kong: Government Printer, 1985–1990.

Huss, William R. (1987). "Forecasting in the Electric Utility Industry." In *The Handbook of Forecasting: A Manager's Guide*, edited by Spyros Makridakis and Steven C. Wheelwright. New York: John Wiley & Sons.

Keane, Michael P. and David E. Runkle (1990). "Testing the Rationality of Price Forecasts: New Evidence from Panel Data." *The American Economic Review*, September, Vol. 80, pp. 714–735.

Mentzer, John T. and James E. Cox (1984). "Familiarity, Application, and Performance of Sales Forecasting Techniques." *Journal of Forecasting*, Vol. 3, pp. 27–36.

Peebles, G. (1988). *Hong Kong's Economy: An Introductory Macroeconomic Analysis*. Hong Kong: Oxford University Press.

Stekler, H. O. "Who Forecasts Better?" *Journal of Business and Economic Statistics*, January, Vol. 5, pp. 155–158.

Wallis, Kenneth F. (1989). "Macroeconomic Forecasting: A Survey." *The Economic Journal*, March, Vol. 99, pp. 28–61.

Zarnowitz, Victor (1984). "The Accuracy of Individual and Group Forecasts from Business Outlook Surveys." *International Journal of Forecasting*, Vol. 3, pp. 11–26.

CHAPTER 6

Inter-industry Response to Business Cycles in Hong Kong[1]

Choi Hak
The Chinese University of Hong Kong, Hong Kong

I. INTRODUCTION

Hong Kong is a very competitive economy, especially for manufacturing industries. Industrial companies receive almost no help from the Government, and they face competition from Japan and other newly developed Asian countries. China has been a big supply base for Hong Kong's resources, but now, more and more, China is becoming Hong Kong's competitor. Because of reliance on foreign supply and markets, and because of competition, manufacturing companies in Hong Kong are subject to great ups and downs in business cycles.

This essay sets out to consider the industry responses to business cycles. In the first instance, business cycles of individual industries of Hong Kong's manufacturing sector are computed. They are then compared with industry-wide business cycles. Reasons for the different degrees of volatility among various industries are then considered.

---

[1] Financial support from the Centre for Hong Kong Studies at The Chinese University of Hong Kong is hereby acknowledged. Assistance from the following students during the earlier stage of this project is also very much appreciated. They are Leung Wai Man, Lin Woon Wang, Ma Kwong Man and Mock Chi Kong.

II. THEORETICAL BACKGROUND

The theoretical background of this essay is a neo-classical production function for each industry. Potential output is computed and compared with actual output. All variables are considered in real and net terms. The Business Cycle Indicator (BCI) is then computed as the percentage deviation of actual output from potential output. Details of the methodology can be found in Choi and Ng (1988), but here is a brief description of the development of the Business Cycle Indicator:

Business Cycle Indicator

According to the capacity utilization principle (Gabisch and Lorenz 1987), the BCI can be measured as follows:

$$BCI = \frac{Y}{\hat{Y}} \dots\dots\dots\dots\dots\dots\dots\dots\dots (1)$$

where Y is the actual output and $\hat{Y}$ is the potential output. Instead of measuring the highest potential output, we measure the mean potential output. Thus our indicator of business cycles is really the deviation from the mean output.

Recall from the neo-classical definition of a production function that:

$$Y = Af(K, L)e^{u} \dots\dots\dots\dots\dots\dots\dots\dots\dots (2)$$

which states that output is a function of capital (K) and labour (L) input. Output is also influenced by technological change and a random fluctuation factor. Potential output is correspondingly defined as follows:

$$\hat{Y} = Af(K, L) \dots\dots\dots\dots\dots\dots\dots\dots\dots (3)$$

The difference between these two is the disturbance term only. Substituting these two definitions into the BCI, we have:

$$BCI = \frac{Af(K, L)e^{u}}{Af(K, L)} \dots\dots\dots\dots\dots\dots\dots\dots\dots (4)$$

$$\frac{Y}{\hat{Y}} = \frac{Ae^{u}}{A} \dots\dots\dots\dots\dots\dots\dots\dots\dots (5)$$

Thus, measuring actual and potential output comes to the same thing as measuring actual and potential productivity, as far as the business cycle indicator is concerned.

We shall name the term Ae^u as in Equation (5) total factor productivity, P. Thus BCI becomes:

$$BCI = \frac{P}{A} \quad \dots \dots \dots \dots \dots \dots \dots \dots \dots \dots \dots \dots \dots \dots \quad (6)$$

Productivity Measurements

The total factor productivity measurement can be derived from a neo-classical production function with the assumption of constant returns to scale and competitive factor markets. In short, we define P as follows:

$$\frac{dP}{P} = \frac{dY}{Y} - W_k \frac{dK}{K} - W_l \frac{dL}{L} \quad \dots \dots \dots \dots \dots \dots \dots \dots \dots \dots \quad (7)$$

Data for industrial output and labour can be obtained from the *Survey of Industrial Production* published by the Hong Kong Government every year, with at least three years' time lag each year. Price Indices are obtained from the *Estimate of GDP*. Capital share is deduced from information in the *Survey of Industrial Production* based on the assumption of constant returns to scale, i.e. the sum of capital and labour shares must be one. Capital data is derived from investment figures using the method described in Choi and Ng (1988).

Source of Productivity Difference

Among different industries, productivity growth can vary a lot. As Denison (1962, 1967, 1974, 1976 and 1979) indicated, the reasons behind productivity growth can be very different. We maintain our view that investment is the vital factor for productivity growth (see Denison). Thus we regress the logarithm of the productivity index on that of investment:

$$lnP = a + blnI + u \quad \dots \dots \dots \dots \dots \dots \dots \dots \dots \dots \dots \dots \dots \quad (8)$$

From the regression result, an expected productivity change can be calculated:

$$\hat{P} = e^a I^b \quad \dots \dots \dots \dots \dots \dots \dots \dots \dots \dots \dots \dots \dots \dots \dots \quad (9)$$

Thus, we have the actual and expected productivity index, and the BCI can be obtained therefrom.

III. EMPIRICAL FINDINGS

General Description

Over the period from 1976 to 1992, the manufacturing industry as a whole experienced a gross output growth of 45.16%, in real terms. Among the sub-industries, the paper industry experienced the highest growth with 252.32%, followed by the basic metal industry with 101.69%. However, some industries experienced negative growth, reflecting a structural change in Hong Kong. These include the leather and plastics industries.

In terms of net output, i.e. gross output minus depreciation, the paper industry also ranks first with a 234.97% increase over a period of 16 years, followed by the basic metal industry with a 101.69% increase.

In terms of productivity, the picture is totally different. Productivity growth is the balance of net output growth over growth of inputs. Thus, while some industries experience a high growth rate in net output, if such high growth is the mere result of growth in inputs, productivity change will then be low. Thus, productivity change reflects the real net growth of the industry. The paper industry becomes the one with the lowest growth rate in productivity over the same period under study. Actually its productivity change is negative, indicating that the high growth of net output is purely the result of more inputs. Capital has increased by 407%, while labour has increased by 65.93%. Both are well above the average figure for the whole manufacturing industry.

The chemical industry becomes that with the highest growth rate of productivity with a 657% increase over the period. However, since this industry experienced a disinvestment, a laying-off of labour and great fluctuations in output, it should be treated separately. The clothing industry is the second highest with a 50% growth rate. Details of the statistics are given in Table 6.1.

The diversity of productivity growth among different industries and the divergence of productivity change from net output indicate the importance of a comparative study of business cycles on the inter-industry level.

Inter-industry Business Cycle Indicators

With the productivity data available, we are now in a position to estimate the volatility of business cycles for each individual industry. The method for calculating the BCI was given in Section II. Accordingly, we regress the productivity index on the level of investment. As the results shall

Table 6.1 Growth Rate of Various Indicators (%)

Industry	Code	Gross Output	Invest-ment	Capital	Labour	Produc-tivity	Net Output
All	1	45.16	44.17	68.67	−26.67	32.74	41.43
Basic metals	2	101.69	119.30	104.15	4.83	43.52	101.69
Electric	4	69.93	157.09	191.55	−44.95	27.27	52.47
Food	5	94.24	194.56	72.61	39.46	21.63	99.32
Leather	6	−33.76	−57.27	18.82	−58.30	−2.53	−39.77
Others	7	35.82	113.18	128.68	−9.54	−5.61	35.82
Paper	8	252.32	461.14	407.47	65.93	−26.58	234.97
Plastics	9	−14.77	−14.16	23.70	−57.42	15.53	−24.94
Textiles	10	13.60	−39.14	31.21	−34.86	28.59	8.38
Clothing	11	8.39	−25.39	−5.95	−35.04	50.48	9.57

reveal, the statistical significance of these regressions is understandably quite low because the two sets of data concerned are both residuals of other economic data. Productivity is the residual of the output change that cannot be explained by the change in inputs. Investment, unlike capital, never obeys any fixed rule and seldom has an obvious trend.

Nevertheless, the regression results help us to find a smoothed path of productivity change. One might as well regress productivity on time, which we think, however, should only be employed when no other way is available. The detailed data and results of the estimate of the BCI for each industry can be obtained from the author. Table 6.2 summarizes the regression result of productivity on investment according to Equation (8).

Table 6.2 Regression of Productivity on Investment

Industry	Code	Coefficient	Standard Error	T-Value	R-Square (%)
All	1	−0.0016	0.1822	−0.0089	0.00
Basic metals	2	0.3406	0.1295	2.6305	31.57
Chemicals	3	−0.0821	0.0688	−1.1935	10.61
Electric	4	0.1100	0.0599	1.8379	18.38
Food	5	0.0952	0.1430	0.6656	2.87
Leather	6	0.1851	0.0523	3.5377	45.49
Others	7	0.2166	0.1053	2.0559	21.98
Paper	8	−0.1375	0.0883	−1.5577	13.92
Plastics	9	0.3707	0.0989	3.7495	48.38
Textiles	10	0.4311	0.1465	2.9423	36.59
Clothing	11	−0.0118	0.1747	−0.0673	0.03

The results presented here are better than expected. Out of 11 industries we have six where the coefficients of the variable are significantly different from zero at a 90% confidence level. Nonetheless, what we want to achieve is nothing more than the smoothing of the data, which can be accomplished by any regression model.

The comparison of actual to expected productivity as implied by the regression results yields the statistics of the BCI. The data were plotted in two graphs (Figures 6.1 and 6.2), each with the manufacturing total as a comparison stick.

Amplitude of Business Cycles

As revealed by Figures 6.1–6.2, most of the industries exhibit similar business cycles to those of the overall industry.

To see the amplitude of business cycles, we use two measures: (a) the Max-Min method, which is defined as the maximum BCI minus the minimum BCI, and (b) the Sum of Absolute Difference method, which should be apparent by its own definition. As expected, the chemical industry ranks first, followed by the paper industry and the food industry (see Table 6.3). Strikingly evident is that both measures produce very similar rankings.

Figure 6.1 Inter-industry Business Cycles (I)

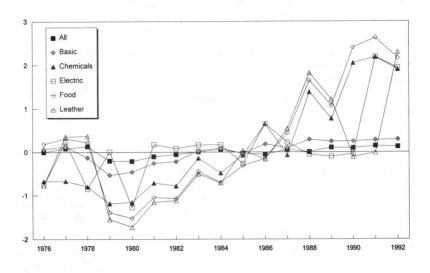

Figure 6.2 Inter-industry Business Cycles (II)

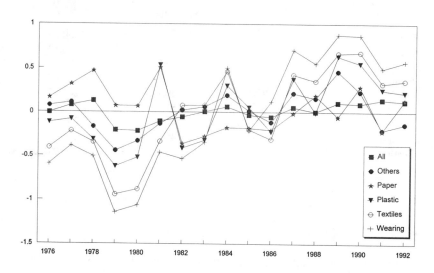

Figure 6.3 Business Cycles and Capital-labour Ratio

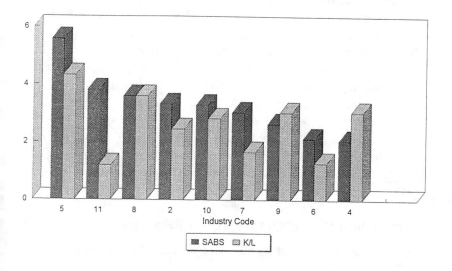

Table 6.3 Amplitude of Business Cycles by Industries

Industry	Code	Max-Min (%)	SABS (%)
Chemicals	3	259.88	1250.53
Paper	8	81.05	246.13
Food	5	77.02	382.85
Basic metals	2	60.68	227.67
Others	7	59.14	208.15
Textiles	10	52.51	225.60
Clothing	11	47.74	261.34
Plastics	9	45.73	180.48
Leather	6	37.41	145.97
Electric	4	36.72	140.84
All	1	35.50	146.15

Relative Volatility

The previous paragraph shows the amplitude of business cycles for each individual industry. There is another way to interpret a business cycle. Here we estimate the relative business cycle volatility of each industry against the manufacturing total. In doing so, we regress the *BCI* of each industry (BCI_i) on the BCI of the manufacturing total (BCI_m). That is,

$$BCI_i = \alpha + \beta BCI_m + u \quad \dots \dots \dots \dots \dots \dots \dots \dots \dots \dots \dots \dots \dots .(10)$$

The coefficient β will indicate how the industry i will respond to a one point change in the BCI of the whole industry. Of course there is no implication of causality. Therefore, the coefficient here really represents the relative position of the individual industry *vis-à-vis* the manufacturing total. The results reveal that in terms of relative volatility, the chemical industry again ranks first, followed by the food industry. Table 6.4 lists the results in descending order of the regression coefficient, together with the significant tests.

When comparing these results and those of the previous section, one notices that the ranking of the industries is quite drastically changed. For example, the paper industry is the one with the highest amplitude in terms of Max-Min, but in terms of relative volatility, it ranks last.

Explanation of Different Business Cycle Behaviour

Most of the theoretical explanations of business cycles apply to one single

Table 6.4 Relative Volatility

Industry	Code	Coefficient	Standard Error	T-Value	R-Square (%)
Chemicals	3	4.433	1.891	2.34	26.80
Food	5	1.685	0.425	3.96	51.17
Textiles	10	1.124	0.278	4.04	52.08
Basic metals	2	1.018	0.293	3.48	44.64
Clothing	11	0.882	0.343	2.57	30.59
Leather	6	0.734	0.179	4.10	52.86
Plastics	9	0.722	0.248	2.91	36.06
Others	7	0.414	0.351	1.18	8.46
Electric	4	0.065	0.242	0.27	0.47
Paper	8	−0.050	0.485	−0.10	0.07

cycle. For comparisons of different business cycles, only the acceleration principle (Clark 1917; Samuelson 1939) seems to offer some hints. According to the theory, industries that produce capital goods are likely to experience larger ups and downs in business cycles than those that produce retail goods. By assumption, industries that produce capital goods should have a higher capital-labour ratio.

We compute the correlation coefficients between each of the amplitude/volatility statistics and the capital-labour ratio on the sub-industry level. The correlations are very high. The coefficient of K/L with Max-Min is 0.97, with SABS it is 0.965, and with Relative Volatility it is 0.894. Figure 6.3 should also confirm this relationship. It also reveals that the food industry turns out to have the highest capital-labour ratio, followed by the paper industry.

V. IN SEARCH OF THE BEST INDUSTRY

Having seen a number of cycles one may wonder what the point of these exercises is. Is it better to be an industry of low volatility or smaller business cycle amplitude? The answer should be positive. However, as usual, there is no gain without pain. There is always a trade-off. The trade-off is that for less fluctuation, productivity might be lower.[2] So the best

---

[2]   What businessmen have in mind is, of course, to be in the industry with the least fluctuation and high profit. We use productivity instead of profit because we do not have data for profit, and because high productivity might imply high profit.

industry to be in should be the one with the smallest fluctuation and the highest productivity growth. To see if there is a trade-off, and to see if there is any indication of the best industry, we plot productivity against business cycle fluctuation (Figure 6.4).

Figure 6.4 Productivity versus Business Cycles

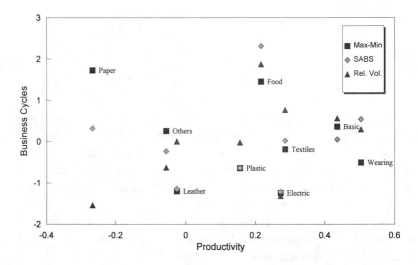

There seems to be a certain kind of trade-off between high productivity and less fluctuation. This is particularly obvious with the relative volatility definition. In terms of best industry, the clothing and electric industries are the most likely industries, with relatively high productivities and low fluctuations, according to this study.

REFERENCES

Choi Hak and Linda F. Y. Ng (1988). "Business Cycles and Investment: The Case of Hong Kong, 1966–1986." *Hong Kong Journal of Business Management*, Vol. VI, pp. 121–139.

Clark, J. M. (1917). "Business Acceleration and the Law of Demand: A Technical Factor in Economic Cycles." *Journal of Political Economy*, Vol. 25, pp. 217–235.

Denison, E. F. (1962). *The Sources of Economic Growth in the United States and the Alternatives before Us*. New York: Committee for Economic Development.

—————— (1967). *Why Growth Rates Differ, Postwar Experience in Nine Western Countries*. Washington, D.C.: The Brookings Institution.

—————— (1974). *Accounting for United States Economic Growth 1929–1969*. Washington, D.C.: The Brookings Institution.

—————— (1976). *How Japan's Economy Grew So Fast, The Sources of Postwar Expansion*. Washington, D.C.: The Brookings Institution.

—————— (1979). *Accounting for Slower Economic Growth*. Washington, D.C.: The Brookings Institution.

Gabisch, Gunter and H. W. Lorenz (1987). *Business Cycle Theory — A Survey of Methods and Concepts*. Lecture Notes in Economics and Mathematical Systems. Berlin: Springer-Verlag.

Samuelson, P. A. (1939). "Interactions between the Multiplier Analysis and Principle of Acceleration." *Review of Economic Statistics*, Vol. 21, pp. 75–78.

CHAPTER 7

Exchange Rate Policies of Hong Kong and Singapore: A Selective Comparison

Kenneth S. Chan[1]
McMaster University, Canada

I. INTRODUCTION

This essay compares the exchange rate policy experiences of Hong Kong and Singapore. Because of the fear of adverse effects of being returned to China in 1997, Hong Kong has adopted an exchange rate pegged to the U.S. dollar since 1983, while Singapore has maintained a flexible exchange rate (a managed float) since 1973. Both economies rely heavily on international trade and have very similar national endowments, history and culture. The similarity of these two emerging economies makes the comparison of the impacts of different exchange rate policies an interesting one.

There is no central bank in Hong Kong, only a Currency Board, and no independent monetary policy. After World War II, the Hong Kong dollar was pegged to sterling at HK$16 per pound. In June 1972, Britain floated the pound against foreign currencies. With the float of the British currency, the Hong Kong dollar could no longer be linked to sterling and was then linked to U.S. dollar instead. Owing to persistent balance of payments

---

[1] I am indebted to Bill Scarth and participants at the international conference on "Challenges and Opportunities for the Three Chinese Economies in the 1990s," 18–19 June 1993, Hong Kong, for comments on earlier drafts, which were titled "Exchange Rate Regimes, Lessons from Some Southeast Asian Economies."

difficulties in the U.S., in the early 1970s the depreciating U.S. dollar finally forced the Hong Kong authorities to abandon its link to the U.S. dollar. From 1974 to October 1983, Hong Kong adopted a flexible exchange rate. The fear of possible adverse effects of Hong Kong being returned to China in 1997 precipitated a confidence crisis in the fall of 1983, resulting in a sharp depreciation of the Hong Kong dollar to a trough of HK$9.60 per U.S. dollar. The exchange rate eventually stabilized in October 1983, when the Hong Kong dollar was linked to the U.S. dollar at a fixed rate of HK$7.8 per U.S. dollar. Since then, Hong Kong has adopted this fixed rate.

The Monetary Authority of Singapore (MAS) conducts monetary policy in Singapore. Immediately after independence in 1967, Singapore adopted a system of interchangeability of currencies between Brunei, Malaysia and Singapore (essentially, a fixed exchange rate system). This tripartite arrangement was terminated in 1973 when Malaysia opted out of it. Singapore has maintained (managed) flexible exchange rates since then. Because of its openness to trade and capital flow, MAS controls inflation and money supply by intervening in the market for foreign exchange, which then influences the domestic interest rate through capital flow. The trade-weighted Singapore dollar is allowed to float within an undisclosed band. MAS reduces inflation by causing the Singapore dollar to appreciate.

This differs from the experience in Europe, where the high inflation country can lower inflation by borrowing "credibility" from the low inflation country through a fixed exchange rate: the inflation rate in Hong Kong is much higher that those of Singapore or the United States. As most of the emerging Southeast Asian economies are undergoing rapid productivity growth, the present essay suggests that such productivity shocks can cause "excessive" price instability and inflation in those economies with a fixed exchange rate policy.

II. SOME COMMON MACROECONOMIC SHOCKS AMONG EMERGING ECONOMIES

There are two types of macroeconmic shock that are common to small open emerging economies. The first type of shock occurs in the financial asset market, which affects capital flow. Examples of this type of shock are speculative attacks on the exchange rate, bubbles, and changes in the political climate which directly affect the demand for domestic financial assets via the stock market.

The second type of common shock among emerging economies originates from their rapid productivity growth, which directly affects the "real" side of the economy.

III. SOME CONVENTIONAL THEORIES[2]

Bela Belassa (1964) first addressed the problem of how productivity growth can lead to inflation for developing countries. Belassa introduced non-traded goods that have a lower productivity growth than traded goods. As productivity grows in the traded goods sector, pulling up money wages, the price of non-traded goods is pushed upwards because the higher money wages cannot be absorbed by the low productivity growth in the non-traded goods sector. Hence, even if two countries are linked by a fixed exchange rate, their inflation rates can differ due to differential productivity growth between their traded and non-traded goods.

In the conventional Mundell–Fleming framework, productivity growth should affect the real side of the economy by shifting the IS-curve to the right, which creates inflationary pressure via the above Belassa mechanism. Hence, under a fixed exchange rate regime, money flows in from abroad (shifting the LM-curve) and verifies the inflationary pressure. However, under a pure flexible exchange rate regime, the exchange rate appreciates, shifting the IS-curve to the left, and dampening the inflationary pressure generated from productivity growth. In other words, with rapid productivity growth, commodity arbitration among tradable goods creates a lot pressure for the domestic wage to rise. And, when the exchange rate appreciates, the upward pressure on the domestic wage is diminished. As for the fixed exchange rate, the short-run price index must rise: although the rise in wages exactly offsets the increase in productivity of the tradable goods, maintaining a constant price in tradable goods, it nonetheless affects the increase in the price of non-tradable goods, where productivity growth remains slow. Hence, during productivity shocks, a flexible exchange rate

---

[2] The implications of the theories in this section continue to hold even when the following fixed price Keynesian framework is replaced by an alternative flexible price framework. The proof of this can be found in an earlier version of this essay available from the author upon request.

regime seems to fare better than a fixed exchange rate regime. The impact of productivity growth is similar to the impact of fiscal policy, which is effective under a fixed exchange rate, but is ineffective under a flexible exchange rate with perfect capital mobility.

As for shocks originating in the financial asset market, they should affect primarily the LM-curve in the Mundell–Fleming model. Under a fixed exchange rate regime, money and capital flow in and out of the economy, neutralizing the financial asset market shocks. As for a flexible exchange rate regime, the exchange rate adjusts to clear the market for foreign exchange, in response to capital flow, which in turn affects the real side (shifts the IS-curve) of the economy. Intuitively, with no variations in exchange rates, domestic and foreign assets are closer substitutes under a fixed exchange rate than under a flexible exchange rate. As a consequence, shocks originating from the financial asset market can be cushioned better under a fixed exchange rate, through asset substitution, than under flexible rates. Hence, a fixed exchange rate regime seems superior for this type of shock. The impact of financial asset market shocks is similar to the impact of monetary policy, which is effective under the flexible exchange rate regime but is ineffective under the fixed exchange rate.

IV. COMPARATIVE LESSONS FROM HONG KONG AND SINGAPORE

Both productivity shocks and financial asset market shocks are present in these two Asian economies. However, due to uncertainty over the political future of Hong Kong, financial asset market shocks are relatively more (less) numerous than productivity shocks for Hong Kong (Singapore). According to the aforementioned theories, it is reasonable for the Hong Kong (Singapore) authorities to adopt a fixed (flexible) exchange rate.

It is often argued that a fixed exchange rate can lower the inflation of a high inflation countries for two reasons. First, a country can borrow "credibility" by pegging its currency to that of a low inflation country (via Purchasing Power Parity). Second, since monetary policy is ineffective under fixed rates, especially in small open economies, this can prevent irresponsible governments from expanding their money supply in order to catch up with "winning" economies that can afford tight monetary policy. A flexible exchange rate is inherently inflationary as it gives monetary autonomy to irresponsible governments that could choose their own rates of inflation. Robert Mundell (1976) opposed flexible exchange rates on the grounds that once governments are free of the discipline of the balance of payments constraint imposed by fixed rates, they will tend to follow a more inflationary and expansionary policy.

The experiences of Hong Kong and Singapore seem to contradict the above presumptions. Singapore has adopted a flexible exchange rate (a managed float) and has a low inflation rate. On the other hand, Hong Kong has pursued a fixed exchange rate (linked to the U.S. dollar) since 1983. The inflation rate in Hong Kong since then has been very high (see Table 7.1).

Driven by rapid productivity growth in the traded sectors, the infrastructures in Hong Kong are often overutilized. Bottlenecks occur which temporarily push up supply prices. This temporary increase in prices becomes permanent under a fixed exchange rate as soon as money flows in from the rest of the world, to verify this type of cost-push inflation. This has been the nature of inflation in Hong Kong since 1986 (see Chen and Wong 1992). In addition to the above mechanism, a high inflation rate also reduces the real rate of interest, as the nominal rate of interest is fixed in the rest of the world. This low real rate of interest (which can be negative) can fuel the demand for non-traded goods, especially the demand for real estate.

Singapore has adopted a more flexible exchange rate policy, which mitigates against real and productivity shocks. An explicit policy goal of the MAS has been to lower the inflation rate by causing the Singapore dollar to appreciate (see Teh and Shanmugaratnam 1991). Hence, for responsible governments, a flexible exchange rate policy seems better than a fixed exchange rate policy in controlling the structural type of inflation (caused by rapid productivity growth).

The choice to peg the Hong Kong dollar to the U.S. dollar was largely due to the political uncertainty in Hong Kong. This type of "political" shock chiefly affects the financial sector of the economy by affecting the demand for financial assets. Under a flexible exchange rate regime, these shocks can cause an excessive outflow of capital, or the exchange rate to "overshoot" (see Dornbusch 1976), or a speculative attack (bubbles) on the exchange rate. Shock originating in the financial market and the exchange market are much more numerous and serious for Hong Kong than for Singapore, which explains the choice for Hong Kong to peg its dollar.

According to a common presumption in relevant literature, a fixed exchange rate regime requires a large stock of international reserves while

Table 7.1 Inflation and Exchange Rates in Hong Kong and Singapore

Year	Inflation Rates (CPI)			Exchange Rates (per U.S. dollars)	
	Hong Kong	Singapore	U.S.A.	Hong Kong	Singapore
1970	7.1	0.4	5.9		3.08
1971	3.5	1.8	4.3	5.71	2.90
1972	6.1	2.1	3.3	5.69	2.82
1973	18.2	26.2	6.2	5.09	2.49
1974	14.6	22.4	11.0	4.91	2.31
1975	2.7	2.6	9.1	5.04	2.49
1976	3.8	−1.9	5.7	4.67	2.46
1977	5.6	3.2	6.5	4.62	2.34
1978	5.8	4.7	7.6	4.80	2.16
1979	11.7	4.0	11.3	4.95	2.16
1980	14.8	8.5	13.5	5.13	2.09
1981	13.8	8.2	10.3	5.68	2.05
1982	10.6	3.9	6.2	6.50	2.11
1983	9.9	1.2	3.2	7.78	2.13
1984	8.5	2.6	4.3	7.82	2.18
1985	3.4	0.5	3.6	7.81	2.11
1986	3.2	−1.4	1.9	7.80	2.18
1987	5.3	0.5	3.7	7.76	2.00
1988	7.4	1.5	4.0	7.81	1.95
1989	9.7	2.4	4.8	7.81	1.89
1990	9.9	3.4	5.4	7.80	1.75
1991	11.0	3.4	4.2	7.80	1.63

Sources: *International Financial Statistics*, IMF, and Census and Statistics Department, Hong Kong Government, various issues.

a flexible exchange rate regime requires little or no international reserves. Once again, the experiences of Hong Kong and Singapore seem at odds with this common presumption. Singapore's stock of international reserves is larger than Hong Kong's. The international reserves of Hong Kong stand at US$28.9 billion, while the reserves of Singapore amount to US$34.1 billion. In terms of exchange reserve funds per capita, Singapore has US$11,376 per capita, while Hong Kong has US$4,962 per capita.[3]

From our earlier theoretical discussions, not only are financial shocks more numerous under a flexible exchange rate regime, but they can also be transmitted easily and excessively to the domestic economy. A large stock of international reserves can help to stabilize financial shocks. With "over-shooting" and speculative attacks on exchange rates, there is a greater need for reserves if central banks want to avert them and still maintain a flexible exchange rate with checks. Speculative bubbles cannot arise if there is enough credible commitment to the exchange rate, usually with enough reserves, which dampens the prospects of capital gain from accelerating departure of the exchange rate.

The exchange rate in Singapore is not entirely market determined; it is stabilized to meet policy-makers' inflation objectives. In order to stabilize the effect of financial market shocks (such as averting speculative bubbles and exchange rate overshoots from "news") on the Singapore economy, the MAS needs to have a large stock of reserves in hand. The comparative experiences of Hong Kong and Singapore suggest that the need for reserves can be quite large as well under a flexible exchange rate regime.

V. TO RECAPITULATE

A fixed (flexible) exchange rate regime typically mitigates financial market (real or productivity) shocks better than a flexible (fixed) exchange rate regime.

Hong Kong has adopted a pegged exchange rate (to the U.S. dollar) primarily because of its international political situation, which tends to generate a lot of financial market shocks to its economy. While the fixed exchange rate has served Hong Kong very well in mitigating financial market shocks, it has not been able to prevent excessive inflation (higher than that in the U.S. and Singapore), a consequence of the rapid produc-tivity growth as in most of the East and Southeast Asian economies. The nature and magnitude of financial market shocks to Singapore do not

---

[3]   Figures released by the Hong Kong Government on 15 July 1992. See *South China Morning Post*, Vol. XLVIII, No. 196, published in Hong Kong on 16 July 1992.

appear as severe as those to Hong Kong. Hence it makes sense for Singapore to adopt a (managed) flexible exchange rate. Inflation in Singapore has been low, mainly due to the use of a flexible exchange rate policy to mitigate inflation. Large international reserves have also helped Singapore to stabilize shock originating in the financial market.

Nowadays, world opinion seems to favour the fixed exchange rate regime over the flexible exchange rate regime, partly because of the excessive volatility of the flexible exchange rate, and partly because a fixed rate can lower inflation through a high inflation country borrowing credibility from a low inflation country. The experiences of Hong Kong and Singapore suggest that this new discourse might merit a second thought. Meanwhile, maintaining a high growth rate with a tolerable rate of inflation will remain the main challenge for the Hong Kong economy until 1997.

REFERENCES

Balassa, Bela (1964). "The Purchasing Power Parity Doctrine: A Reappraisal." *Journal of Political Economy*, December, pp. 584–596.

Chen, Edward K. Y. and Po-Wah Wong (1992). "Exchange Rate Regimes and Economic Development in the Asia-Pacific in a Changing Regional Environment: An Analysis with a Case Study of Hong Kong." *Asian Club Papers*, No. 3, Tokyo Club Foundation for Global Studies, April, pp. 183–204.

Dornbusch, Rudiger (1976). "Expectations and Exchange Rate Dynamics." *Journal of Political Economy*, Vol. 84, pp. 1161–1176.

Census and Statistics Department. *International Financial Statistics*, Hong Kong Government, various issues.

Mundell, Robert A. "Can Flexible Exchange Rates Stop Imported Inflation?" Paper delivered to McMaster Conference on Inflation in Open Economies, 5 March 1976.

Teh, Kok Peng and Tharman Shanmugaratnam (1991). "Exchange Rate Policy: Philosophy and Conduct over the Past Decade." Monetary Authority of Singapore (mimeo).

CHAPTER 8

An Econometric Study of a Trade-oriented Economy: Policy Simulation and Forecasts for Taiwan

Joan C. Lo
Institute of Economics, Academia Sinica, Taiwan

Lee Kai-Cheong
Lingnan College, Hong Kong, and Institute of Economics, Academia Sinica, Taiwan

I. INTRODUCTION

Taiwan is a small but highly open economy. Its population is just over 20 million, about 0.4% of the world population, yet the volume of its trade amounts to approximately 2.2% of total world trade, ranking it as the twelfth largest trading country in 1989.

The land area of Taiwan is rather small and its natural resources are relatively scarce. Foreign trade influences Taiwan's economy not only through contributing to GDP, but also through importation of machinery and raw materials that are needed for production.

Though Taiwan's trade components, in terms of the SITC code, have changed over the years, manufactured products are still the island's major export, while raw materials are the major import.

Since Taiwan's economy can hardly be considered self-supporting, foreign trade is, therefore, an indispensable activity. Heavy reliance on foreign trade, however, has made Taiwan's economic performance subject to its trading partners' economic fluctuations.

In order to understand the quantitative effects that possible policy changes would have on the economy as well as on the balance of trade between Taiwan and its trading partners, a trade-oriented macro-econometric model is a necessary tool for analysis.

Macroeconometric models are also useful for making forecasts. By making certain reasonable assumptions about the future course of exogenous variables specified in the model, we can generate a quantitative forecast for the future development of the economy with the help of the model. A forecast so generated, the "baseline" forecast as it is generally called, can be further utilized as a basic of comparison with other simulated forecasts which incorporates not only the results of the baseline assumptions about exogenous variables, but also the results of some specific changes of economic policy to be enacted at home or abroad.

The main purpose of this essay is, by studying the trade linkages between Taiwan and its major partners, to identify the effects that foreign policy changes (economic fluctuations) will have on Taiwan's economy in the next few years (1991–1996). For that purpose, a baseline forecast will be prepared and then several simulated forecasts with different policy packages will be generated and compared. The whole analysis is based on the operation of a macroeconometric model built for Taiwan with the sample period running from 1971 to 1989.

The order of the essay is as follows. Section II provides an overview of the development of foreign trade in Taiwan. Section III explains the structure of the econometric model used in this essay. A baseline forecast and two simulated forecasts are presented in Section IV. Concluding remarks are given in Section V. The essay also includes an annex which explains the meanings and definitions of each variable appearing in the econometric model.

II. THE IMPORTANCE OF FOREIGN TRADE FOR TAIWAN

Taiwan has benefited to a large extent from foreign trade. Its exports in terms of US dollars has grown more than 300 fold over the last 30 years. Ample foreign demand for Taiwan's products compensated for limited domestic demand and brought Taiwan's economic development (performance) to a remarkable level.

Table 8.1 shows that, in 1961, Taiwan's balance of foreign trade was still in the red. Since 1971 it has been in the black except for 1974, 1975, and 1980 — the three years in which the price of oil soared.

In the early 1970s, Taiwan's trade surplus was only around 5% of GDP. It gradually increased and reached its highest level in 1986, amounting to almost 20% of GDP. In recent years, however, owing to the drastic

Table 8.1   Trade Statistics of Taiwan

Year	X	M	X–M	%(X–M)	(X–M)/ GDP*100	EXR
1961	245.08	369.20	–124.13	n/a	–7.09	40.00
1962	262.45	365.38	–102.93	17.1	–5.34	40.00
1963	390.93	415.90	–24.98	75.7	–1.15	40.00
1964	509.28	489.90	19.38	NM	0.76	40.00
1965	544.28	628.60	–84.33	NM	–3.00	40.00
1966	688.05	679.33	8.73	NM	0.28	40.00
1967	807.15	881.78	–74.63	NM	–2.05	40.00
1968	1,031.70	1,152.50	–120.80	–61.9	–2.84	40.00
1969	1,322.73	1,358.33	–35.60	70.5	–0.72	40.00
1970	1,718.65	1,721.50	–2.85	92.0	–0.05	40.00
1971	2,344.40	2,182.20	162.20	NM	2.46	40.00
1972	3,340.25	2,846.68	493.58	204.3	6.24	40.00
1973	5,065.49	4,496.50	568.99	10.2	5.30	38.25
1974	6,352.50	7,473.11	–1,120.61	NM	–7.75	38.00
1975	6,150.03	6,658.08	–508.05	54.7	–3.27	38.00
1976	8,848.10	8,446.47	401.63	NM	2.16	38.00
1977	10,671.95	9,608.37	1,063.58	164.8	4.88	38.00
1978	14,056.08	12,325.20	1,730.88	58.2	6.45	36.95
1979	17,710.72	17,335.19	375.53	–78.9	1.13	36.00
1980	21,757.56	22,250.72	–493.17	NM	–1.19	36.00
1981	25,031.80	24,047.38	984.43	NM	2.04	36.79
1982	24,347.42	21,847.50	2,499.92	170.0	5.15	39.12
1983	27,815.73	23,286.90	4,528.83	85.5	8.64	40.06
1984	33,252.95	26,629.28	6,623.68	44.6	11.20	39.62
1985	33,649.10	25,082.08	8,567.06	30.1	13.80	39.86
1986	43,824.15	28,892.15	14,932.00	65.5	19.80	37.85
1987	58,218.04	40,601.38	17,616.66	–0.7	17.42	31.87
1988	66,916.74	53,434.53	13,482.21	–31.3	11.03	28.61
1989	73,958.99	62,462.63	11,496.37	–21.3	7.83	26.41
1990	75,206.62	65,761.54	9,445.08	–16.3	5.99	26.91

Notes: X   : Exports of goods and services
M   : Imports of goods and services
%(.) : Percentage change from a year ago
EXR: The exchange rate (NT$/US$)

Source: *National Income of the Republic of China*, Directorate-General of Budget, Accounting and Statistics, Executive Yuan.

appreciation of the N.T. dollar, the reduction of import tax rates, as well as the liberalization of import demand, the value of Taiwan's exports has not increased as fast as the value of the country's imports, which, in turn, has caused the trade surplus share of GDP to decline. It was 7.8% in 1989 and decreased further to 6% in 1990.

Though the level of trade has expanded tremendously over the years, regional expansion has been disproportionate. Among the eight regions listed in Table 8.2, export to North America ranked at the top for all years except 1990; its share, however, has been declining in recent years.

Asia was Taiwan's second largest export market prior to 1990 and became number one in 1990. The export share of Asia, on average, has been around 30% for the last 10 years.

Besides Asia, Europe is the most promising area for Taiwan's exports. The export share of Europe has almost doubled over the last five years. The increased shares of Asia and Europe have compensated for losses in other areas, especially North America, the Middle East and the Near East, and Africa.

Basically Taiwan's import share tells the same story. Imports from Asia and Europe have increased, while imports from Africa and the Middle and Near East have decreased.

Although, relatively speaking, Central America and Africa are two areas with which Taiwan does not have a very active trading relationship, Taiwan's trade balance with them has been positive for the past ten years, as shown in Table 8.3. Taiwan's trade balances with the Middle East and the Near East, and South America were all negative due to the island's heavy energy and raw materials imports.

Taiwan's trade balance with Asia and Oceania was mixed, while that with North America and Europe was positive. Its favourable trade balance with Europe has been increasing, while that with North America has been displaying a decreasing trend in recent years. This phenomenon demonstrates that Taiwan's efforts to diversify its export markets by turning from North America to Europe have been successful.

As to the trade shares of specific countries which Taiwan does most of its trading with, the figures are shown in Table 8.4. Its major trading partners and their relative importance have been very stable over the years. Taiwan's trade is depicted by exports, mainly to the U.S., and imports mainly from Japan. The U.S., Japan, and Hong Kong are the top three areas

Table 8.2 Export and Import Share by Regions

Unit: %

Export Share

Year	Africa	Asia	Central America	Europe	Middle & Near East	North America	Oceania	South America
1981	4.87	29.01	2.35	12.77	5.49	38.61	3.56	2.03
1982	3.98	27.36	2.10	11.65	6.96	41.74	3.46	1.30
1983	2.71	25.80	1.47	10.99	5.95	48.01	2.99	0.53
1984	2.30	25.07	1.40	10.06	4.39	51.83	3.09	0.52
1985	1.82	27.20	1.60	9.75	3.66	51.16	2.94	0.54
1986	1.86	25.94	1.66	11.98	3.23	50.89	2.62	0.67
1987	2.02	28.21	1.41	14.71	2.74	47.04	2.50	0.58
1988	2.25	32.82	1.19	16.30	2.43	41.29	2.71	0.50
1989	1.90	35.29	1.33	16.53	2.17	38.90	2.76	0.49
1990	1.87	38.22	1.38	18.20	2.08	34.67	2.29	0.64
Average	2.56	29.49	1.59	13.29	3.91	44.41	2.89	0.78

Import Share

Year	Africa	Asia	Central America	Europe	Middle & Near East	North America	Oceania	South America
1981	3.43	37.60	0.60	9.35	20.04	23.74	3.13	1.82
1982	2.86	34.31	0.52	11.16	18.70	25.83	3.85	2.53
1983	2.67	36.64	0.42	11.19	18.13	24.69	3.84	2.11
1984	2.30	39.83	0.80	10.84	15.12	24.78	4.00	2.13
1985	2.65	38.52	0.55	12.21	13.90	25.45	4.39	2.17
1986	2.49	44.56	0.47	13.39	8.28	24.42	4.09	1.90
1987	2.93	45.00	0.53	15.09	7.30	23.69	3.30	1.67
1988	2.54	42.15	0.50	16.10	5.16	28.10	3.07	2.14
1989	2.25	44.52	0.48	16.04	5.39	24.86	3.54	2.68
1990	2.23	43.59	0.33	17.52	6.04	24.58	3.41	2.11
Average	2.63	40.67	0.51	13.29	11.81	25.03	3.66	2.13

Source: *Monthly Statistics of Exports and Imports*, Taiwan Area, Republic of China, Department of Statistics, Ministry of Finance.

Table 8.3 Trade Balance by Regions

Unit: Million US$

Year	Africa	Asia	Central America	Europe	Middle & Near East	North America	Oceania	South America
1981	372.87	-1,411.37	403.51	904.84	-3,008.47	3,697.19	139.66	73.97
1982	344.66	-405.39	367.58	478.59	-1,986.90	4,389.07	41.40	-188.09
1983	139.22	-950.47	284.54	491.08	-2,184.71	7,053.45	-27.69	-294.13
1984	195.01	-1,110.32	252.03	683.52	-1,984.69	10,342.06	64.16	-309.11
1985	28.42	612.70	381.57	542.89	-1,669.58	10,603.03	19.66	-269.88
1986	141.71	-431.70	547.36	1,537.65	-716.60	14,376.06	58.26	-190.77
1987	57.74	-607.09	567.90	2,611.72	-1,087.17	16,937.93	184.52	-276.15
1988	101.66	-1,042.88	475.34	1,880.60	-1,086.26	11,057.70	114.03	-763.34
1989	80.98	103.46	630.18	2,561.45	-1,383.58	12,761.95	-17.01	-1,073.35
1990	36.60	1,842.78	745.72	2,647.59	-1,906.30	9,854.10	-325.06	-725.54

Source: *Monthly Statistics of Exports and Imports*, Taiwan Area, Republic of China, Department of Statistics, Ministry of Finance.

Table 8.4   Export Share by Countries (Goods Only)

Unit: %

Country	1970–1974	1975–1979	1980–1984	1985–1989	1990
OECD Countries					
USA	39.04	37.00	40.72	42.97	32.35
Japan	14.48	12.96	10.60	12.77	12.41
West Germany	4.76	4.94	3.86	3.46	4.76
Canada	4.23	3.07	2.61	2.89	2.32
United Kingdom	1.90	2.51	2.40	2.75	2.95
Australia	2.12	2.59	2.77	2.25	1.90
The Netherlands	2.07	2.07	1.68	2.02	2.76
France	0.46	0.92	1.06	1.29	1.68
Italy	0.96	0.90	0.96	1.13	1.47
Belgium	0.63	0.71	0.63	0.66	0.72
Sweden	0.35	0.45	0.38	0.49	0.61
Spain	0.14	0.28	0.24	0.51	0.88
Switzerland	0.11	0.36	0.27	0.37	0.55
New Zealand	0.11	0.14	0.22	0.31	0.29
Denmark	0.08	0.15	0.16	0.22	0.24
Austria	0.02	0.10	0.11	0.23	0.39
Greece	0.00	0.00	0.00	0.15	0.20
Ireland	0.04	0.04	0.11	0.14	0.17
Norway	0.04	0.08	0.08	0.12	0.17
Portugal	0.01	0.03	0.04	0.08	0.17
Turkey	0.02	0.02	0.02	0.08	0.26
Iceland	0.01	0.01	0.01	0.01	0.01
Luxembourg	—	0.00	0.00	0.01	0.00
Finland	—	—	—	0.11	0.15
OECD Total	71.58	69.33	68.93	75.02	67.41
Asian Countries					
Hong Kong	7.44	7.00	7.33	8.62	12.73
Singapore	2.48	2.54	2.75	2.70	3.28
South Korea	1.82	1.26	1.02	1.22	1.80
Indonesia	2.37	2.68	1.81	1.04	1.85
Thailand	1.48	1.16	0.92	1.03	2.12
Philippines	0.84	1.21	0.98	0.92	1.21
Malaysia	0.75	0.75	0.87	0.69	1.64
Asia Total	17.18	16.60	15.68	16.22	24.63

Source: *Monthly Statistics of Exports and Imports*, Taiwan Area, Republic of China. Department of Statistics, Ministry of Finance.

that Taiwan exports goods to, and Japan, the U.S. and West Germany are the top three countries which Taiwan imports goods from.

Exporting to the U.S. has long accounted for about two-fifths of Taiwan's total exports, as shown in Table 8.4. It increased to 43% during the period from 1985 to 1989. Exports to Japan have accounted for over one-tenth of total exports. From 1985 to 1989, exports to the U.S., Japan and Hong Kong together accounted for 64% of Taiwan's total exports of goods. During the same period, West Germany, Canada, the United Kingdom and Singapore absorbed 12% of the total value of the island's exports in goods.

Since the U.S., Japan, West Germany, Canada and the United Kingdom are member countries of the OECD, Taiwan's exports of goods to OECD countries have accounted for well over 70% of total exports of goods. This share climbed even higher, to 75%, during the period from 1985 to 1989.

Taiwan's imports of goods basically come from those countries to which Taiwan exports most. However, their relative importance is different. Japan has been Taiwan's largest supplier of goods. Goods from Japan accounted for over two-fifths of Taiwan's imports of goods during the period from 1970 to 1974, as shown in Table 8.5. Though Japan's share dropped in the following decade, it still amounted to more than one-quarter of the market. The U.S. is Taiwan's second largest supplier of goods. The U.S's share was very stable in the periods that we studied, and occupied more than one-fifth of Taiwan's imports of goods. Imported goods from OECD countries accounted for 75% of the total value of imported goods in the period from 1985 to 1989.

The trade pattern in 1990 was basically in line with past experience. However, there were three major export shifts which deserve our attention. First, exports to the U.S. declined tremendously. They dropped to more than 25% less than the previous period. Secondly, the export share of Hong Kong increased tremendously, from 8.62% to 12.73%, and thirdly, the export share of other Asia countries also increased quite sharply.

The decrease in exports to the U.S. was due primarily to the appreciation of the N.T. dollar, while the increase of exports to Hong Kong was due to demand increases in mainland China. The vast exports surge to other Asian countries resulted on the other hand from Taiwan's huge investment in that region.

Since Asia has become Taiwan's largest trading area, and since the trade volume with this area is expected to grow fast, we will model the

Table 8.5   Import Share by Countries (Goods Only)

Unit: %

Country	1970–1974	1975–1979	1980–1984	1985–1989	1990
OECD Countries					
USA	23.37	23.78	23.24	23.40	23.05
Japan	39.75	31.60	27.46	31.23	29.24
West Germany	4.85	4.43	3.57	4.65	4.96
Canada	0.93	0.85	1.56	1.91	1.53
United Kingdom	1.80	2.12	1.44	1.81	2.11
Australia	2.91	2.72	3.14	3.26	3.03
Netherland	0.97	0.80	0.88	1.36	1.33
France	0.55	0.89	1.18	1.35	2.07
Italy	0.78	0.84	0.95	1.28	1.49
Belgium	0.73	0.53	0.37	0.58	0.72
Sweden	0.21	0.44	0.47	0.66	0.91
Spain	0.09	0.09	0.18	0.34	0.25
Switzerland	0.88	0.65	0.71	1.31	2.19
New Zealand	0.25	0.38	0.37	0.37	0.35
Denmark	0.14	0.14	0.21	0.26	0.22
Austria	0.10	0.09	0.08	0.21	0.24
Greece	0.00	0.00	0.00	0.04	0.02
Ireland	0.04	0.04	0.13	0.11	0.08
Norway	0.04	0.10	0.14	0.19	0.14
Portugal	0.06	0.02	0.02	0.03	0.04
Turkey	0.07	0.23	0.05	0.18	0.28
Iceland	0.00	0.00	0.00	0.01	0.01
Luxembourg	0.00	0.00	0.01	0.02	0.06
Finland	—	—	—	0.16	0.18
OECD Total	78.52	70.74	66.16	74.72	74.50
Asia Countries					
Hong Kong	2.12	1.54	1.50	2.68	2.64
Singapore	0.60	0.75	0.98	1.49	2.57
South Korea	0.83	1.17	1.13	1.60	2.46
Indonesia	1.80	3.02	1.99	1.55	1.68
Thailand	1.97	0.92	0.52	0.68	0.82
Philippines	1.33	0.48	0.52	0.53	0.43
Malaysia	1.64	1.67	2.34	2.03	1.83
Asia Total	10.29	9.55	8.98	10.56	12.43

Source: *Monthly Statistics of Exports and Imports*, Taiwan Area, Republic of China, Department of Statistics, Ministry of Finance.

import and export structure for each country in this region separately except for Hong Kong. We will also model trading relationships with the eight OECD countries where mutual trade amounted to more than 1% of Taiwan's total trade volume.

III. A TRADE-ORIENTED MACROECONOMETRIC MODEL

The annual macroeconometric model of Taiwan used in this essay is basically a Keynesian-type model. It is comprised of a commodity market, a money market, a labour market and a price sector. There are 68 behaviour equations, 63 identities and 39 exogenous variables. The sectoral modules and their interrelationships are exhibited in Figure 8.1.

The price sector in this model has the most correlation with the other sectors. The Consumer Price (CPI) influences the price deflators for all consumer goods and government consumption, and also influences the manufacturing wage and the deflator for service exports. The Wholesale Price (WPI) influences price deflators as well as the levels of investment and inventory; it also influences the deflator for goods exports.

The driving force behind the Wholesale Price is the price deflator for imports. The rationale behind this specification is that approximately 90% of imports are capital goods or raw materials needed for production.

Unit manufacturing labour costs, as defined in the labour market block, affect the Consumer Price, Wholesale Price, and price deflators for all investment in the service sector.

The financial sector is connected with the other sectors mainly by interest rates. Interest rates influence the demand for consumer durables, investment, inventory, as well as the Consumer Price. Normally, we would expect the price level, especially the Consumer Price, to influence the lending rate rather than vice-versa. Nevertheless, in Taiwan, financial liberalization has not been common practice. The Central Bank of China has great power in the determination of the interest rate, which is often used to restrict the money supply so as to curb inflation.

Within each expenditure module, the level of real expenditure of the various components was first determined, and then the corresponding deflators. Total nominal expenditures and the general deflator were defined last. Money demand in this sector is influenced by GDP, the summation of private consumption, government consumption, gross investment, and net exports.

Figure 8.1 The Sectoral Modules and their Interrelationships

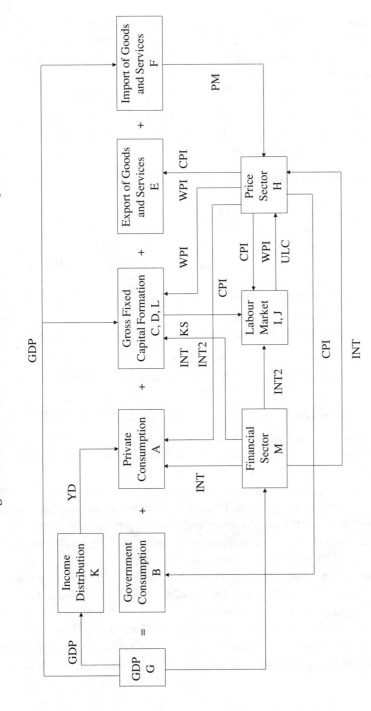

Note: "A" through "K" inside the boxes represent the section label of the documentations.

Since this model is aimed also at measuring the macroeconomic linkages between Taiwan and its major trading partners, a great emphasis has been placed on the economic interdependence between Taiwan and these countries.

The trade equations specified in this model are as follows:

$$Xi = f(Yi, PX/EXR*EXRi/WPIi, PX/EXR*EXRj/PXj) \text{ for all } i, i>(<)j$$
$$Mi = g(Y, PXi/EXRi*EXR*(1+IMPORT\ TAX/M)/WPI,$$
$$PXi/EXRi*EXRj/PXj \qquad\qquad\qquad \text{for all } j, j>(<)i$$

Where i indicates the ith country
        j indicates the jth country
        Xi is Taiwan's export of goods to country i
        Mi is Taiwan's import of goods from country i
        M is Taiwan's total import of goods and services
        Y is GNP or aggregate demand (AD, AD = GNP + M)
        PX is the export price
        WPI is the wholesale price index
        EXR is the exchange rate
        IMPORT TAX/M is Taiwan's average import tax rate

Due to space limitation, the whole set of model equations is not presented here. Variable descriptions are, however, given in Annex 8.1.

IV. BASELINE FORECAST AND SIMULATED FORECAST

After the model is built, estimated and tested, it is used as a tool to make a baseline forecast for the period 1991 to 1996. The results are summarized and presented in Table 8.7.

This forecast is prepared under a set of assumptions regarding the future course of certain policy variables. It is assumed that there will be strong investment demand originating from the government sector and the public enterprise sector. The former will increase by 18% each year and the later by 15%. On the employment side, the wage increase in the government sector will be maintained at 8% each year while the labour force will increase by 1.5% in 1991 and 1992, by 2% in 1993 and 1994, and by 2.5% in the last two years. The rediscount rate, on the other hand, will increase slowly from 7.35% in 1991 and 1992 to 7.75% in 1995 and 1996.

With regard to the group of variables representing foreign economic activities, it is assumed first of all that the price of oil will be stable in the next few years, at US$20 per barrel. Furthermore, it is assumed that price inflation in West Germany, Japan and the United States will be mild during most of the forecast period, ranging from 3% to 4.5%. In the meantime, GNP growth for those countries is also encouraging, and there will be, on average, a 2.5% increase for the United States, 2.9% for West Germany, and 4.3% for Japan. As to foreign exchange rates, the New Taiwan dollar is assumed to become even stronger than before during the next few years. It will appreciate against the U.S. dollar, the German mark, and the Japanese yen. All relevant assumptions regarding these and other exogenous variables are given in Table 8.6.

Table 8.6 Exogenous Variables

Unit: Level

	1991	1992	1993	1994	1995	1996
EXR	26.722	26.160	25.663	25.381	25.102	24.826
EXR@GE	1.710	1.638	1.577	1.560	1.543	1.526
EXR@JA	130.173	127.049	119.299	115.482	113.057	110.682
IMPTAXRT	8.500	8.500	8.500	8.500	8.500	8.500
POIL$	20.000	20.000	20.000	20.000	20.000	20.000
RDISC	7.350	7.350	7.500	7.500	7.750	7.750
DRG	0.020	0.020	0.020	0.020	0.020	0.020
DRM	0.088	0.088	0.088	0.088	0.088	0.088
DRP	0.070	0.070	0.070	0.070	0.070	0.070
DRPE	0.060	0.060	0.060	0.060	0.060	0.060

Unit: Growth Rate

	1991	1992	1993	1994	1995	1996
GCNW86	10.55	10.00	10.00	10.00	10.00	10.00
GCW86	8.00	8.00	8.00	8.00	8.00	8.00
CONWIND	12.00	12.00	12.00	12.00	12.00	12.00
GNP85@GE	2.96	2.60	2.60	3.20	2.70	3.30
GNP85@JA	3.30	3.80	4.70	4.70	4.70	4.40
GNP85@US	1.64	2.20	2.50	3.00	2.60	2.80
HH	2.50	2.50	2.50	2.50	2.50	2.50
IG86	18.04	18.00	18.00	18.00	18.00	18.00
IPE86	11.86	15.00	15.00	15.00	15.00	15.00
LF	1.50	1.50	2.00	2.00	2.50	2.50
WPI@GE	3.80	3.30	3.20	2.90	2.90	2.70
WPI@JA	−0.20	2.00	1.80	1.50	1.80	1.90
WPI@US	1.80	2.50	3.30	7.20	4.20	4.50
XS86	11.08	5.00	5.00	5.00	5.00	5.00
X86OTH	10.00	10.00	10.00	10.00	10.00	10.00

Baseline Forecast

The results of the baseline forecast are encouraging. As shown in Table 8.7, the economy will generate a GDP growth of about 7.4% each year on average. The growth path is supported by 7.2% growth in private consumption, 12% growth in fixed capital formation, and 6% growth in total exports. In the meantime, the economy generates faster growth for imports (8.7%) than exports (6.1%). The resulting persistent surplus in the current account, will become smaller and smaller until it goes down to almost zero in 1996.

Turning to the price side, inflation is mild and decreasing. The Consumer Price increases by about 4% in 1991 and 1992; yet the rate of change decreases to about 2.3% in 1995 and 1996. The Wholesale Price presents a similar pattern, and the export rate of change is much smaller, below 2% throughout. Manufacturing wages, on the other hand, increase rapidly, by about 10.5% each year. Unemployment remains low and stable in the meantime.

Simulated Forecast

In this section, we will present the spill-over effects of foreign policy (impulses) on Taiwan's economy. All of the foreign policy changes are measured by the resulting changes in incomes, export prices and import prices. Evaluations of the various effects on Taiwan are made primarily by looking at the changes in the composition of GDP, and changes in the various price deflators, and unemployment rates. Two cases are discussed below.

Case 1: (a) Main assumption: U.S. Government spending falls by 1% of real GDP.

(b) Other assumptions:

(1) U.S. income falls by 1.00%, 0.75%, 0.50%, 0.35%, 0.20%, 0.10%.

(2) U.S. Wholesale Price and export prices fall by 0.10%, 0.30%, 0.30%, 0.25%, 0.15%, 0.10%.

(3) Japan's (Canada, Australia, France, West Germany, Italy, United Kingdom) income falls by 0.25%, 0.30%, 0.25%, 0.15%, 0.15%, 0.05%, 0%.

(4) Japan's (Canada, Australia, France, West Germany, Italy,

Table 8.7 Baseline Solutions, 1991–1996

Unit: Million NT$

	1991	1992	1993	1994	1995	1996
Real Expenditure						
Private Consumption	2,239,363.00 (7.54)	2,430,122.00 (8.52)	2,614,139.00 (7.57)	2,789,134.00 (6.69)	2,952,750.00 (5.87)	3,151,006.00 (6.71)
Government Consumption	687,376.00 (9.17)	748,770.00 (8.93)	815,716.00 (8.94)	888,722.00 (8.95)	968,344.00 (8.96)	1,055,188.00 (8.97)
Fixed Investment	955,772.00 (9.56)	1,075,656.00 (12.54)	1,220,927.00 (13.51)	1,369,922.00 (12.20)	1,526,602.00 (11.44)	1,711,211.00 (12.09)
Export of Goods and Services	2,435,608.00 (9.31)	2,591,460.00 (6.40)	2,758,478.00 (6.44)	2,870,298.00 (4.05)	2,999,773.00 (4.51)	3,175,952.00 (5.87)
Import of Goods and Services	2,155,887.00 (11.87)	2,363,812.00 (9.64)	2,569,904.00 (8.72)	2,736,987.00 (6.50)	2,924,402.00 (6.85)	3,179,592.00 (8.73)
GDP	4,176,822.00 (7.55)	4,502,584.00 (7.80)	4,857,093.00 (7.87)	5,202,497.00 (7.11)	5,549,668.00 (6.67)	5,948,947.00 (7.19)
Price Deflators						
Private Consumption	115.53	121.05	125.77	129.63	133.18	136.33
Government Consumption	123.52	130.74	136.00	140.28	143.78	147.14
Fixed Investment	112.79	114.06	114.82	116.41	119.52	123.92
Export of Goods and Services	91.58	94.11	97.29	99.47	100.58	101.32
Import of Goods and Services	94.10	94.97	96.78	100.38	103.72	106.85
GDP	113.38	119.35	124.06	126.93	129.42	132.05
Consumer Price Index	115.32 (4.18)	120.29 (4.32)	124.36 (3.38)	127.59 (2.60)	130.59 (2.35)	133.44 (2.18)
Wholesale Price Index	96.14 (1.95)	97.34 (1.25)	99.05 (1.75)	100.54 (1.50)	101.77 (1.23)	102.96 (1.17)
Unemployment Rate (dif)	1.47	1.56	1.37	1.26	1.63	1.64
Manufacturing Average Wage	24,656.00	27,581.00	30,723.00	34,055.00	36,967.00	40,625.00
Interest Rate: One-year	8.79	8.84	9.01	9.10	9.46	9.51
Oil Prices* (US$/barrel)	20.00	20.00	20.00	20.00	20.00	20.00
Exchange Rates* (NT$/US$)	26.27	26.16	25.66	25.38	25.10	24.83

* Exogenous variable.

Note: Growth rates in parentheses.

United Kingdom) Wholesale Price and export prices fall
by 0.20%, 0.25%, 0.20%, 0.15%, 0.10%, 0.05%.

(5) Japan's (Canada, Australia, France, West Germany, Italy,
United Kingdom) currency value appreciates by 3.00%,
2.70%, 2.40%, 2.10%, 1.80%, 1.50%.

A fall in foreign demand resulting from foreign income reduction
would decrease Taiwan's exports, GDP, private consumption, fixed investment and imports, and increase the rate of unemployment, which, in turn,
would push prices down, and in later years offset the lower demand.

Foreign currency appreciation relative to the N.T. dollar, however,
would result in higher import prices, manufacturing wages, and Wholesale
Price and Consumer Price levels in Taiwan.

The decrease in GDP would push down the short-run interest rate and
increase the demand for money in the initial period. The decrease in GDP
and the Consumer Price would further depress the demand for money in
later years (see Table 8.8).

Case 2: (a) Main assumption: 5% permanent monetary contraction in
Japan, the U.S. and the other OECD countries.

(b) Other assumptions:

(1) U.S. income falls by 2.50%, 1.50%, 0.80%, 0%, 0%, 0%.

(2) U.S. Wholesale Price and export prices fall by 1.30%,
1.30%, 1.00%, 0.75%, 0.50%, 0.25%.

(3) Japan's income falls by 2.00%, 0.80%, 0%, 0%, 0%, 0%.

(4) Japan's Wholesale Price and export prices fall by 1.30%,
1.30%, 0.50%, 0%, 0%, 0%.

(5) Incomes in Canada, Australia, France, West Germany,
Italy, United Kingdom fall by 2.50%, 1.50%, 0.80%, 0%,
0%, 0%.

(6) The Wholesale Price and export prices in Canada,
Australia, France, West Germany, Italy, United Kingdom
fall by 1.30%, 1.30%, 1.00%, 0.75%, 0.50%, 0.25%.

Due to monetary contraction, in all the developed countries, income
and prices would fall. As a result Taiwan's export and import prices would
also both fall immediately, which would cause GDP, fixed investment,
private consumption and imports to decrease, and the unemployment rate to
increase.

Table 8.8 Case 1: U.S. Government Spending Fall by 1% of Real GDP

Unit: % difference from the baseline

	1991	1992	1993	1994	1995	1996
Real Expenditure						
Private Consumption	0.068	-0.231	-0.334	-0.310	-0.202	-0.134
Government Consumption	0.000	0.000	0.000	0.000	0.000	0.000
Fixed Investment	0.091	-0.312	-0.521	-0.421	-0.209	-0.074
Export of Goods and Services	-0.134	-0.342	-0.467	-0.375	-0.268	-0.224
Import of Goods and Services	0.172	-0.066	-0.170	-0.130	-0.006	0.032
GDP	-0.023	-0.340	-0.471	-0.427	-0.308	-0.234
Price Deflators						
Private Consumption	0.896	0.700	0.364	0.205	0.209	0.209
Government Consumption	0.870	0.748	0.475	0.311	0.267	0.227
Fixed Investment	0.648	0.575	0.397	0.269	0.195	0.125
Export of Goods and Services	1.025	0.903	0.584	0.363	0.263	0.175
Import of Goods and Services	1.008	1.022	0.789	0.518	0.288	0.099
GDP	0.893	0.680	0.365	0.210	0.238	0.251
Consumer Price Index	0.926	0.726	0.384	0.218	0.223	0.224
Wholesale Price Index	1.017	0.901	0.597	0.384	0.277	0.175
Unemployment Rate (dif)	0.015	0.088	0.143	0.132	0.086	0.049
Manufacturing Average Wage	0.652	0.234	-0.225	-0.310	-0.139	-0.005
Interest Rate: One-year	0.000	-0.004	-0.007	-0.007	-0.006	-0.005

Since Taiwan's Wholesale Price is influenced primarily by import prices, lower foreign prices would push domestic prices downward. The money supply would also decrease due to lower prices and income.

The foreign monetary contractions would also have a negative impact on the trade balance of the G-7 countries (see Table 8.9).

V. CONCLUDING REMARKS

The increasing interdependence among countries has motivated people to improve their understanding of international linkages. The development of international macroeconometric models, with a global point of view, definitely serves this purpose. However, in order to gain a broad picture, many details had to be sacrificed. We therefore developed an econometric model to study the economic relationship between Taiwan and its trading partners from Taiwan's point of view.

Due to the limitations associated with using the capital account, all the analyses were done using trade flows. Taiwan has benefited a great deal from foreign trade. Taiwan's trade surplus was once 20% of GDP; however, it dropped to 6% in 1990. Its imports of goods come mainly from Japan, the U.S. and West Germany, while its exports of goods go mainly to the U.S., Japan and Hong Kong. Exports to OECD countries in general have very high income and price effects. The policies of both Taiwan and of OECD countries, therefore, have significant impact on Taiwan's balance of trade.

Income and price effects on exports to Asian countries in general are not so large as those of the OECD countries, and, when coupled with smaller market shares, result in weaker impacts resulting from policy changes.

REFERENCES

Beenstock, M. and A. P. L. Minford (1976). "A Quarterly Econometric Model of World Trade and Prices, 1955–71." In *Inflation in Open Economies*, edited by M. Parkin and G. Zis, pp. 85–125. Manchester: Manchester University Press.

Cline, Willam R. (1989). "United States External Adjustment and the World Economy." Institute for International Economics, Washington D.C.

Fair, R. C. (1983). "An Outline of a Multicountry Econometric Model." *Global*

Table 8.9 Case 2: 5% Permanent Monetary Contraction in Japan, U.S. and Other OECD Countries

Unit: % difference from the baseline

	1991	1992	1993	1994	1995	1996
Real Expenditure						
Private Consumption	-1.074	-1.437	-0.809	-0.342	-0.131	-0.216
Government Consumption	0.000	0.000	0.000	0.000	0.000	0.000
Fixed Investment	-1.959	-2.457	-1.191	-0.041	0.327	0.248
Export of Goods and Services	-3.570	-2.555	-1.668	-0.845	-0.904	-0.794
Import of Goods and Services	-2.532	-2.239	-1.302	-0.632	-0.470	-0.566
GDP	-1.564	-1.776	-1.026	-0.395	-0.197	-0.207
Price Deflators						
Private Consumption	-1.422	-3.008	-3.214	-2.793	-2.495	-2.642
Government Consumption	-1.161	-2.525	-2.907	-2.767	-2.663	-2.864
Fixed Investment	-0.789	-1.654	-1.941	-1.956	-1.971	-2.106
Export of Goods and Services	-1.202	-2.596	-3.000	-2.921	-2.878	-3.088
Import of Goods and Services	-0.685	-1.583	-2.264	-2.580	-2.743	-2.838
GDP	-1.227	-2.964	-3.095	-2.722	-2.383	-2.615
Consumer Price Index	-1.440	-3.066	-3.316	-2.922	-2.643	-2.825
Wholesale Price Index	-1.224	-2.614	-3.048	-2.998	2.982	-3.188
Unemployment Rate (dif)	0.536	0.685	0.515	0.259	0.149	0.127
Manufacturing Average Wage	-3.001	-4.740	-4.341	-3.154	-2.553	-2.615
Interest Rate: One-year	-0.017	-0.024	-0.019	-0.010	-0.006	-0.004

International Economic Models, edited by B. G. Hickman, pp. 85–95. Amsterdam: North-Holland.

——— (1979). "On Modelling the Economic Linkages among Countries." In *International Economic Policy: Theory and Evidence*, edited by R. Dornbusch and J. A. Frenkel, pp. 209–245. Baltimore: Johns Hopkins University Press.

Hughes, A. J. Hallett (1987). "The Impact of Interdependence on Economic Policy Design: The Case of the USA, EEC and Japan." *Economic Modelling*, Vol. 4, No. 3, pp. 377–396.

Hickman, B. G. (1983). "A Cross-section of Global International Economic Models." In *Global International Economic Models*, edited by B. G. Hickman, pp. 3–26. Amsterdam: North-Holland.

Lee, Kai-cheong (1983). "A Trade-oriented Econometric Model of Taiwan (1961–81)." Conference on Pacific Area Economic Models of LINK, 11–12 July. The Institute of Economics, Academia Sinica, Taipei, Taiwan.

Minford, A. P. (1985). "The Effects of American Policies — A New Classical Interpretation." In *International Economic Policy Coordination*, edited by W. H. Buiter and R. C. Marston, pp. 84–130. Cambridge: Cambridge University Press.

Minford, Patrick, Pierre-Richard Agnor and Eric Nowell (1986). "A New Classical Econometric Model of the World Economy." *Economic Modelling*, Vol. 3, No. 3, pp. 154–174.

Warner, D. L. (1983). "A Model of Trade and Exchange Rates." *Global International Economic Models*, edited by B. G. Hickman, pp. 297–313. Amsterdam: North-Holland.

Lo, Joan C., Hung-Yi Li and Tzong-Shian Yu (1990). "A Study on the Macro-economic Linkages between Taiwan and Its Major Trading Partners." Monograph Series No. 27, Chung-Hua Institution for Economic Research.

ANNEX 8.1

Variable Descriptions:

TYPE	MNEMONIC	VARIABLE DESCRIPTION	UNITS	SOURCES
I	ALLEMP	Total Employment	1,000 persons	2
B	CD86	Private Consumption — Durable Goods	Million 1986 NT$	1
B	CND86	Private Consumption — Non-Durable Goods	Million 1986 NT$	1
E	CONWIND	Construction Workers Wage Index	1986=100	2
I	CP	Private Consumption	Million NT$	1
I	CP86	Private Consumption	Million 1986 NT$	1
I	CPI	Consumer Price Index	1986=100	3
B	CPINOSE	CPI — Non-Service	1986=100	6
B	CPISER	CPI — Service	1986=100	6
B	CSD86	Private Consumption — Semi-Durable Goods	1986=100	1
B	CS86	Private Consumption — Services	Million 1986 NT$	1
B	CURR	Money Supply — Currency in Circulation	Million NT$	3
I	D	Total Depreciation	Million NT$	1
B	DD	Money Supply — Checking Account and Passbook Deposits	Million NT$	3
I	DG86	Depreciation of Government Sector	Million 1986 NT$	1
I	DM86	Depreciation of Manufacturing Sector	Million 1986 NT$	1
I	DP86	Depreciation of Private Sector	Million 1986 NT$	1
I	DPE86	Depreciation of Public Enterprise	Million 1986 NT$	1
B	DPS	Money Supply — Passbook Savings Deposits	Million NT$	3
E	DRG	Depreciation Rate for Capital Stock in Government Sector	(%)	1
E	DRM	Depreciation Rate for Capital Stock in Manufacturing	(%)	1
E	DRP	Depreciation Rate for Capital Stock in Private Sector	(%)	1
E	DRPE	Depreciation Rate for Capital Stock in Public Enterprise	(%)	1
E	DUM86	Dummy	1986=1	
E	D74	Dummy	1974=1	
E	D75	Dummy	1975=1	
E	D80	Dummy	1980=1	
E	D88	Dummy	1988=1	
E	D8485	Dummy	1984ín1985=1	
E	D8588	Dummy	1985ín1988=1	
E	D8789	Dummy	1987ín1989=1	
E	D8889	Dummy	1988ín1989=1	
B	EMP	Manufacturing Employment	1,000 persons	2
I	EUS	Exchange Rate Index (NT$/US$)	1986=100	2
E	EXR	Exchange Rate (NT$/US$)		1
I	G	Government Consumption	Million NT$	1
I	G86	Government Consumption	Million 1986 NT$	1

I	GCNW	G — other	Million NT$	1
E	GCNW86	G — other	Million 1986 NT$	1
I	GCW	G — Compensation of Employees	Million NT$	1
E	GCW86	G — Compensation of Employees	Million 1986 NT$	1
I	GDP	Gross Domestic Product	Million NT$	1
I	GDP86	Gross Domestic Product	Million 1986 NT$	1
I	GNP	Gross National Product	Million NT$	1
I	GNP86	Gross National Product	Million 1986 NT$	1
E	HH	Number of Households	1,000 households	4
I	I	Total Fixed Investment	Million NT$	1
I	I86	Total Fixed Investment	Million 1986 NT$	1
I	IG	Government Fixed Investment	Million NT$	1
E	IG86	Government Fixed Investment	Million 1986 NT$	1
B	IM86	Manufacturing Fixed Investment	Million 1986 NT$	1
I	IMPTAX	Import Tax Revenue	Million NT$	1
E	IMPTAXRT	Import Tax Rate	(%)	1
B	INT	1-Year Time Deposit Rate	(%)	3
B	INT2	1-Month Time Deposit Rate	(%)	3
E	IPE86	Public Enterprise Fixed Investment	Million 1986 NT$	1
B	IP86	Private Fixed Investment	Million 1986 NT$	1
I	KSG86	Government Capital Stock	Million 1986 NT$	1
I	KSM86	Manufacturing Capital Stock	Million 1986 NT$	1
I	KSNM86	Non-Manufacturing Capital Stock	Million 1986 NT$	1
I	KSP86	Private Capital Stock	Million 1986 NT$	1
I	KSPE86	Public Enterprise Capital Stock	Million 1986 NT$	1
E	LF	Labour Force	1,000 persons	2
I	LPRODM	Labour Productivity in Manufacturing		
I	LPRODNM	Labour Productivity in Non-Manufacturing		
I	M	Import of Goods and Services	Million NT$	1
I	M86	Import of Goods and Services	Million 1986 NT$	1
I	MG	Import of Goods	Million NT$	1
B	MOIL	Oil Imports	Million NT$	5
I	MG86	Import of Goods	Million 1986 NT$	1
I	MS	Import of Services	Million NT$	1
B	MS86	Import of Services	Million 1986 NT$	1
B	MWAGE	Average Wage in Manufacturing Sector	NT$/Month	2
I	M1A	Money Supply — M1A	Million NT$	B
I	M1B	Money Supply — M1B	Million NT$	B
I	M2	Money Supply — M2	Million NT$	1
E	NFI	Net Factor Income from Abroad	Million NT$	1
E	NFI86	Net Factor Income from Abroad	Million 1986 NT$	1
B	NMEMP	Non-Manufacturing Employment	1,000 persons	2
I	NQM	Non-Manufacturing Output	Million 1986 NT$	2
B	PCD	Deflator for CD	1986=100	1
I	PCNS	Deflator for CD+CND+CSD	1986=100	1
B	PCND	Deflator for CND	1986=100	1
I	PCP	Deflator for CP	1986=100	1
B	PCS	Deflator for CS	1986=100	1
B	PCSD	Deflator for CSD	1986=100	1

I	PG	Deflator for G	1986=100	1
I	PGDP	GDP Deflator	1986=100	1
B	PGNW	PG — Other	1986=100	1
B	PGW	PG — Compensation of Employees	1986=100	1
I	PI	Deflator for Fixed Investment	1986=100	1
B	PIG	Deflator for Government Fixed Investment	1986=100	1
B	PIP	Deflator for Public Enterprise Fixed Investment	1986=100	1
B	PIPE	Deflator for Private Fixed Investment	1986=100	1
I	PM	Deflator for Import of Goods and Services	1986=100	1
I	PMGNO	Deflator for Non-Oil Imports	1986=100	
B	PMG	Deflator for Import of Goods	1986=100	1
I	PMG2	Import Tax Adjusted Deflator	1986=100	1
E	PMS	Deflator for Import of Services	1986=100	1
I	POIL	Price of Importing Oil per Barrel	NT$	5
E	POIL$	Price of Importing Oil per Barrel	US$	5
I	POILIND	Oil Price Index	1986=100	
B	PV	Deflator for Inventory Change	1986=100	1
I	PX	Deflator for Export of Goods and Services	1986=100	1
B	PXG	Deflator for Export of Goods	1986=100	1
B	PXS	Deflator for Export of Services	1986=100	1
B	QM	Manufacturing Output	Million 1986 NT$	1
B	QMON	Money Supply — Quasi-Money	Million NT$	3
E	RDISC	Rediscount Rate	(%)	3
B	TAXDHI	Household Direct Tax — Income Tax	Million NT$	1
B	TAXDHNI	Household Direct Tax — Other	Million NT$	1
B	TAXDNH	Business Profit Tax	Million NT$	1
B	TAXIDNT	Indirect Tax — Non-Import Tax	Million NT$	1
I	TAX	Total Taxes	Million NT$	1
I	TD86	Total Demand	Million 1986 NT$	1
I	TR	Import Tax Factor		1
I	ULCM	Unit Labour Cost Index — Manufacturing	1986=100	2
I	UR	Unemployment Rate	(%)	2
I	V	Inventory Change	Million NT$	1
B	V86	Inventory Change	Million 1986 NT$	1
B	WPI	Wholesale Price Index	1986=100	3
I	X	Export of Goods and Services	Million NT$	1
I	X86	Export of Goods and Services	Million 1986 NT$	1
I	XG	Export of Goods	Million NT$	1
I	XG86	Export of Goods	Million 1986 NT$	1
I	XS	Export of Services	Million NT$	1
E	XS86	Export of Services	Million 1986 NT$	1
I	Y	Household Income	Million NT$	
I	YD	Household Disposable Income	Million NT$	1
I	YD86	Household Disposable Income	Million 1986 NT$	1
E	YEAR	Year		
E	YGAP	Gap Between YD and NNP-Tax	Million NT$	1
B	X@ii86	Real Export to Country ii	Million 1986 NT$	5
B	M@ii86	Real Import from Country ii	Million 1986 NT$	5

E	GDP85@ii	Real GDP of Country ii in Local Currency (Singapore is expressed in Million $)	Billion 1985 $	7
E	GNP85@ii	Real GNP of Country ii (L_u)	Billion 1985 $	7
I	ER@ii	Exchange Rate Index of Country ii (L_r)	1986=100	7
E	EXR@ii	Exchange Rate of Country ii (L_r)		7
E	PX@ii	Price Deflator of Country ii's Goods Export (L_u)	1986=100	7
E	UM@ii	Unit Value Index of Country ii's Goods Import (L_u)	1986=100	7
E	UX@ii	Unit Value Index of Country ii's Goods Export (L_u)	1986=100	7
E	WPI@ii	WPI of Country ii	1986=100	7
I	XG86SUM	Sum of Exports to Specified Countries	Million 1986 NT$	
E	X86OTH	Real Exports to Other Countries	Million 1986 NT$	
I	MG86SUM	Sum of Imports from Specified Countries	Million 1986 NT$	
B	M86OTH	Imports from Other Countries	Million 1986 NT$	
I	MGSUM	Sum of Imports from Specified Countries	Million NT$	
I	PMGSUM	Weighted Prices of Imports (Oil included)	1986=100	
	ii	Country		
	AU	Australia		
	CA	Canada		
	FR	France		
	GE	Germany		
	IN	Indonesia		
	IT	Italy		
	JA	Japan		
	KO	South Korea		
	MA	Malaysia		
	PH	Philippines		
	SI	Singapore		
	TH	Thailand		
	UK	United Kingdom		
	US	United States		

Type:
   I: Identity
   B: Behaviour Equation
   E: Exogenous

Notes:
   (a) In Local Currency
   (b) Local Currency/US$

Sources:
1. *National Income of the Republic of China*, Directorate-General of Budget, Accounting and Statistics, Executive Yuan, Republic of China.
2. "Quarterly National Economic Trends, Taiwan Area, Republic of China." DGBAS
3. "Financial Statistics Monthly, Taiwan District, Republic of China." Economic Research Department, The Central Bank of China.

4. "Monthly Statistics of The Republic of China." DGBAS.
5. *Monthly Statistics of Exports and Imports*, Taiwan Area, Republic of China, Department of Statistics, Ministry of Finance.
6. "Commodity-Price Statistics Monthly in the Taiwan Area of the Republic of China." DGBAS.
7. "International Financial Statistics." IMF.

CHAPTER 9

Taiwan-United States Trade: From Complementary to Competitive Relations

Lee Maw-Lin
University of Missouri–Columbia, U.S.A.
Ben C. Liu
Chicago State University, U.S.A.

I. INTRODUCTION

The persistent problem of trade imbalance between Taiwan and the U.S. has been a topic of interest for scholars, politicians and the public for many years. In this essay, we discuss this problem from a structural perspective. We suggest that it is not possible to use the exchange rate mechanism alone to fully correct the trade imbalance problem between Taiwan and U.S. because the two economies have a complementary rather than competitive relationship.[1] This complementary relationship exists because the two countries have been at different stages of development, i.e. the U.S. is a mature economy while Taiwan has been in a relatively early stage of its development process. In fact, it is the structural problem of a mature (U.S.) economy which offers the opportunities for Taiwan (and other Pacific Rim countries) to expand its exports, facilitating the growth of its economy. However, we also note that, in its relations with the U.S. economy, Taiwan is departing from the complementary era and is entering a new age of competitiveness.

---

[1] Impacts of exchange rate changes on international trade have been the subject of studies by many authors. See, for example, Baldwin and Krugman (1989), Dornbusch (1987), Feinberg (1989), Fisher (1989), Mann (1986), and Meade (1988).

Our approach to considering the structural factors in Taiwan-U.S. trade relations is to compare and contrast the relevant consumption and production spaces of the two countries.

II. COMPOSITION OF TAIWAN-U.S. TRADE

Taiwan's commodity trade has expanded rapidly since the late 1950s. In this trade expansion, the U.S. has been Taiwan's principal partner. As shown in Table 9.1, Taiwan's exports to the U.S. amounted to 3.5% of its total exports in 1952. The percentage was 48.8 in 1985, and 32.2 in 1990. Taiwan's imports from the U.S. accounted for 45.7% of its total imports in 1952. This percentage decreased to 23 in 1990.

Table 9.1 Taiwan's Commodity Trade (in US$ million)

	1952	1960	1965	1970	1975	1980	1985	1990	1991
Total exports	116	164	450	1,481	5,309	19,811	30,726	67,214	76,178
Percent to U.S. (%)	3.5	11.5	21.3	38.1	34.3	34.1	48.8	32.4	29.3
Total imports	187	297	556	1,524	5,952	19,733	20,102	54,716	62,861
Percent from U.S. (%)	45.7	38.1	31.7	23.9	27.8	23.7	23.0	23.0	22.4
Export–Import	−71	−132	−106	−43	−643	77	10,624	12,498	13,317

Source: *Taiwan Statistical Data Book 1992.*

The exchange rate between the NT$ and the US$ has undergone several important changes during the past 40 years. In the 1950s, the exchange rate was fixed, but there were different exchange rates for different commodity groups. Between 1961 and 1971, the exchange rate was fixed at 40 to 1. This rate was fixed at 37.95 between 1973 and 1977, but ranged from 35.95 to 40.22 during the period 1978–1983. Since 1984, the rate declined sharply from 39.42 to the recent low of around 25 New Taiwan dollars for each U.S. dollar.

The composition of exports to and imports from the U.S. has also undergone important changes.[2] As shown in Table 9.2, agricultural and

---

[2] See, for example, Hervey (1990), for an interesting discussion of changing patterns of U.S. foreign trade.

**Table 9.2 Composition of Taiwan's Exports to the United States
by Commodity Groups**

	1972	1975	1978	1981	1984	1987	1990	1991
Total (in US$ million)	1,251	1,823	5,010	8,158	14,868	23,685	21,746	22,321
Total percent	100	100	100	100	100	100	100	100
Canned food, sugar	3.0	5.1	2.0	1.1	0.6	0.1	0.2	0.0
Textile products	31.5	28.2	27.5	22.3	17.0	12.0	12.3	13.2
Plastic, rubber	4.2	12.6	11.6	11.4	10.6	11.7	6.1	5.9
Metal, metal products	2.4	3.0	5.3	6.9	8.5	9.2	8.9	8.8
Machinery, electrical	—	—	—	27.0	29.2	30.9	34.8	36.5
Dolls, toys, etc.	—	2.1	2.6	4.8	5.0	4.4	2.4	2.1
Others	58.9	49.0	51.0	26.6	29.2	31.7	35.6	24.5

Source: *Taiwan Statistical Data Book 1992.*

textile products were the most important commodities exported to the U.S. in the 1950s. In recent years, the most important products exported to the U.S. have been manufactured goods which accounts for roughly one-third of the total value of exports. Table 9.3 shows that the importation of agricultural products as a percentage of total imports from the U.S. decreased from 33.7 in 1972 to 6.0 in 1990. The importation of chemicals as a percentage of total imports from the U.S. was 7.9 in 1972, 20.8 in 1984, and 13.4 in 1990.

**Table 9.3 Composition of Taiwan's Imports from the United States
by Commodity Groups**

	1972	1975	1978	1981	1984	1987	1990	1991
Total (in US$ million)	543	1,652	2,376	4,766	5,042	7,467	12,611	14,114
Total percent	100	100	100	100	100	100	100	100
Agricultural products	33.7	26.4	20.4	13.3	13.8	9.2	6.0	
Machinery	29.0	33.1	27.8	30.0	23.4	24.3	28.9	
Chemicals	7.9	11.3	12.3	17.8	20.8	20.1	13.4	
Transportation	8.5	4.4	6.7	3.2	0.7	1.7	7.8	
Basic metals	5.8	6.5	3.8	4.9	5.1	10.4	6.0	
Others	15.2	18.0	29.0	30.8	36.3	34.4	37.9	

Source: *Taiwan Statistical Data Book 1992.*

III. A DEFINITION OF PRODUCTION AND
CONSUMPTION SPACES

To develop the concepts of state-dependent production and consumption spaces which we use to discuss structural factors, we assume that the state of an economy is represented by the stocks of its human and non-human capital, and its environment. We use two functional relations to define the limits which the capital stocks and the environment place on the production and consumption spaces. One functional relation, named the activity generating function, is implied by Stigler and Becker's (1977) observation that "the investment required simply to maintain the capital stock intact would increase as the stock increased." A relationship of this form is also suggested by the recent findings that there is a status quo and that it limits economic rationality.[3] The other functional relation we use is the activity production function.

Both producers and consumers are economic agents who make decisions about combinations of commodity inputs with human and non-human capital stocks to produce human activity. A single basic concept of the state-dependent choice set can therefore be developed for application in the definition of the state-dependent consumption set and production set. We assume that there is a meaningful way to "aggregate" individual consumption and production sets to obtain aggregate consumption and production spaces for an economy.

To develop a definition of the state-dependent choice set, let R be the agent's capital stock and environment. We assume that:

(a) There are capital stocks which require and generate a particular activity A, to maintain the state of functional equilibrium. These are called generating capital, r_G. For instance, a certain characteristic of being a technological leader is that a capital stock determines the requirements for research and development activities. We also assume that in the subset R_G of R which contains capital stocks r_G such that r_G generate activity A, there is defined a positive real-valued function G_A measuring the requirements for the activity A, called the activity generating function.

Definition (Equilibrium set for Activity A): the set of zeros of the

---

[3]   These findings, for example, by Tversky and Kahneman (1991), indicate that there is a reference state which contradicts the traditional assumption about preferences and global rationality.

activity generating function is called the equilibrium set for activity A and is denoted by E_A.

$$E_A = \{r_G \; \varepsilon \; r_G \,/\, G_A(r_G) = 0\}$$

That is, when the generating capital stocks lie within the equilibrium set, the status quo is maintained and the associated activity is neither required nor generated.

(b) Similarly, there are capital stocks which enable activity A to take place. These are called production capital, r_P. For example, an instrumental laboratory enables experiments to take place. In addition, there are activity production functions which measure the transformation of commodity bundles and production capital into capital stocks, through the flow of the activity A, i. e.

$$P_A: Q \times R_G \times R_P \rightarrow R_G \times R_P$$

where Q is usual commodity space. Specifically, the production function P_A transforms a point (q, r_G, r_P) into a point (r'_G, r'_P), where q is in Q, r_G and r'_G are in the generating capital stock set R_G, and r_P and r'_P are in the production capital stock set R_P of R which contains capital stocks r_P such that r_P enables activity A to take place.

We develop the following definition of the state-dependent choice set:
Definition: For a given activity A and capital stocks (r_G, r_P),

$$C = \{q \; \varepsilon \; Q \,/\, P_A(q, r_G, r_P) \; \varepsilon \; E_A \times R_P\}$$

That is the state-dependent choice set at (r_G, r_P) where

$$E_A = \{r_G \; \varepsilon \; R_G /\, G_A(r_G) = 0\}$$

That is, the state-dependent choice set C of the agent at (r_G, r_P) consists of those commodity points q for which (q, r_G, r_P) produces, through the activity A, a point (r'_G, r'_P) whose generating capital stocks lie within the equilibrium set with respect to A. Figure 9.1 provides an illustration of the choice set:

In Figure 9.1, P_A is an activity production function and we assume that its inverse, P_A^{-1}, exists. Define the function:

$$h_A = P_A^{-1}/E_A \times R_P : E_A \times R_P \rightarrow Q \times R_G \times R_P$$
$$g : h_A(E_A \times R_P) \rightarrow Q$$

where g is the canonical projection from $h_A(E_A \times R_P) \; \varepsilon \; Q \times R_G \times R_P$ into

Figure 9.1 The State-dependent Choice Set

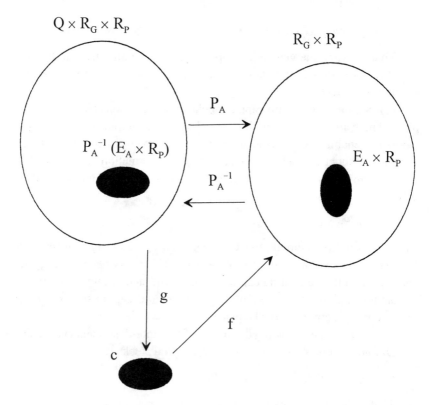

usual commodity space Q, and f is defined as $f = goh_A$. Thus, the choice set depends upon two state parameters representing generating and production capitals, respectively, at the time.

For the consumer, the relevant choice set is his state-dependent consumption set and for producer, it is his state-dependent production set. We assume that an economy's consumption space is a combination of its individuals' consumption sets. The economy's production space is a combination of its individuals' production sets.

IV. ERA OF COMPLEMENTARITY

It is a historical fact that as a country goes through its development processes, its consumption and production spaces undergo systematic changes, i.e. they both expand and shift. But there are important differences in the patterns of change in the consumption and production spaces as economic development proceeds. In the case of consumption space, the basic necessities of life, such as clothing and shoes, will continue to remain an important part of the consumption space even though the quality of products may change. The production space, however, is different in that some industries may simply cease to exist. Others will be added. Such differential changes in production and consumption spaces over time explain why the U.S. and Taiwan have had complementary, rather than competitive, trade relations. For each country, the production space does not match the consumption space. Moreover, a portion of Taiwan's production space matches a portion of U.S. consumption space. More importantly, for several decades extending to recent years, there has been little intersection in the production spaces of Taiwan and the United States.

It is true that free trade between nations is complementary in the sense that it is frequently motivated by differences in factor endowments. But we suggest that differential changes in consumption and production spaces have played a particularly important part in the expanding trade relations of the U.S. with Taiwan and other Pacific Rim countries from the 1960s through the 1980s.

For Taiwan, its development processes began in the 1950s. The United States was an important source of the capital goods needed to expand its productive capacity, funds needed to finance the importation of capital goods, raw materials for its industrial processes, and education for its future scientists, engineers, and managers. The U.S. was also an important market for the consumer goods which Taiwan produced in its early stage of development.

The recent economic history of the U.S. is different. As a major industrial nation that was not damaged by World War II, the U.S. became the most important supplier of manufactured and capital goods. The cold war in general, and the Korean War and the war in Vietnam in particular, caused the U.S. to devote a large proportion of its resources to its own defence and to the production of military and other goods and services for other countries. This caused resources to be directed to the military and defence sector, and away from low-tech industries producing basic necessities.

The growing importance of the defence and manufacturing sectors in the U.S. was accompanied by structural changes in the economy associated with the technological revolution brought about by computer automation, and the development of relatively inexpensive and readily accessible transportation and communication networks. These caused important changes in both production and consumption spaces, leading to changes in demand and supply.

There are several factors which account for the shift in the pattern of demand that was observed in the United States. Among these must be the high rates of inflation which the U.S. consumers experienced during the period which extended from the 1960s through the early part of the 1980s. Confronted with the problem of inflation, consumers resisted price increases. They sought less expensive substitutes for many products to protect their standard of living. For example, the obvious shift in consumer demand from low gasoline mileage to high mileage automobiles in the 1970s was a result of the increases in the price of gasoline generated by the oil crisis.

A second factor which explains a part of the shift in demand results from the rise of the service industry. The low wage rates that were paid to workers in these industries had the effect of making income distribution more unequal. That is, the real income for some groups fell because

Table 9.4 Consumer Price Index

Year	All items	Apparel*	Year	All items	Apparel*
1967	100.0	100.0	1980	246.8	178.2
1968	104.2	105.3	1981	272.4	186.9
1969	109.8	111.4	1982	289.1	191.8
1970	116.3	116.1	1983	298.4	196.5
1971	121.3	119.8	1984	311.1	200.2
1972	125.3	122.2	1985	322.2	205.9
1973	133.1	126.7	1986	328.4	207.6
1974	147.7	136.1	1987	340.4	216.9
1975	161.2	142.2	1988	354.5	226.3
1976	170.5	147.5	1989	371.6	232.5
1977	181.5	154.1	1990	391.4	243.3
1978	195.4	159.6	1991	408.0	252.4
1979	217.4	166.5	1992	416.1	258.7

Note: * including upkeep
Source: Based on data reported in the *Economic Report of the President* (1993).

nominal wages had not kept pace with consumer prices. Finally, there has been a growing acceptance of products based on quality rather than the origin of the products. This acceptance was facilitated by the development of transportation and communication.

While the pattern of consumer demand changed much during the period 1960s through the 1980s, many domestic firms did not respond quickly to these demand shifts. In other words, production space did not shift in response to changes in consumption space. There are several reasons for this slow response.

Many products for which demand continues to remain at a high level produce low profit margins given the prevailing U.S. wage rates. These products have a common feature in that there are few cost-reducing technological innovations in these industries. Textiles, apparel and shoes are examples of such products. The initial response by U.S. firms was to move to the southern U.S., and then overseas.

Supply shift responsiveness is also limited because well-established and mature industries have a limited ability to adapt to new conditions. The slow response by the American automobile industry to increased demand for high mileage cars exemplifies this lack of adaptability. Historically, the production and consumption spaces for automobiles in the U.S. were for large cars. When gasoline prices rose sharply in the 1970s, the consumption space expanded to include small cars. U.S. producers were both unwilling and unable to shift their production space from large to small cars. Japan's production and consumption spaces for automobiles were for small cars. The inability of the U.S. producers to shift their production space enabled Japanese producers to expand and penetrate the U.S. market quite easily.

Industries in mature countries may also be relatively inflexible with respect to design, when domestic markets are large enough to permit the complete exploitation of economies of scale. Domestic markets which are large relative to existing technology permit producers to tailor products to specific large-scale national markets. Such markets do exist in the United States with the result that producers do not normally need to approach foreign markets aggressively.

Technical considerations, of course, determine feasible factor mixtures. Nonetheless, it is convenient to speak of industries being high-cost because of high domestic factor prices. High wage rates and high interest rates have contributed to high costs of production in the United States.

It is well known that Americans are paid high wages, and these wages have increased over the years. High wages and wage increases are related to the level of and changes in labour productivity. The consequences of wage agreements which exceed increases in labour productivity are particularly acute for industries which already experience low profit margins. As shown in Table 9.5, wage rate settlements ranged from 6.1 to 9.1% increases from 1969 to 1981. It is unlikely that such large wage increases were matched by comparable increases in labour productivity. It is perhaps because of this that imported products gained important positions in U.S. markets.

Table 9.5 U.S. Wage Rate Settlements

Year	Percentage (%)	Year	Percentage (%)	Year	Percentage (%)
1969	8.2	1977	6.2	1985	2.7
1970	9.1	1978	6.3	1986	1.6
1971	8.8	1979	6.6	1987	2.6
1972	7.4	1980	7.1	1988	2.5
1973	6.1	1981	8.3	1989	3.4
1974	7.8	1982	2.8	1990	3.4
1975	8.1	1983	3.0	1991	3.1
1976	6.6	1984	2.8	1992	3.1

Sources: *Statistical Abstract of the United States*, various issues.

The recent history of domestic U.S. interest rates is shown in Table 9.6 below. Rising interest rates in the 1960s and the high rates in the 1970s through the 1980s were brought about by a shortage of capital associated with a low rate of savings, a high demand for funds generated by the computer revolution, a large federal deficit, and by mergers and acquisitions.[4] The high rates were also due to the Federal Reserve System's programme of controlling inflation.

These high interest rates, whether due in part to a low rate of domestic savings or due to a high demand for funds, are undoubtedly partly responsible for the low rate of capital formation experienced within the U.S. in the recent past. Data bearing upon this point can be found in Table 9.7. Low

---

[4] During most of the past decade, the annual federal deficit has been in excess of $200 billion.

Table 9.6   Interest Rate Trend (3-Year T-Bonds)

Year	Percentage (%)	Year	Percentage (%)	Year	Percentage (%)
1965	4.2	1974	7.8	1983	10.5
1966	5.2	1975	7.5	1984	11.9
1967	5.0	1976	6.8	1985	9.6
1968	5.7	1977	6.7	1986	7.1
1969	7.0	1978	8.3	1987	7.7
1970	7.3	1979	9.7	1988	8.3
1971	5.7	1980	11.6	1989	8.6
1972	5.7	1981	14.4	1990	8.3
1973	7.0	1982	12.9	1991	6.8
				1992	5.3

Source: *Economic Report of the President* (1993).

rates of capital formation are particularly detrimental to productivity when industries are mature and well stocked with vintage capital at a time when technology is changing rapidly. Development in the computer and artificial intelligence fields had led to particularly rapid capital obsolescence.

In summary, the shifts in consumer demand and the relative inability of U.S. industries to respond to these demand changes have provided unusual market opportunities for foreign producers. These market opportunities were in principle open to all countries. That Taiwan and other Pacific Rim

Table 9.7   Capital Formation as a Percentage of GDP

Region	1965– 1969	1970– 1974	1975– 1979	1980– 1984	1985– 1989	1990– 1991
South Korea	22.1	23.7	28.0	29.7	29.7	—
U.S.A.	17.7	17.8	16.8	16.8	17.0	16.4
Japan	32.3	34.7	30.7	29.6	27.9	—
Taiwan	17.5	23.1	26.9	26.4	20.2	22.5

Sources: For Taiwan, *Taiwan Statistical Data Book 1992*; For South Korea, *Economic Statistics Yearbook*, 1990; For the U.S., *Economic Report of the President*, 1993; For Japan, *Statistical Yearbook for Asia and the Pacific, United Nations*, various issues.

countries have been more successful in exploiting these markets than other countries can be explained by borrowing Dornbusch and Park's observation that "Korea's labour force is better trained and works harder. Its people save more and borrow wisely."[5]

V. NEW AGE OF COMPETITIVENESS

We have argued that Taiwan-U.S. economic relations developed quickly because these two economies are complementary. Because access to large markets was vital to economic development, this complementarity played an important role in facilitating the remarkable growth rates displayed by the Taiwanese economy. Equally important, this complementarity also enabled U.S. consumers to maintain their standard of living at a time when U.S. industries were not responsive to demand changes. Complementarity, therefore, figures prominently in any discussion focused upon the prospects for Taiwan-U.S. economic relations. The degree of complementarity, however, has been decreasing over time.

Wage increases which exceeded productivity growth in the United States also played a role in the pattern and level of trade between these two partners. However, there has been moderation in such wage settlements in recent years. If this continues, trade driven by these considerations will tail off. Furthermore, one would expect that, over a decade or less, wage rates in excess of labour productivity will lead to readjustments within the affected industries either by slower wage increases or changes in the industries' capital structures which will bring labour productivity into line with pay rates.

In part, trade differences were driven by high United States interest rates. These were tied to inflation, partly through policy decisions. With the moderation of inflation, real interest rates fell. Nevertheless, the U.S. still seems to be dogged by a low savings rate. And with still substantial federal and trade deficits, we may continue to see rather low rates of capital formation. This problem is moderated to some extent by investment programmes undertaken by countries with trade surpluses with the United States.

In conjunction with these forces, we expect to find the competitive

---

[5] This observation by Dornbusch and Park (1987) of South Korea is equally applicable to Taiwan.

position of U.S. firms improving as a consequence of active reinvestment programmes designed to replace ageing plants and equipment with new production processes. We see an example of this in the U.S. steel and automobile industries. Furthermore, the issue of product quality has been brought home to U.S. industry, the automobile industry being a strong case in point, and programmes designed to improve product quality will begin to exert an influence upon foreign trade.

The developments described above are internal to the U.S. Taiwan, at the same time, will be subject to forces which will help shape trade flows between these countries. Rising wages associated with rising real incomes within Taiwan will lead to the gradual removal of some products, such as textiles and shoes, from the set of products which it is economically feasible to export to the U.S. That these products will find new markets in other developing countries is irrelevant to this argument. Furthermore, rising wages will make it less attractive for U.S. firms to produce certain product lines there.

As Taiwan's industries continue to develop, it is to be expected that the geographical distribution of Taiwan exports will continue to broaden. This will necessarily mean less dependence upon the U.S. market as an outlet for its industrial products. Investing in mainland China and in Southeast Asia reflects Taiwan's diversification.

Furthermore, product diversification will continue to develop in Taiwan industry. Unquestionably, Taiwan firms will continue to expand into product lines which require more and more technological sophistication, both in terms of human and physical capital. As this occurs, Taiwan firms will find they have a less and less complementary relationship with U.S. firms and markets and that they will move to a more and more competitive position. Such complementarity as exists will tend to reflect human resource endowments more and more clearly, and will reflect less and less strongly differences related to overall industrial maturity. There is already evidence of this shift in the fact that an increasing proportion of Taiwan's exports are goods with high technology contents.

VI. SUMMARY AND CONCLUSIONS

The fact that economic relations between Taiwan and the United States continue to expand despite the intensification of trade disputes indicates that both countries derive important net benefits from these exchanges.

Difficulties inherent in the negotiations undertaken to resolve such trade disputes, however, are exacerbated because the economic benefits of this external trade are more visible to Taiwanese than to Americans. This is related to the fact that many of the benefits to the United States are qualitative and that trade deficits are on the United States side. Even so, we can identify some of the major economic benefits to the U.S. from this trade relationship. These include the fact that imports from Taiwan and other Pacific Rim countries have contributed substantially to the moderation of inflation in the U.S. economy. The extent to which imports have moderated price inflation is difficult to ascertain. Nevertheless, evidence exists which indicates that specific categories of imports contributed to relatively moderate rate of inflation. For example, as shown in Table 9.4, while the consumer price index as a whole increased from 100 in 1967 to 328.4 in 1986, the index for apparel prices for men and boys increased from 100 to only 199.7 over the same period. It can not be doubted that part of this performance is related to the fact that imports accounted for an increasing percentage in this category of products of total U.S. supply.

By their exports to the U.S., foreign producers put competitive pressures not only on prices but also on the quality of the products which U.S. firms produce. While we see this most obviously in the U.S. automobile industry, efforts at quality improvements by U.S. firms in other industries have had considerable impact already, and their quality can be expected to improve. Such product improvement, which has considerable efficiency and welfare implications, would have materialized more slowly had it not been for the competition generated by imports.

A beneficial consequence of this trade is the closely related improvement we find in the efficiency of U.S. industries. These production line and inventory control improvements contribute to moderation in cost-push inflation. Some of this increased efficiency can be attributed to the competitive pressure exerted by foreign producers.

Unquestionably, competitive pressures force industry negotiators to "hold the line" more forcefully when negotiating new wage contracts. We refer, of course, to wage increases which are in excess of productivity increases. Foreign competition, then, helps hold down cost-push inflation just as effectively as domestic competition does. At least, this is the case so long as trade barriers are not erected in the place of more carefully considered wage increases.

We often hear the case made that imports contribute to unemployment.

This may be true in the short run. But workers affected by increased importation are in general able to shift to other industries or occupations. Moreover, importation facilitates exports which create employment. Employment in an economy is likely to be greater with than without trade, even if there is a trade deficit.

In conclusion, we quote McInerney and White (1993) who write in their book *Beating Japan* that "Americans love to hate the Japanese, the best excuse we have for failure." The authors also suggest that in order to succeed, U.S. firms must structurally dismantle and rebuild their businesses so they can be competitive with Japan, and must live and breathe the customers, no matter where in the world they are discovered. These insights are also applicable if U.S. firms are to strengthen their trading relations with other Pacific Rim countries.

REFERENCES

Baldwin, Richard and Paul Krugman (1989). "Persistent Trade Effects of Large Exchange Rate Shocks." *Quarterly Journal of Economics*, November, Vol. 104, pp. 635–654.

Dornbusch, Rudiger (1987). "Exchange Rates and Prices." *American Economic Review*, March, Vol. 77, pp. 93–104.

Dornbusch, Rudiger and Yung Chul Park (1987). "Korean Growth Policy." *Brookings Papers on Economic Activities*, Vol. 2, pp. 389–444.

Feinberg, Robert M. (1989). "The Effects of Foreign Exchange Movements on U.S. Domestic Prices." *Review of Economics and Statistics*, August, Vol. 71, pp. 505–511.

Hervey, J. L. (1990). "Changing U.S. Trade Patterns." *Economic Perspectives*, Federal Reserve Bank of Chicago, Vol. 14, pp. 2–12.

Fisher, Eric N. (1989). "A Model of Exchange Rate Pass-through." *Journal of International Economics*, February, Vol. 26, pp. 119–137.

Mann, Catherine L. (1986). "Prices, Profit Margins and Exchange Rates." *Federal Reserve Bulletin*, June, Vol. 72, pp. 366–379.

McInerney, Francis and Sean White (1993). *Beating Japan*. New York: Truman Talley Books.

Meade, E. E. (1988). "Exchange Rates, Adjustment and the J-Curve." *Federal Reserve Bulletin*, October, Vol. 74, pp. 633–644.

Stigler, George J. and Gary S. Becker (1977). "De-Gustibus Non Est Disputandum." *American Economic Review*, March, Vol. 67, pp. 76–90.

Tversky, Amos and Daniel Kahneman (1991). "Loss Aversion in Riskless Choice: A Reference-Dependence Model." *Quarterly Journal of Economics*, November, Vol. 106, pp. 1039–1061.

CHAPTER 10

Financial Policies in a Maturing Taiwan Economy

Christina Y. Liu
The National Taiwan University, Taiwan

I. INTRODUCTION

Since financial liberalization and internationalization were adopted as national policies in Taiwan in the early 1980s, the financial market has become an increasingly important sector. The recent development of Taiwan's financial market has not only generated strong effects on its macroeconomy but also induced a much tighter link between the capital market in Taiwan and the global capital market.

This essay presents an analysis of the financial policies in the recent maturing Taiwan economy. The effect of the financial policies of liberalization and internationalization is examined. The essay proceeds as follows: Section II provides a background of the financial deregulation in Taiwan; Section III examines domestic money market liberalization, focusing on the interest rate liberalization in the 1980s; Section IV presents foreign exchange liberalization and some related issues, including the appreciation of the N.T. dollar starting in 1986, the relaxation of restrictions on cross-border capital flows since 1987, and also presents statistical evidence of a lesser extent of Central Bank intervention in the 1990s; Section V presents statistical evidence regarding the link between the securities market in Taiwan and the macroeconomy of the Pacific-Basin region and of the world; finally, Section VI summarizes and concludes the essay.

II. BACKGROUND OF THE FINANCIAL DEREGULATION IN THE 1980s

The order and speed of economic liberalization have received great attention in both academic and policy-making circles in recent years. In general, it is suggested in the literature that both stable prices and a balanced fiscal budget are essential preconditions for financial liberalization. Moreover, a country's domestic financial market should be liberalized prior to its international capital market, and its international trade sector should be liberalized prior to its international capital sector.[1]

Based on the above suggestions, it is clear that the timing of financial liberalization programmes implemented in Taiwan was very favourable. The country recorded a high savings rate, a sound government budget, and a low inflation rate in the early 1980s. The necessary conditions for financial liberalization were hence satisfied. In addition, since liberalization in the trade sector was continuously emphasized long before the 1980s, the economy was in every respect ready for financial liberalization at the beginning of the 1980s.[2]

On the other hand, there was an increasing demand for financial deregulation in Taiwan at the same time. Due to the huge trade surplus in the 1980s, there were massive foreign reserves and a rapid growth in the money supply in Taiwan. To absorb those increased foreign reserves and money supplies, it was very important for the economy to rely on more flexible interest rates and foreign exchange rates. The financial liberalization programme hence received great attention in Taiwan in the 1980s. The process and effects of liberalization in interest rates and in foreign exchange rates are analysed below in Sections III and IV, respectively.

III. INTEREST RATE LIBERALIZATION

The money market in Taiwan was officially established in 1976. The

---

[1] For the order and speed of liberalization, see Balassa (1982), Edwards (1984), Frenkel (1982), Harberger (1984), Krueger (1984), McKinnon (1982, 1986), among others.

[2] See Kuo (1983) for an extensive analysis of the Taiwan economy, and see Kuo (1992), Kuo (1992, 1993), and Ranis (1992), for the most recent economic developments in Taiwan.

money market instruments consist of commercial papers, bankers' acceptances, negotiable certificates of deposit, and treasury bills. Deregulation of the money market was the first step in interest rate liberalization in Taiwan. In November 1980, the Central Bank of China promulgated the Essentials of Interest Rate Adjustment, which permitted a wider range in the difference between maximum and minimum loan rates and also allowed for a free setting of interest rates on certificates of deposit and on some other money market instruments.

One of the most important effects of this first-step liberalization programme was that it led official interest rates to move closer to the market-determined money market rate. During the period from November 1980 to September 1982, the official interest rates were adjusted as many as ten times to keep up with the movement of money market rates and that of interbank call rates.

The second stage of the interest rate liberalization programme started in 1985. Starting in March 1985, each depository bank was asked to make a daily announcement of its prime rate. Differences in prime rates among banks were not only officially recognized, but actually encouraged. At the same time, the Central Interbank Call Rate System was abolished to give each bank complete freedom in the determination of its own call rate.

In September 1985, the Regulations for Interest Rate Management were also abolished, which helped to widen the range of maximum and minimum loan rates. In January 1986, deposit categories were reduced from thirteen to four, which greatly expanded the free zone of banking activities.[3] Lastly, the revision of the Banking Law in 1989 removed controls on all deposit and loan rates. Overall, the interest rate liberalization programme has been implemented smoothly and successfully, and interest rates in Taiwan are now determined mostly by market forces.[4]

---

[3] According to the Banking Law at that time, the Central Bank determined the maximum interest rate for "each kind" of deposits. Therefore, while thirteen categories of deposits lead to the restrictions of thirteen maximum rates, the classifying of deposits into only four categories reduces those restrictions.

[4] See Kuo (1990), Liu and Kuo (1990) for details of the process and effect of interest rate liberalization in Taiwan in the 1980s. Also, Chiu (1992), and Shea (1990), analyse the effect of monetary policy on prices under financial liberalization.

IV. FOREIGN EXCHANGE LIBERALIZATION AND RELATED ISSUES

This section presents the process and effects of the recent foreign exchange liberalization in Taiwan, focusing particularly on the appreciation of the N.T. dollar starting in 1986, the relaxation of restrictions on cross-border capital flows starting in 1987, and also presents statistical evidence of the lesser degree of Central Bank intervention in the 1990s.[5]

Appreciation of the N. T. Dollar Starting in 1986

The foreign exchange system was officially changed from a fixed exchange rate regime to a flexible regime in February 1979. The currency value had remained quite stable during the 1981–1985 period, but appreciated by more than 40% relative to the U.S. dollar over the 1986–1987 period. The extensive appreciation of the N.T. dollar was initiated by the huge trade surplus generated in Taiwan in the 1980s. Since 1985, the current account balance in Taiwan had increased drastically, mainly due to the fact that savings have far exceeded the investment demand of the economy. For example, the gross savings/GNP ratio generally was higher than 30% in the 1980s (it reached 37.7% in 1986, and 38.5% in 1987), and the investment/GNP ratio only ranged between some 15 to 20% over the 1985–1987 period. As a result, the current account balance accounted for 15.5% of GNP in 1985, and this share increased to 22.4% and 20.7% of GNP in 1986 and 1987, respectively. During the same period, the G-5 meeting in 1985 induced a depreciation of the U.S. dollar against most of the major currencies in the world. Both of the above factors created a natural tendency for the N.T. dollar to appreciate against the U.S. dollar in 1985.

The appreciation of the N.T. dollar over the 1986–1987 period, however, did not occur by just following market forces. Instead, there were intensive Central Bank intervention operations during that period. Even though the general public in Taiwan believed that the appreciation of the

---

[5] The sub-sections "Appreciation of the N.T. Dollar Starting in 1986" and "Relaxation of Restrictions on Cross-border Capital Flows" draw on Liu (1992a). For more detailed analysis of the liberalization of foreign exchange rates in Taiwan, see Kuo (1990), and Liu (1992b). Also, see Liang and Hou Liang (1988), among others, for financial policies.

N.T. dollar was inevitable, there was still strong pressure on the Central Bank to intervene in the foreign exchange market.[6] The general concern of the community and of the government sector was that any drastic appreciation of the N.T. dollar would involve high adjustment costs, which might be too painful for the export and importing-competing sectors to bear. Reflecting this philosophy, the Central Bank in the 1986–1987 period frequently intervened in the foreign exchange market to absorb the excess supply of U.S. dollars, leading to the huge foreign exchange reserves held in the Central Bank in Taiwan.

While Central Bank intervention is common in most countries, the particular Central Bank intervention in Taiwan during the 1986–1987 period might have induced a serious violation of a fundamental international capital market equilibrium condition. That is, the interest rate parity condition was violated during this period.[7] In particular, since the Central Bank in that period intervened in such a way that the N.T. dollar was appreciating "gradually" and "smoothly", the market continuously expected a further appreciation of the N.T. dollar. As a result, this expectation induced a huge speculative capital inflow into the economy (the statistical evidence for the above point is presented below in "A Lesser Extent of Intervention in the 1990s — Statistical Evidence"). Those speculative capital flows fuelled the initial problem created by the trade surplus and further induced inflation in the stock and real estate markets in Taiwan in the late 1980s.

---

[6]   In addition to the consideration of high adjustment costs for the trade sector, another reason for public pressure on the Central Bank in the 1986–1987 period was the concern for the deviation of the short-run equilibrium from the long-run equilibrium. In particular, after N.T. dollar had appreciated by some 20% in early 1987, the currency level did not seem too far away from the long-run level indicated by the real effective exchange rate level in Taiwan. Based on this real effective exchange rate indicator, some believed that the N.T. dollar was already "overshooting" its long-run level. For a formal empirical examination of this, see Liu and He (1991a), Liu and Kuo (1991b). For a theoretical model of overshooting, see Dornbusch (1976).

[7]   The work in Liu (1992a) presents an empirical test of the interest rate parity condition. It was shown in the essay that the uncovered interest parity condition was significantly violated over a period from January 1986 to March 1988.

Relaxation of Restrictions on Cross-border Capital Flows

Direct capital movement by the general public was greatly restricted in Taiwan before July 1987. However, there were official channels for capital flows long before that time. Specifically, according to the foreign exchange regulations, commercial banks have been allowed to borrow foreign exchange from abroad, and any importer/exporter has been eligible to borrow foreign exchange through commercial banks and to sell it on the foreign exchange market for N.T. dollars, long before 1987.

Foreign liabilities outstanding in commercial banks increased drastically starting in 1986, especially between the last quarter of 1986 and the first quarter of 1987. Actually, within that short six-month period, the foreign liabilities outstanding in commercial banks went up from just a little over US$5 billion to a level of US$13.8 billion. These huge capital inflows were mainly speculative capital flows, and which were induced to capture the excess profit existing in the foreign exchange market in Taiwan at that time.[8]

Towards the end of May 1987, market expectations for further appreciation of the N.T. dollar remained strong, attracting even larger capital inflows than before. To put a stop to the continuing capital inflow, the Central Bank announced a freeze on the level of foreign liabilities outstanding at the existing level of US$13.8 billion on 31 May 1987. In addition, foreign exchange controls were largely relaxed to allow and to encourage direct capital outflow by the non-bank private sector. Specifically, on 31 May 1987, the maximum amount of outward remittance for each adult per year was dramatically expanded to US$5 million, while the maximum amount of inward remittance for each adult per year was increased only to US$50,000. This was a significant step in the direction of liberalization of capital outflow. Because of the continued expectation of an appreciation of the N.T. dollar at that time, however, no immediate net capital outflow was observed in the wake of this capital movement liberalization programme.

With the freeze on the foreign debt of commercial banks, the link between capital inflow and the expectation of currency appreciation was broken. Termination of the continuous huge capital inflow helped to moderate further currency appreciation and to reduce the current account surplus for the following reasons.

---

[8]   Empirical evidence of the connection between foreign liabilities of commercial banks and the expectation of currency appreciation is provided in Liu (1992a).

While there existed a speculative profit opportunity during the 1986–1987 period, capital movement was not officially permitted the general public until June 1987. Exporters in Taiwan, however, had official channels for capital flows, and therefore took the most advantage of that speculative opportunity. In fact, since many exporters charged their foreign customers the same foreign currency price as before the N.T. dollar had appreciated and covered the trade loss with their speculative profits, the trade surplus remained high even after the N.T. dollar had greatly appreciated. After the Central Bank imposed controls on foreign liabilities, exporters in Taiwan lost this speculative profit opportunity, forcing them to charge prices which truly reflected their rising costs. As a result, the trade surplus declined, reducing the pressure of further appreciation on the N.T. dollar.

During the 1989–1993 period, since the pressure on the N.T. dollar to appreciate was reduced, the capital inflow restrictions were also significantly relaxed. The permitted maximum capital inflow for each adult per year was first increased to US$200,000 in June 1989; to US$500,000 in September 1989; to US$1 million in November 1989; to US$2 million in July 1990; and then to US$3 million in March 1991. Starting in October 1992, each adult has been allowed to remit outwardly or inwardly up to a maximum of US$5 million per year, without Central Bank approval and without restrictions on the use of the funds remitted. With such high ceilings, limitations on international capital flows have been removed almost completely. Moreover, for portfolio or direct investment, the remittance amount is not even restricted by this limit.

Appropriate timing was the key factor contributing to the smooth and successful process of liberalization of international capital movements. In particular, the capital outflow restriction was relaxed most at the time when the market had no intention of moving capital outward; and the capital inflow restrictions were gradually removed while the market had little intention of moving capital inward. As a result, there was no objection within the economy at the time liberalization was taking place.

A Lesser Extent of Intervention in the 1990s — Statistical Evidence

As pointed out in Mussa (1990), the empirical assessment of the effectiveness of official intervention has taken on renewed policy importance since the Louvre Accourd of February 1987. It is now widely accepted in academia that it is crucial to examine whether and how the market responds to news of intervention, rather than merely paying attention to how frequently the Central Bank intervenes in the market. This is because the effects of intervention could be totally different if the market has a different perception regarding the same intervention behaviour. In addition, it is also important to examine whether Central Bank intervention leads to any serious disequilibrium in its foreign exchange market, which will normally induce some additional adverse effects on the economy.

In view of the above, this section presents statistical study results regarding the effects of Central Bank intervention in Taiwan for the overall sample period (1981–1992), and also for each of the three sub-sample periods (1981–1985, 1986–1987, and 1988–1992). The report in this section is based on the work in Liu (1993).

The examination in Liu (1993) addresses the following three questions. First, do we observe a disequilibrium in the foreign exchange market in Taiwan in any statistically significant way? Second, has Central Bank intervention in Taiwan induced any market disequilibrium? Third, how does the market in Taiwan perceive the Central Bank's intervention? In particular, has the market expected intervention to be effective and hence perceived it as "credible" intervention?[9]

In general, the ex post excess return in the foreign exchange market is defined as the realized profit a trader can make by borrowing in one currency and lending in another currency simultaneously. If the foreign exchange market is efficient and if the international capital market is in equilibrium, the ex post excess return should average out at zero. That is, one should not have the continuous profit opportunity of borrowing in one currency and investing in another currency. In contrast, if the market is not in equilibrium, one may observe a consistent profit opportunity of transferring funds between two currencies, which in turn will induce huge speculative capital movements between countries.

Excess Profits in the Foreign Exchange Market?

Based on the above rationale, the ex post excess profit in the foreign

---

[9]   For Central Bank intervention operations, see Borenztein (1987), Dominguez (1990), Liu (1989), Mussa (1990), Moreno and Yin (1992), among others.

exchange market in Taiwan, by borrowing U.S. dollar and investing in N.T. dollar assets, was first calculated following Equation (1):

$$Profit_{t+1} = (I_{t,t+1} - I^*_{t,t+1}) - [log(S_{t+1}) - log(S_t)] \dots\dots\dots\dots\dots (1)$$

where $profit_{t+1}$ is the one-month ex post excess profit realized at time $t+1$; $I_{t,t+1}$ is the one-month deposit rate in the N.T. dollar asset at time t; $I^*_{t,t+1}$ is the one-month Eurodollar rate at time t; S_t and S_{t+1} are spot exchange rates at time t and $t+1$, respectively, both defined as the unit value of the U.S. dollar in terms of the N.T. dollar.

It was first found in the essay that, on average, there is no statistical evidence of excess profits for either the overall sample period (1981–1992), or for the third sub-sample period (1988–1992), which implies that there is no sign of disequilibrium in the foreign exchange market in Taiwan in recent years. In contrast, there was statistically significant evidence of positive excess profit, or market disequilibrium over the period of 1986–1987, which confirms the analysis presented earlier in "Appreciation of the N.T. Dollar Starting in 1986".

The second question addressed in the essay is whether the excess profit was affected by Central Bank intervention. To answer this question, the excess profit was examined from an ex ante, instead of an ex post point of view. The test results support the conjecture that the Central Bank intervention operation over the 1986–1987 period indeed contributed to the market disequilibrium during that period. In contrast, there is no evidence of that sort of disturbance from Central Bank intervention in Taiwan in recent years.

"Credible" or "Effective" Intervention Operations?

The essay also presents statistical evidence regarding the issue of market perceptions of the Central Bank intervention operation. By examining the sign of a particular estimated coefficient in a testing equation, the essay derives implications on whether the market perceives intervention as "credible", that is, whether the market believes intervention can actually influence the currency in an effective way.

It is found in the essay that generally, the market in Taiwan perceives the Central Bank's behavioural "credible", except for the heavy intervention period of 1986–1987. This finding also supports our explanation earlier regarding the market expectation for further appreciation of the N.T.

dollar over the 1986–1987 period. That is, for the period of 1986–1987, even though the Central Bank intervened significantly in the market to prevent the N.T. dollar from appreciating, the market believed that a larger extent of appreciation was inevitable, and did not believe that the Central Bank's intervention could prevent it from happening. As a result, the Central Bank intervention could not prevent the N.T. dollar from appreciating and thus became "ineffective" over that period of time.

In contrast, the essay presents a different picture for the more recent period of 1988–1992. Unlike the 1986–1987 period, there is no sign of disequilibrium or distortion in the foreign exchange market. In addition, Central Bank intervention in the recent years has not only been relatively mild, but has also been more credible than in the 1986–1987 period.

V. TAIWAN STOCK RETURNS AND THE WORLD PACIFIC-BASIN MACRO VARIABLES

Globalization of the securities market was an international trend in the 1980s. Several factors contributed to this trend. Basically, the prominence of international trade and the development of multinational companies led to huge foreign holdings by individuals. In addition, technological innovation played an important role in the globalization process. For example, electronic fund transfer, automatic trading systems, and the cross-listing of securities by exchanges of different countries have all hastened the pace of globalization of the securities market.

In view of the trend towards globalization in the world, and also in view of recent volatilities in the Taiwan stock-market, globalization of the securities market in Taiwan has been adopted as a major goal by the Government in the past few years. This section presents empirical findings on the influence of macroeconomic factors upon the returns of Taiwan securities investment.

There is now increasing empirical evidence of equity market returns containing a component which can be predicted by some macroeconomic variables. For example, it is shown in Bekaert and Hodrick (1992) that some U.S. macroeconomic instrumental variables have predictive power on the returns of several important equity markets in the world. Campbell and Hamao (1992) present evidence of common movements in expected excess the returns across the U.S. and Japanese equity portfolios, and Hamao (1988), Brown and Otsuki (1990), Harvey (1991), Solnik (1991), and

Ferson and Harvey (1992), among others, present additional evidence of changes in expected country stock returns having a predictable component. They have found that variables such as yield spreads on government long-term bonds, short-term interest rates, and dividend yields have forecastability in national stock-markets.

Based on the above studies, the paper in Liu and He (1993) constructs three alternative sets of macroeconomic variables as predictors for the Taiwan stock-market return. To be in line with other studies, the stock return is measured as a U.S. dollar-denominated return, as given in Equation (2):

$$R_t = [I_t * X_t - I_{t-1} * X_{t-1}] / (I_{t-1} * X_{t-1}) \dots\dots\dots\dots\dots\dots\dots \quad (2)$$

where R_t is the exchange rate adjusted return from investment in the Taiwan stock-market from time $t-1$ to time i; I_t is the weighted stock index in Taiwan at time t; and X_t is the spot foreign exchange rate at time t, defined as the unit value of the N.T. dollar in terms of the U.S. dollar.

The monthly foreign exchange rate adjusted stock return over the period from January 1981 to December 1991 was regressed alternatively on the one-period lagged value of the following three sets of macro variables. The first set of data includes three country-specific macro variables: the short-term interest rate, the monthly change in the money supply, and the monthly change in foreign reserves held in the Central Bank in Taiwan. The second set of data contains five Pacific-Basin regional variables, including the excess return on the MSCI (Morgan Stanley Capital International) Pacific stock index, dividend yields, and the short-term and long-term interest rates in Japan. The third set of data consists of seven global macro instrumental variables, including the MSCI world stock index, dividends, short-term and long-term interest rates, and the default premium. The estimation equations using the three alternative sets of macro variables are thus given as:

(1) using country-specific macroeconomic variables:

$$E_{t-1}(R_t) = a_1 + a_2 TBOP_{t-1} + a_3 TMS_{t-1} + a_4 TTB_{t-1} \dots\dots\dots\dots\dots \quad (3)$$

(2) using Pacific-Basin regional macroeconomic variables:

$$E_{t-1}(R_t) = b_1 + b_2 PRET_{t-1} + b_3 PDY_{t-1} + b_4 JTERM_{t-1} + b_5 JTB_{t-1} + b_6 PRET*PDY_{t-1} \dots\dots\dots\dots\dots\dots\dots\dots\dots\dots\dots\dots \quad (4)$$

(3) using world-wide macroeconomic variables:

$$E_{t-1}(R_t) = c_1 + c_2 WRET_{t-1} + c_3 WDY_{t-1} + c_4 TED_{t-1} + c_5 TERM_{t-1} +$$
$$c_6 PREM_{t-1} + c_7 TB_{t-1} + c_8 WRET^*WDY_{t-1} \dots\dots\dots\dots (5)$$

where R_t is as given in Equation (2), $E_{t-1}(.)$ denotes the expectation of (.) formed at time $t-1$, and a detailed description of the variables adopted above is given in the Appendix.

Table 10.1 presents the test results, with the coefficients for each variable reported in the main entries, and the heteroscedasticity-adjusted standard errors given in parentheses. The test results first show that among the country-specific variables examined, the change in the money supply has the strongest effect on stock return, which confirms the conjecture in Liu (1992a) that the stock-market in Taiwan in the 1980s was highly influenced by its domestic money market.

It is also found in this essay that, like other industrialized countries, the exchange adjusted stock-market return in Taiwan contains a predictable component which is linked with each of the three alternative sets (country-specific, regional, and world) of macroeconomic variables. It is particularly interesting to note that even though the process of globalization of the stock-market in Taiwan did not officially take place until the late 1980s, the test results indicate a reasonably close link between the stock return in Taiwan and the macroeconomy of the Pacific-Basin region and of the world. In view of the long and tight link with the world through its commodity trading position, the above finding may be due to the possible substitutability between the commodity trade and the financial trade.[10] Moreover, based on the test results of where either the interest rate term premium or dividend yield was used, it is found that the conditional expected stock return in Taiwan is more closely linked with the economic situation of the Pacific-Basin region than with the world economic environment.

VI. SUMMARY AND CONCLUDING REMARKS

Liberalization and globalization of the financial market have been strongly emphasized in Taiwan in recent years. Deregulation in the domestic capital market, foreign exchange market, securities market, and banking

---

[10] See Cole and Obstfeld (1991) for the theoretical analysis of this substitutability.

Table 10.1   Predictability of Taiwan Equity Market Returns
Exchange-Rate-Adjusted, January 1981 to December 1991

Panel A: Using Country-Specific Macroeconomic Variables

$$R_t = (I_t X_t - I_{t-1} X_{t-1}) / (I_{t-1} X_{t-1})$$

$$E_{t-1}(R_t) = a_1 + a_2 TBOP_{t-1} + a_3 TMS_{t-1} + a_4 TTB_{t-1}$$

TBOP	TMS	TTB	R^2
−0.43	0.45*	1.47	0.07
(0.28)	(0.22)	(0.92)	

Panel B: Using Pacific-Basin Regional Macroeconomic Variables

$$E_{t-1}(R_t) = b_1 + b_2 PRET_{t-1} + b_3 PDY_{t-1} + b_4 JTERM_{t-1} + b_6 PRET*PDY_{t-1}$$

PRET	PDY	JTERM	JTB	PRET*PDY	R^2
0.02*	1.09*	−0.54*	−0.49*	−0.07*	0.12
(0.01)	(0.49)	(0.18)	(0.01)	(0.03)	

Panel C: Using World-wide Macroeconomic Variables

$$E_{t-1}(R_t) = c_1 + c_2 WRET_{t-1} + c_3 WDY_{t-1} + c_4 TED_{t-1} + c5TERM_{t-1} +$$
$$c_6 PREM_{t-1} + c_7 TB_{t-1} + c_8 WRET*WDY_{t-1}$$

WRET	WDY	TED	TERM	PREM	TB	WRET*WDY	R^2
0.025*	0.05	−0.03	0.01	0.10*	−0.07	−0.07*	0.11
(0.012)	(0.16)	(0.07)	(0.30)	(0.05)	(0.05)	(0.03)	

(Heteroscedasticity-adjusted standard errors are in parentheses, and * denotes statistical significance at the 1% level.)

industry took place in Taiwan in the late 1980s. In particular, the relaxation of restrictions on capital movements in the 1987–1991 period formed the necessary foundation for globalization, and the revised *Banking Law* of July 1989 contributed greatly to both the liberalization and globalization processes.

Overall, deregulation in the domestic money market and in capital movements have been quite successful, and the globalization of the securities market and of the banking system have advanced smoothly. Currently, the long-term goal of financial policies is to establish Taipei as a regional financial centre in Asia, and efforts continue toward further liberalized and globalized capital markets.

To become a maturing financial economy, Taiwan needs to establish a sound and complete set of financial institutions and markets, in order to provide combinations of various financial instruments. For example, a multinational firm in a maturing economy should be able to use currency futures or options to hedge its foreign exchange risk, or to use interest rate futures or Eurodollar deposits to avoid interest rate risk.

A complete set of financial markets generally includes domestic and foreign money markets, bond and stock markets, and other derivative markets, such as futures, options, and swap markets. Correspondingly, a complete set of financial institutions includes a banking system and other thrift institutions, financial conglomerates, investment companies, pension funds, and insurance companies.

Given the financial policy goal of establishing Taipei as a regional financial centre, and evaluating current financial development in Taiwan, several areas will need to be strengthened. It is also clear that to establish a complete set of financial institutions and markets, further liberalization, institutionalization, and internationalization in various aspects of the financial industry are urgently needed.

REFERENCES

Balassa, Bela (1982). *Development Strategies in Semi-Industrial Economies*. Baltimore: Johns Hopkins University Press.

Bekaert, Geert and Robert J. Hodrick (1992). "Characterizing Predictable Components in Excess Returns on Equity and Foreign Exchange Markets." *Journal of Finance*, Vol. 47, No. 2, pp. 467–509.

Borensztein, Eduards R. (1987). "Alternative Hypotheses about the Excess Return on Dollar Assets, 1980–84." IMF Staff Papers, pp. 29–59.

Brown, S. and T. Otsuki (1990). "A Global Asset Pricing Model." Working Paper, New York University.

Brunner, Allan D., John V. Duca and Mary M. McLaughlin (1992). "Recent Developments Affecting the Probability and Practices of Commercial Banks." In *The Commercial Bank Management Reader*, edited by Robert W. Kolb. Miami, Florida: Kolb Publishing Company.

Campbell, John and Yasushi Hamao (1992). "Predictable Stock Returns in the United States and Japan: A Study of Long-Term Capital Market Integration." *Journal of Finance*, Vol. 47, No. 1, pp. 43–69.

Chiu, Paul C. H. (1992). "Money and Financial Markets." In *Taiwan: From Developing to Mature Economy*, edited by Gustav Ranis, pp. 121–193. Boulder, Colorado: Westview Press.

Cole, Harold L. and Maurice Obstfeld (1991). "Commodity Trade and International Risk Sharing." *Journal of Monetary Economics*, Vol. 28, pp. 3–24.

Corrigan, E. Gerald (1992a). "Reforming the U.S. Financial System: An International Perspective." In *The Commercial Bank Management Reader*, edited by Robert W. Kolb. Miami, Florida: Kolb Publishing Company.

———— (1992b). "Trends in International Banking in the United States and Japan." In *The Commercial Bank Management Reader*, edited by Robert W. Kolb. Miami, Florida: Kolb Publishing Company.

Dominguez, Kathryn Mary (1990). "Market Responses to Coordinated Central Bank Intervention: Comment." In *Carnegie-Rochester Conference Series on Public Policy*, Vol. 32, pp. 121–171.

Dornbusch, Rudiger (1976). "Expectation and Exchange Rate Dynamics." *Journal of Political Economy*, 84, No. 6, pp. 1161–1176.

Edwards, Sebalstian (1984). "The Order of Liberalization of the External Sector in Developing Countries." *Essays in International Finance* (Princeton University), No. 156.

Fei, John C. H. (1992). "Taiwan's Economic Development and Its Relation to the International Environment." In *Taiwan's Enterprises in Global Perspective*, edited by N. T. Wang. New York: M. E. Sharpe, Inc.

Ferson, Wayne E. and Campbell Harvey (1992). "The Risk and Predictability of International Equity Returns." Working paper, Duke University.

Frenkel, Jacob A. (1982). "The Order of Economic Liberalization: Discussion." In *Economic Policy in a World of Change*, edited by K. Brunner and A. H. Meltzer. Amsterdam: North-Holland.

Frankel, Allen B. and Paul B. Morgan (1993). "Deregulation and Competition in Japanese Banking." In *The International Finance Reader*, edited by Robert W. Kolb. Miami, Florida: Kolb Publishing Company.

Hamao, Yasushi (1988). "An Empirical Examination of the Arbitrage Pricing Theory: Using Japanese Data." *Japan and the World Economy*, Vol. 1, pp. 45–61.

Harberger, Arnold C. (1984). "Welfare Consequences of Capital Inflows." Paper presented at the World Bank Conference.

Harvey, Campbell (1991). "The World Price of Covariance Risk." *Journal of Finance*, 46, pp. 111–157.

Hirtle, Beverly (1993). "Factors Affecting the Competitiveness of Internationally Active Financial Institutions." In *The Financial Institutions and Markets Reader*, edited by Robert W. Kolb. Miami, Florida: Kolb Publishing Company.

Krueger, Anno O. (1984). "Problems of Liberalization." In *World Economic Growth*, edited by A. C. Harberger. San Francisco, California: Institute for Contemporary Studies.

Kuo, Shirley W. Y. (1983). *The Taiwan Economy in Transition*. Boulder, Colorado: Westview Press.

———— (1990). "Liberalization of the Financial Market in Taiwan in the 1980s." In

Pacific-Basin Capital Market Research, edited by Gustar Ranis, pp. 7–26. Boulder, Colorado: Elsevier Science Publishers.

———— (1991). "Key Factors for High Growth with Equity: The Taiwan Experience, 1952–1990." Presented in a symposium on "High Growth Performance Experiences of Dynamic Developing Economies." Paris: OECD.

———— (1993). "The Taiwan Economy in the 1990s." Presented in the Conference on "Taiwan in the Asia Pacific in the 1990s," Australia.

Lee, Sheng-Yi (1993). "Taipei as a Financial Centre." Presented in the conference on "Taiwan in the Asia-Pacific in the 1990s," Australia.

Liang, Kuo-Shu and Hou Liang Ching (1988). "The Financial System and Financial Policy." Council for Economic Planning and Development (text in Chinese), Taipei.

Liu, Christina Y. (1989). "Expected Excess Returns under Central Bank Intervention." Presented at the First Annual Pacific-Basin Finance Conference.

———— (1992a). "Money and Financial Markets: The International Perspective." In *Taiwan: From Developing to Mature Economy*, edited by Gustav Ranis, pp. 195–221. Boulder, Colorado: Westview Press.

———— (1992b). "Liberalization and Globalization of the Financial Market." In *Taiwan's Enterprises in Global Perspective*, edited by N. T. Wang, pp. 123–149. New York: M. E. Sharpe, Inc.

———— (1993). "Managed Exchange Rate Regime: New Taiwan Dollar/U.S. Dollar." Presented in a special finance conference on "Managed Exchange Rate Regimes — Yen, Dollar and ECU" at the Federal Reserve Bank of Atlanta, Atlanta.

Liu, Christina Y. and He Jia (1991a). "Permanent or Transitory Deviations from Purchasing Power Parity: An Examination of Eight Pacific-Basin Countries." In *Pacific-Basin Capital Markets Research* (Vol. 2), edited by S. Ghon Rhee and Rosita P. Chang, pp. 413–436. Amsterdam, North-Holland: Elsevier Science Publishers.

———— (1991b). "Do Real Exchange Rates Follow Random Walks? A Heteroscedasticity-Robust Autocorrelation Test." *International Economic Journal*, Vol. 5, No. 3, pp. 39–48.

———— (1993). "Predictability of Taiwan Stock Returns Using World, Pacific-Basin, and Country-Specific Macro Variables." *American Asian Review* (forthcoming).

Liu, Christina Y. and Shirley W. Y. Kuo (1990). "Interest Rates and Foreign Exchange Liberalization in Taiwan in the 1980s." In *Essays on Economic Development in Asia*. Honolulu, Hawaii: Hawaii University Press.

McKinnon, Ronald I. (1982). "The Order of Economic Liberalization: Lessons from Chile and Argentina." *Carnegie-Rochester Conference Series on Public Policy*, Vol. 17, pp. 159–186.

———— (1986). "Financial Liberalization in Retrospect: Interest Rate Policies in LDCs." Policy Paper, Center for Policy Research.

Moreno, Ramom and Yin Norman (1992). "Exchange Rate Policy and Shocks to Asset Markets: The Case of Taiwan in the 1980s." In *Economic Review*, Federal Reserve Bank of San Francisco, No. 1, pp. 14–34.

Mussa, Michael (1990). "Market Responses to Coordinated Central Bank Intervention; Comment." In *Carnegie-Rochester Conference Series on Public Policy*, Vol. 32, pp. 121–171.

Pavel, Christine and John N. McElravey (1992). "Globalization in the Financial Services Industry." In *The Commercial Bank Management Reader*, edited by Robert W. Kolb. Miami, Florida: Kolb Publishing Company.

Ranis, Gustav, ed. (1992). *Taiwan: From Developing to Mature Economy.* Boulder, Colorado: Westview Press.

Shea, Jia-Dong (1990). "Financial Development in Taiwan: A Macro Analysis." Presented in a Conference on Financial Development in Japan, Korea and Taiwan, The Institute of Economics, Academia Sinica, Taipei, Taiwan.

Shieh, Samuel C. (1992). "Financial Liberalization and Internationalization: The Development of Taipei as a Regional Financial Center in Asia." Delivered in a meeting sponsored by the Royal Institute of International Affairs, London.

———— (1993). "Foreign Banking Institutions' Role in the R.O.C.'s Advance to Regional Financial Center." Delivered at the Citibank Pan-Asia Journalism Award Ceremony, Taipei.

Solnik, Bruno (1991). "Using the Predictability of International Asset Returns." Working Paper, Group HEC-School of Management.

Yang, Ya-Hwei (1990). "A Micro Analysis of the Financial System in Taiwan," Presented in a conference on "Financial Development in Japan, Korea and Taiwan," The Institute of Economics, Academia Sinica, Taipei, Taiwan.

ANNEX 10.1

Detailed Descriptions of the Variables Adopted in Section V.

The first set of the data includes the following three country-specific macro variables:

TTB:	The 90-day interest yield in Taiwan.
TMS:	The monthly percentage change in the money supply.
TBOP:	The monthly percentage change in the balance of payments (foreign reserves held in the central bank in Taiwan).

The second set of the data contains five Pacific-Basin regional variables, including the excess return on the MSCI (Morgan Stanley Capital International) pacific stock index, dividend yields, and the short-term and long-term interest rates in Japan. These variables are defined as:

PERT:	The excess return on the Morgan Stanley Capital International (MSCI) Pacific stock index. In constructing this index, the MSCI used the value-weighted stock index from five Pacific-Basin countries (Australia, Hong Kong, Japan, and Singapore/Malaysia), and it excludes the market value of investment companies and of foreign domiciled companies to avoid double-counting.
PDY:	The dividend yield on the Pacific Stock Index.
JTERM:	The interest rate spread, defined as the difference between the yield on the Japanese Central Government bonds with maturity of five years or more and the three-month short-term Gensaki rate. The short-term and the long-term rates are obtained from Citibase.
JTB:	The 30-day Treasury Bill yield from Japan.
PRED*PDY:	An interaction variable defined as the product of PRED and PDY variables.

The third set of the data consists of seven global macro instrumental variables, including the MSCI world stock index, dividends, short-term and long-term interest rates, and the default premium. The variables are defined as:

WERT:	The excess return on the MSCI world stock index, where the index contains value-weighted stock indices from 18

countries in the world. In constructing this index, the MSCI excludes the market value of investment companies and of foreign domiciled companies to avoid double-counting.

WDY: The dividend yield on the MSCI world index.

TED: The spread between the Eurodollar deposit rate and the Treasury yield.

TERM: The difference between the CRSP long-term government bond return and the short-term U.S. Treasury Bill rate.

PREM: The default premium calculated as the difference in returns between the low grade bonds and CRSP long-term government bonds. From January 1981 through December 1987, low grade bonds were rated under Baa; from January 1988 through December 1991, the Merrill Lynch All High Yield Bond Index was used.

TB: The 30-day Treasury Bill yield.

WRET*WDY: An interaction variable defined as the product of WRET and WDY variables.

CHAPTER 11

An Evaluation of the Effectiveness of Government Automation Promotion Schemes in the Electrical Component Industry in Taiwan

Lan Ke-Jeng
National Chung Cheng University, Taiwan

I. INTRODUCTION

Motivation and Purpose

In recent years, Taiwan's products have been facing increasing challenges from the sharp appreciation of the N.T. dollar; growing labour disputes; the awareness of environmental protection; the entrepreneur's unwillingness to invest; and also from the impingement of internationalization and of liberalization. Additionally, due to the cheap labour cost in newly flourishing Southeast Asian countries and mainland China and the improving quality of the developing countries' products, Taiwan's products are losing their competitiveness, thus leading to a worsening exporting situation.

Thus, how to promote both production efficiency and the quality of products for them to be competitive, and to be in accordance with the coming economic environment are important subjects.

To achieve the goals stated above, production automation is an important strategy. Therefore, in July of 1990, the Science and Technology Group of the Executive Yuan took charge of co-ordinating all the related departments to launch the R.O.C. Industrial Automation Programme, and at the end of that year enacted the "Statute for Industrial Upgrading and Promotion" (SIUP) to replace the "Statute of Investment Encouragement" (SIE). SIUP has been in effect since January 1991, and intends to encourage enterprises to speed up production automation. What have been the effects of Government automation promotion schemes? Do they need to be improved when carried out in the future? These questions deserve to be explored. This essay primarily studies the induced effects of the Government's promotion schemes, such as investment tax credit, accelerated depreciation, exemption from tariffs, and low-rate loans, on automation. In doing so, this essay can help highlight the difficulties of the enterprises who are adopting production automation, and can also serve as a reference to further help the Government review the effect of its promotion schemes.

Scope of the Study

Automation promotion is a type of industrial policy, and hence the scope of the study is the context of the promotion schemes policy, a specific industry, and a firm involved, as shown in Figure 11.1.

Promotion Schemes

In the tax exemption regulation of SIUP, there are several important schemes such as investment tax credit and accelerated depreciation;[1] additionally, customs tariff exemption and low-rate loans offered by the banks are regarded as kinds of promotion schemes.[2] Because these promotion schemes are supposed to influence the decisions of manufacturers, this study will focus upon the following four schemes: investment tax credit; accelerated depreciation; exemption of tariffs; and low-rate loans, to show how different combinations of the four schemes may influence automation investment decisions of firms.

Specific Industry

Owing to the numerous industries in the manufacturing sector, the study

---

[1] Regulations related to investment tax credit are contained in Article 2 (Sections 5 to 20) of SIUP; only Sections 5 and 6 are directly related to automation investment.

[2] Customs Import Regulations state that to apply for an exemption from tariffs on automation equipment requires the approval from the Ministry of Economic Affairs and that the equipment must be unavailable from domestic suppliers.

Figure 11.1 Scope of the Research

	Promotion Schemes
I. Government SIUP and Related Practices ⟶	(1) Investment Tax Credit (2) Accelerated Depreciation (3) Exemption from Tariffs (4) Low-rate Loans

	Category	Electronics Industry
II. Industry	Standardization of Occupation and Industry ⟶	Electrical Component Industry (3607)

III. Firm Performance	Reactions ⟶	(1) Magnitude of Investment Intention (2) Magnitude of Investment (3) Improvement of Firm (4) Obstacles and Suggestions

bases its investigation upon the electronics industry, which has a relatively higher awareness of automation than most other industries.[3]

According to R.O.C. occupational standard quadruple-codes, electronics includes electrical products and electrical components. Electrical components are usually regarded as the major force of the information industry and contribute a great deal to the production amount. For example, electrical components amounted to a total value of NT$180 billion; far higher than any other production items. In order to improve the homogeneity and the precision of the analysis, the study further narrows down its focus to the electrical component industry.

Aspects of the Firm

This essay first aims to find out to what degree the intention of the manufacturers is to invest in automation due to the promotion schemes. In this light, the study explores the inducement effect of the promotion

---

[3] According to the Automation Execution Group of the Ministry of Economic Affairs (1989), 40% of firms in the electronics industry recognize the need for automation and 60% of these have a willingness to invest in automation, and both figures are higher than for other manufacturing industries.

schemes set up by the Government. Secondly, the study is to find out how the firms' production performances and their ability to adjust to market change are improved after they have invested in automation. Finally, difficulties in adopting automation will be discussed and some suggestions will be proposed to improve the practices in the future.

Structure

This essay is divided into four sections: Section I is a brief introduction; Section II describes the methodology used in the research; Section III analyses the results of surveys on firms; and Section IV provides a conclusion along with some suggestions for further study.

II. METHODOLOGY

Basically, the purpose of the promotion schemes set up by the Government is to induce the firm to react correspondingly so that the Government can achieve its pre-set goals. However, enterprises have differences, and they may react differently. To determine the induced effects of promotion schemes, the study has focused upon two aspects: first, exploring the awareness of the firm of the promotion schemes, which is equivalent to exploring how their investment intention may be influenced; second, exploring the firm's behavioural reaction to the promotion schemes. Therefore, the magnitude and the effectiveness of the promotion schemes on the firm will be understood.

Framework of the Concepts

Figure 11.2 indicates the research concepts of the cause-effect relationships. The stimulation of the firm's reactions comes from automation promotion schemes. The firm owner in the electrical component industry first shows his investment intention concerning automation. Following this approach, what the study calls the "first inducement effect" is the influence of promotion schemes on the investment intention of firms. Secondly, we ask whether those who increased automation investment in 1991 were influenced by the combination of promotion schemes. If that is so, the consideration weight is explored. To put it another way, if part of the promotion schemes were cancelled, how much investment would be taken away by the firm? Therefore, the "second inducement effect"

Figure 11.2 Concept Framework of the Research

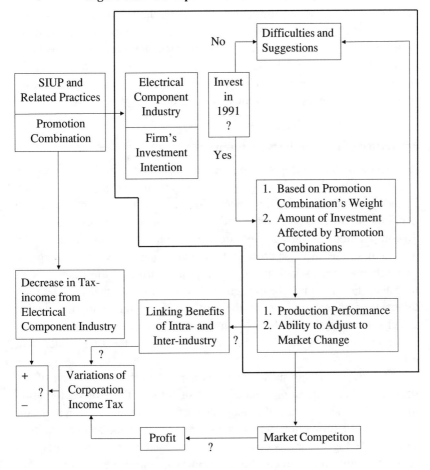

concerns how much of the firm's automation investment can be attributed to the promotion schemes. Further, the study explores the differences in and reasons behind the firm's purchasing behaviour regarding domestic and foreign automation equipment as a result of different promotion schemes.

Moreover, after adopting automation, the firm's production performance and adjustment ability to market change are supposed to be improved; therefore, the "third inducement effect" refers to the improvement magnitude of the firm's production performance and the ability to adjust to market change.

Benefits which come from the firm's improvement as stated above will enhance the firm's competitiveness. However, the profits and the linking effect among firms may be affected by causes too complex to analyse. In addition, whether tax revenue is increased or whether the increased value is higher than the tax credit sacrificed due to the promotion schemes is incapable of being precisely calculated. Thus, the study has to narrow down its scope to within the limits indicated in Figure 11.2.

Structure of the Analysis Framework

According to the concepts mentioned above, Figure 11.3 expresses the structure of the analysis. In Figure 11.3, the first part of the surveyed data, including the firm's priorities concerning the four promotion schemes in deciding automation investment and the firm's investment intention under 16 combinations of the schemes, are utilized through the log-linear model and the multiple response probability model, to show how various promotion schemes are ranked and how they have affected the intentions of investors. Furthermore, the existence of promotion schemes may be used to examine the magnitude of their influence on automation in which the characteristics of the firm (such as firm size, asset density and profit ratio) will be taken into account. These belong to the first inducement effect.

Moreover, through means analysis applied to the second part of the data, including 12 questions related to the situation of the firm's automation investment, one can learn the magnitude of the investment increment induced by the promotion schemes in 1991 (second inducement effect). Through the log-linear model, one can learn why the firm prefers foreign to domestic equipment even though domestic purchases enjoy an advantageous tax credit. Following this, we can use means analysis again to make sure automation equipment and technology have influenced the performance of the enterprise. Furthermore, the Tobit model and the binary Probit model are used to measure the input-output effect of firms (third inducement effect). Meanwhile, this essay also uses the multiple response probability model to explore how the firm's investment was affected by the promotion schemes in 1991. The final step is to use means analysis as well as frequency analysis to gather information about the difficulties and problems encountered by firms, and then provides some suggestions for the promotion schemes.

Figure 11.3 Analysis Framework of the Research

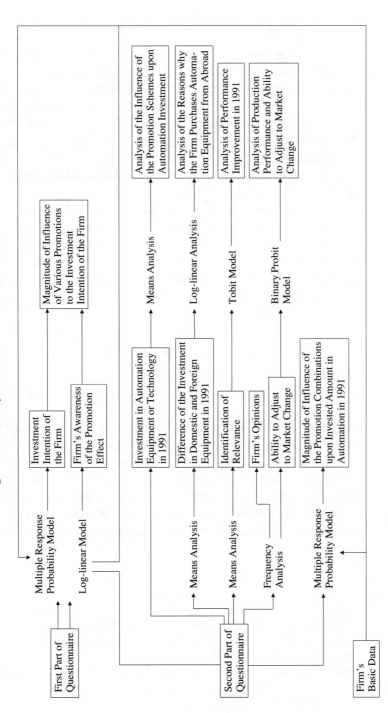

Design of Sampling

Frequently used random sampling techniques include Simple Random Sampling, Systematic Random Sampling, Stratified Random Sampling and Cluster Sampling. Simple Random Sampling and Systematic Random Sampling become difficult when a population is too big or unknown. And Stratified Random Sampling is more appropriate than Cluster Sampling when the difference among various groups is big. Because the firms in the electrical component industry are great in number, and they have characteristics of their own, this study uses Stratified Random Sampling with capital amount as its base.

The sampling population comes from the member list of the Electrical Equipment Association of the Taiwan Area. The firms involved in electrical components amount to 1,894, and at least 320 had to be sampled, to be within a 5% error and 95% confidence interval.[4] The 320 firms were sampled first according to population stratified by capital amount, and then Simple Random Sampling was used.[5]

III. ANALYSIS OF THE SURVEY RESULTS

Before analysing the survey results, we first describe the response rate and distribution so that we can assess the inference reliability of the survey data.

There were 124 effective responses out of the 320 firms sampled. The capital amounts of these sampled firms are indicated in Table 11.1. The retrieved samples were mostly from those firms with a larger capital amount. As a whole, the retrieved samples are of 38.75% of those sampled, which is inadequate for expected inference.[6] However, since the relatively large firms may gain better advantages from the promotion schemes, the surveyed results thus can still provide important information.

---

[4]   When the size of the data population is known, the sampling method is different from the case of an infinite population. See Cochran (1977), p. 75.

[5]   The stratification of capital amount follows the standard of the Electrical Equipment Association of the Taiwan Area.

[6]   With 124 samples, the inference has 8% error and 92% confidence interval.

Table 11.1   Distribution of Sampled Firms by Capital Amount

Capital Amount (NT$ million)	No. of Sampled Firms (%)	Retrieved Samples (%)
<2	30 (9.5)	3 (2.4)
2–5	108 (33.8)	26 (21.0)
5–10	65 (20.4)	23 (18.5)
10–30	60 (18.7)	26 (21.0)
30–50	14 (4.3)	9 (7.3)
50–100	14 (4.2)	11 (8.9)
>100	29 (8.9)	26 (21.0)
Total	320 (100)	124 (100)

Influence of the Promotion Schemes on the Investment Intention of the Firms

To understand the induced effects of various promotion schemes on a firm's investment intention, 16 possible combinations using the variables of up to four schemes were chosen (and this went all the way down to zero chosen), and are shown in Table 11.2. The first type includes all four

Table 11.2   Types of Combination of the Promotion Schemes

Types of Combination	Contents of Combination			
1	[1]	[2]	[3]	[4]
2	[1]	[2]	[3]	
3	[1]	[2]		[4]
4	[1]		[3]	[4]
5		[2]	[3]	[4]
6	[1]	[2]		
7	[1]		[3]	
8	[1]			[4]
9		[2]		[4]
10		[2]	[3]	
11			[3]	[4]
12	[1]			
13		[2]		
14			[3]	
15				[4]
16				

Note: [1] exemption from tariffs; [2] accelerated depreciation; [3] investment tax credit; [4] low-rate loans.

promotion schemes; the second to the fifth include three of the schemes; the sixth to the eleventh include two of the schemes; the twelfth to the fifteenth include only one of the schemes; and the sixteenth type is an empty set. These types of combinations can be analysed with the multiple response probability model so that the various intentions of the firms under each type can be detected. The results are displayed in Table 11.3.[7]

Table 11.3 shows that the investment intention of the firms under the first type of combination is strong (a "great intention" of 0.703). If low-rate loans, investment tax credits, accelerated depreciation or exemption from tariffs are cancelled individually, the investment intention of the firms declines to "some intention" of 0.519, 0.473, 0.535 and 0.468 respectively. Among them, the cancellation of investment tax credit and exemption from tariffs are particularly influential upon the investment intention of the firms. This observation is consistent with the ninth type which excludes both promotion schemes and has a "slight intention" of 0.516. Moreover, the magnitude of "no intention" for the ninth type is 5.02 and 4.86 times that of the third and the fifth types respectively. If, in addition, low-rate loans are cancelled, the investment intention of the firms becomes "no intention" of 0.662; that is, the possibility of no intention to invest by the firms is substantially increased.

---

[7]   The model estimation corresponding to Table 11.3 is the following:

$y = 1.3094^{**}D_1 + 3.6713^{**}D_2 + 6.0749^{**}D_3 - 6.9530^{**}X_1 - 5.3227^{**}X_2$
        (0.3067) (0.3277) (0.3560) (0.4337) (0.4165)
        $-4.0201^{**}X_3 - 5.0332^{**}X_4 - 3.9836^{**}X_5 - 2.6464^{**}X_6 - 3.6889^{**}X_7$
        (0.4037) (0.4133) (0.4046) (0.3968) (0.4036)
        $-3.0808^{**}X_8 - 2.1032^{**}X_9 - 2.7641^{**}X_{10} - 3.0286^{**}X_{11} - 1.6319^{**}X_{12}$
        (0.3990) (0.3939) (0.3974) (0.4000) (0.3928)
        $-0.6345X_{13} - 1.6995^{**}X_{14} - 1.1499^{**}X_{15} - 0.0014^{**}TA$
        (0.4057) (0.3915) (0.3955) (0.0004) .... (3.1)

where $\chi^2 = 463.662$, d.f. $= 16$, $p < 0.01$; standard errors are in parentheses; ** represents the case of $p < 0.01$; y is the log value of odds, whose value is transformed into probability (magnitude of not to invest); D_i's are dummy variables and represent the magnitude of investment intention; X_i's represent the 16 promotion combinations. For example, the probability of no intention to invest of the sixteenth type has a y-value of 1.3094, which is transformed into a 0.787 probability value. Lastly, TA represents total asset value (NT\$ million), whose negative coefficient expresses a higher degree of investment intention for larger firms.

Table 11.3 Various Investment Intention of Firms

Types of Combination \ Magnitude of Intention	No Intention	Slight Intention	Some Intention	Great Intention
1	0.004	0.033	0.260*	0.703**
2	0.018	0.143	0.519**	0.321*
3	0.062	0.351**	0.473**	0.114
4	0.023	0.180	0.535**	0.261*
5	0.064	0.358*	0.468**	0.110
6	0.208	0.529**	0.233*	0.031
7	0.085	0.411*	0.420**	0.084
8	0.145	0.498**	0.309*	0.048
9	0.311*	0.516**	0.154	0.019
10	0.189	0.523**	0.253*	0.035
11	0.145	0.503**	0.300*	0.045
12	0.420*	0.465**	0.104	0.012
13	0.622**	0.292*	0.042	0.004
14	0.403*	0.474**	0.109	0.012
15	0.539**	0.386*	0.067	0.007
16	0.787**	0.188*	0.022	0.002

Notes: 1. The numbers in the Table are probability values, meaning "possibility".
2. ** and * indicate the maximum and the second maximum intention respectively.
3. For the estimation result of the corresponding models, please see Equation (3.1) (previous page).

The above situation can be understood by contrasting the twelfth to the fifteenth combination types with the sixteenth. Among these, the thirteenth and fifteenth (both have no investment tax credit and exemption from tariffs schemes), similar to the sixteenth, are inclined to make the firm hold its investment (the degree of "no intention" is 0.662, 0.539 and 0.787). And the twelfth and fourteenth types indicate a slight investment intention of the firm (the degree of "slight intention" is 0.465 and 0.474).

In contrast to the sixteenth type, the fifteenth indicates a higher degree of slight investment intention from 0.188 to 0.386 and a lower degree of no intention from 0.787 to 0.539, which are better than that of the thirteenth type.[8] All these show that low-rate loans influence the firm more than accelerated depreciation does.

---

[8] Equation (3.1) reveals that the coefficient of the fifteenth type is significant, while the coefficient of the thirteenth type is insignificant.

Generally speaking, the more the promotion, the larger the induced effect on the firm. Among the various combinations of promotion schemes, the types without investment tax credit or exemption from tariffs have a greater influence upon the decreasing of the intention of the firm than the types with low-rate loans or accelerated depreciation. Concerning the individual schemes, investment tax credit and exemption from tariffs have the largest effect, while accelerated depreciation has the smallest effect. In other words, among the four promotion schemes, the investment tax credit and exemption from tariffs have the largest effect (where significant difference is not discernible between these two), then low-rate loans, and then accelerated depreciation. However, if only accelerated depreciation is cancelled, there is still an influence upon the investment intention of the firm. When the scale of the firm (in terms of capital amount) is considered, we find that the bigger the firm, the stronger the investment intention of the firm.[9]

Furthermore, the influence of various schemes may be measured by the firm's awareness of them, as we can see in Table 11.4. This table shows that the order of the first priority is the exemption from tariffs, investment tax credit, low-rate loans, and accelerated depreciation. Conversely, the order of the last priority is accelerated depreciation, low-rate loans, exemption from tariffs, and investment tax credit.

Table 11.4 Rank of Awareness of the Firm

Promotion Schemes / Rank	Exemption from Tariffs	Accelerated Depreciation	Investment Tax Credit	Low-rate Loans
1	41	9	38	29
2	21	28	40	28
3	28	34	29	26
4	27	46	10	34

To explore the significance of their differentials, the following log-linear model is utilized:

---

[9]   From the estimation result of Equation (3.1), one can tell that the coefficient of total asset value (TA, NT$ million) is significant.

$$\ln m_{ij} = \mu_j + \lambda_{ij}, \quad \sum_{i=1}^{4} \lambda_{ij} = 0 \quad \supset_j \dots\dots\dots\dots\dots\dots (3.2)$$

where m_{ij} represents the expected frequency of ith promotion scheme in the jth rank, μ is the mean value, and λ measures the degree of inconsistency.

Table 11.5 shows the result of λ's, where investment tax credit takes the first position, then exemption from tariffs and low-rate loans, and accelerated depreciation takes fourth place. The result confirms the information derived from Table 11.3.

Table 11.5 Differential Test of Promotion Schemes

Promotion Schemes \ Rank	1	2	3	4
Exemption from Tariffs	0.4846*	−0.3050	−0.0388	0.1175
Accelerated Depreciation	−1.0317**	−0.0172	0.1554	0.5903**
Investment Tax Credit	0.4087*	0.3394*	−0.0037	−0.9358*
Low-rate Loans	0.1384	−0.0172	−0.1129	0.2880
χ^2 (d.f. = 3)	18.35**	6.25	1.18	20.44**

Note: ** and * represent relative probability that is smaller than 0.01 and 0.05 separately.

"Behavioural" Reaction of the Electrical Component Firms under the Combination of Promotion Schemes

This section will discuss the actual actions of the firm in the first year of SIUP. Three aspects will be analysed:

(a) Is the firm's investment in automation influenced by promotion schemes? If so, what is the degree of proportion being taken into account by the enterprise?

(b) The purchase of domestic automation equipment enjoys more encouragement than the purchase of foreign equipment. Yet, is the former significantly more common than the latter? And what are the reasons that the firms purchase automation equipment from abroad?

(c) If some of the promotion schemes are cancelled, what percentage will investment drop by?

Before exploring the above questions, the automation investment in the electrical component industry in 1991 is described. In the retrieved surveyed samples, there were 77 who had invested in automation and the percentage is 62.1 (77 out of 124). Table 11.6 indicates the results. It shows that automation investment is biased to the equipment relative to the technology.

Whether or Not and the Degree of Consideration for the Promotion Schemes

Of those who had invested in automation equipment or technology, their consideration factors are divided into practical needs, the four promotion schemes, and other factors. Ten points are assigned for evaluation.

The results are shown in Table 11.7, which indicates that investment in automation equipment or technology in 1991 is primarily based upon practical needs, with an average point level of 7.247. On the other hand, the four promotion schemes have an influence of 1.857 points. To test whether the consideration exists, namely, to see if the result is bigger than zero, we apply the Z-test to it, and come out with a Z-value of 8.76, whose corresponding probability is smaller than 0.05. This shows that the set of

Table 11.6 Distribution of Automation Equipment or Technology

Item	Automation	Production Equipment	Technology
	Whole Factory or Whole Assembly Line	Non-whole Factory or Non-whole Assembly Line	
Number	22	41	18
%	28.57	53.25	23.38

Note: There were four firms who invested both in the equipment and the technology.

Table 11.7 Point Evaluation of Factors in Automation Decision

Factors of Consideration	Average Points	Standard Error
Practical Needs	7.247	2.34
Promotion Schemes	1.857	1.86
Other Factors	0.896	1.65
Total	10.000	—

promotion schemes is truly another factor that the firms take into account. In short, during 1991, the purchase of automation equipment or technology by the firms was obviously under the influence of the government promotion schemes.

A Comparison of the Firm's Purchase of Domestic or Foreign Automation Equipment

Automation equipment is either purchased from domestic sources or from abroad, and in the case of a domestic purchase there is better promotion for the firm according to SIUP.[10] This sub-section explores the difference of investment in domestic and foreign equipment, and finds out the reasons why firms purchase from abroad.

From Table 11.8, we know that in 1991, domestic equipment was favoured by firms; however, the average purchase amount of domestic equipment per firm is less than that of foreign equipment, though the difference is insignificant (t-value = 0.233, $p > 0.05$). That is, under advantageous promotion, firms have invested more in domestic equipment than in foreign items; but the average amounts are only slightly different.

Table 11.8   Differences between Purchase of Domestic and Foreign Equipment

Source of Automation Equipment	Total Amount (NT$ million)	Average Amount (NT$ million)	t-value
Domestic (N = 50)	941.150 (80.50)*	18.823	0.233
Foreign (N = 35)	834.505 (97.755)*	23.843	

Note: * The invested amount in whole factory or whole assembly line.

The reasons why firms favour foreign equipment in spite of the benefits for domestic procurement are examined by frequency analysis and the log-linear model similar to Equation (3.2). The results are shown in Table 11.9.

---

[10] Domestically produced automation equipment has a 15% investment tax credit and foreign equipment has a 10% investment tax credit, but the whole assembly line automation may apply for to up to a 20% investment tax credit.

Table 11.9 shows that the primary reasons for purchasing foreign equipment are "no such equipment is available domestically" and "foreign equipment has a better quality." These two reasons and the exemption from tariffs may offset the advantages for a firm to purchase domestic equipment.

Influence of Promotion Combinations upon Invested Amount

This section will study how different combinations of promotion schemes may affect the firm's invested amount (in percentage terms). Out of the 16 types in Table 11.2, the first type is omitted, because that was the status in 1991, which is the base type for comparison. Therefore, there are only 15 types left, which correspond to the types from the second to the sixteenth combinations in Table 11.2. The multiple response probability model is applied again to the information and the results are in Table 11.10.[11]

From Table 11.10, it is obvious that the more promotions are cancelled, the less probability of zero reduction of the invested amount by enterprises. The line drops from 0.579 to 0.108. In other words, if all four promotion schemes are cancelled, the possibility of the invested amount being influenced could increase to 0.892, which accounts for the inevitable influence of promotion combinations.

---

[11] The model estimation corresponding to Table 11.10 is the following:

$$y = -2.1059^{**}D_1 - 1.6786^{**}D_2 - 1.0682^{**}D_3 - 0.6591^{*}D_4 - 0.3060D_5$$
$$\quad (0.2826) \qquad (0.2763) \qquad (0.2741) \qquad (0.2719) \qquad (0.2707)$$
$$\quad + 0.1646D_6 + 0.5501^{*}D_7 + 1.0631^{**}D_8 + 1.7063^{**}D_9 + 2.9280^{**}D_{10}$$
$$\quad (0.2707) \qquad (0.2727) \qquad (0.2792) \qquad (0.2966) \qquad (0.3791)$$
$$\quad + 2.4240^{**}X_1 + 1.2925^{**}X_2 + 2.0697^{**}X_3 + 1.8631^{**}X_4 + 1.4571^{**}X_5$$
$$\quad (0.4075) \qquad (0.3825) \qquad (0.3975) \qquad (0.3948) \qquad (0.3872)$$
$$\quad + 0.8167^{*}X_6 + 1.2659^{**}X_7 + 0.8065^{*}X_8 + 1.2793^{**}X_9 + 0.6280X_{10}$$
$$\quad (0.3808) \qquad (0.3847) \qquad (0.3833) \qquad (0.3849) \qquad (0.3798)$$
$$\quad + 0.2940X_{11} + 0.7873^{*}X_{12} + 0.4466X_{13} + 0.3455X_{14} + 0.0210^{*}PROF$$
$$\quad (0.3739) \qquad (0.3782) \qquad (0.3791) \qquad (0.3788) \qquad (0.0098)$$
$$\quad + 0.0005TA$$
$$\quad (0.0004)$$

where $\chi^2 = 86.366$, d.f. = 16, $p < 0.01$; standard errors are in parentheses; ** and * represent the corresponding p-values which are smaller than 0.01 and 0.05 respectively; definitions of y, D, X and TA are similar to Equation (3.1), but y represents the magnitude of investment reduction here, and PROF represents (pre-tax) profit ratio.

Table 11.9 Reasons for the Firm Purchasing Foreign Equipment

Reason	Number (%)	Estimated value by log-linear model
(1) No such equipment is available domestically	35 (87.5)	2.226**
(2) Foreign equipment has a better quality	22 (55.0)	1.762**
(3) Costs are lower	1 (2.5)	−1.329
(4) Better service	1 (2.5)	−1.329
(5) Others	1 (2.5)	−1.320

Note: 1. This is a multiple-choice question.
2. ** means the corresponding probability value is smaller than 0.01.

If the accelerated depreciation scheme is cancelled (the third type in Table 11.10), the probability of zero reduction of the invested amount is 0.579; if the investment tax credit is cancelled (the second type), the probability is 0.307; if low-rate loan programme is cancelled (the first type), the probability is 0.491; if exemption from tariffs is cancelled (the fourth type), the probability is 0.439, etc. From this information, the rank of influence of the four promotion schemes is investment tax credit, exemption from tariffs, accelerated depreciation, and low-rate loans.

Further, if two promotions are cancelled, the possibility of zero reduction in investment will decrease. However, if all the promotions are cancelled, the firms would still invest because of practical needs.

From Table 11.10 we may measure an approximate amount (an expected value) of investment reduction according to each type of promotion combination. To show what the expected value is, we assume that an enterprise has invested NT$1 million, and that the investment has decreased to a certain extent under the circumstance of the cancellation of some promotions. Table 11.11 shows the outcome.

Table 11.11 reveals that if the investment tax credit is cancelled, each NT$1 million investment would decrease by NT$0.2816 million; if the exemption from tariffs is cancelled, the decreased amount would be NT$0.2006 million; if the low-rate loan programme is cancelled, the decreased amount would be NT$0.1764 million; if the accelerated depreciation is cancelled, the decreased amount would be NT$0.1371 million.

Table 11.10 Influences of the Promotion Combinations on the Reduction of Automation Investment

(−)% Type	0	1–10	11–20	21–30	31–40	41–50	51–60	61–70	71–80	81–90	91–100
1	0.491	0.106	0.135	0.072	0.050	0.050	0.029	0.026	0.019	0.016	0.007
2	0.307	0.097	0.151	0.097	0.075	0.083	0.052	0.050	0.039	0.033	0.014
3	0.579	0.099	0.117	0.059	0.039	0.037	0.021	0.019	0.014	0.011	0.005
4	0.439	0.106	0.143	0.080	0.057	0.058	0.034	0.031	0.023	0.019	0.008
5	0.186	0.073	0.132	0.101	0.087	0.108	0.076	0.080	0.067	0.061	0.028
6	0.304	0.097	0.151	0.098	0.075	0.083	0.053	0.051	0.040	0.033	0.015
7	0.214	0.081	0.140	0.102	0.086	0.103	0.070	0.071	0.059	0.052	0.023
8	0.216	0.081	0.141	0.102	0.086	0.102	0.069	0.071	0.058	0.051	0.023
9	0.302	0.097	0.151	0.098	0.076	0.084	0.053	0.051	0.040	0.034	0.015
10	0.343	0.102	0.151	0.093	0.070	0.075	0.046	0.044	0.034	0.028	0.012
11	0.147	0.062	0.118	0.095	0.087	0.115	0.085	0.094	0.083	0.077	0.036
12	0.160	0.066	0.124	0.098	0.088	0.113	0.082	0.087	0.077	0.071	0.033
13	0.211	0.080	0.139	0.102	0.086	0.103	0.071	0.072	0.060	0.053	0.023
14	0.140	0.060	0.115	0.094	0.087	0.116	0.087	0.096	0.086	0.081	0.038
15	0.108	0.049	0.098	0.085	0.083	0.117	0.093	0.109	0.103	0.103	0.051

Notes: 1. Same as Note 1 of Table 11.3.
2. See Note 11 for the corresponding models.

Table 11.11 Estimation of Decreased Investment per Million

Type	Expected Decreased Amount
1	0.1764 (3)
2	0.2816 (1)
3	0.1371 (4)
4	0.2006 (2)
5	0.3909
6	0.2850
7	0.3613
8	0.3587
9	0.2868
10	0.2566
11	0.4296
12	0.4211
13	0.3640
14	0.4491
15	0.4999

Note: The estimation in the table is the maximum expected value.

One thing worth noticing is that under the eighth or fifteenth type, the possibility of reducing 50% of investment is relatively high, whereas reducing by 90% is a small possibility (see Table 11.10). The result means that automation investment is based on promotion, on practical needs and on the other factors.

To analyse the content of the practical needs, we consider two variables, the firm's scale (total asset value) and (pre-tax) profit ratio, as possible elements of "other factors" that the firm would consider in their investment decision. The analysis shows that the higher the two variables, the smaller the probability of firms reducing investment, but the firm's scale is insignificant.[12] This implies that profit is an important "other factor".[13]

---

[12] The estimation result of Note 11 shows that the (pre-tax) profit ratio (PROF) has a significant coefficient, while the total asset value (TA) has an insignificant coefficient.

[13] Other factors include: (a) Small amounts and multiple variety orders; automation cannot achieve an economy of scale; (b) Enterprise management has some defects; (c) Technical information on specific machines is not sufficient; (d) Bank loans have some difficulty and the application procedure is too slow.

Improvement of Production Performance and Market Adjustment Ability under the Promotion Schemes

Automation promotion is used to encourage investment in automation by enterprises which may then improve production performance and reinforce their ability to adjust to changes in the market, and finally to expand profit. This section will explore firms' improvements in production performance and their ability to adjust to the market, since the implementation of automation in 1991.

Improvement of Production Performance

To understand the influence of automation equipment or technology upon production performance, we asked firms' relevant personnel to comment, and the data are analysed by means of frequency analysis and means analysis. Table 11.12 shows the results.

From Table 11.12, we know that most of the enterprises are influenced by the instalment of automation equipment. Among these enterprises, the following aspects have been influenced by more than 50%: 67.7% of output increase; 53.8% of the reduction of manufacturing costs; 53.8% of the reduction of the defect rate; and 52.2% of the saving of direct labour.[14] Consequently, we know that in production performance, output increase is the most influenced and the saving of direct labour the least influenced.

However, according to the degree of influence over nine points (almost totally being affected), a different rank appears; that is, 35.4% of output increase, 23.0% of the saving of direct labour, 16.9% of the reduction of manufacturing costs, and 15.4% of the reduction of defect rates. And from the evaluation of average points of influence, the output increase is the highest with 6.8%, while the reduction of manufacturing costs is the lowest with 5.5%. By means of the Scheffe multiple comparison technique, we can further distinguish the differences. Table 11.13 shows the results.

Table 11.13 indicates that on average, the various production performance indicators are influenced with an insignificant difference; in other words, the influence upon those indicators is regarded as the same.

To understand the influence of automation equipment upon marginal

---

[14] These figures are derived by summing up the proportion of responding firms with more than five points of influence in each category.

Table 11.12 Influences of Automation Investment upon Production Performance

Point \ Indicators	Output Increase (%)	Reduction of Manufacturing Costs (%)	Reduction of Defect Rate (%)	Direct Labour Saved (%)
No Influence (0)	2 (3.1)	4 (6.2)	6 (9.2)	1 (1.5)
1	1 (1.5)	2 (3.1)	2 (3.1)	3 (4.6)
2	6 (9.2)	9 (13.8)	4 (6.2)	9 (13.8)
3	2 (3.1)	4 (6.2)	3 (4.6)	7 (10.8)
4	1 (1.5)	1 (1.5)	3 (4.6)	3 (4.6)
5	9 (13.8)	10 (15.4)	12 (18.5)	8 (12.3)
6	5 (7.7)	9 (13.8)	6 (9.2)	5 (7.7)
7	7 (10.8)	7 (10.8)	9 (13.8)	5 (7.7)
8	9 (13.8)	8 (12.3)	10 (15.4)	9 (13.8)
9	6 (9.2)	3 (4.6)	5 (7.7)	6 (9.2)
Complete Influence (10)	17 (26.2)	8 (12.3)	5 (7.7)	9 (13.8)
Mean	6.82	5.54	5.62	5.77
Standard Error	2.93	2.98	2.92	2.99

Table 11.13 Differential Comparison of Influence upon Production Performance

Performance Indicators	Output Increase	Manufacturing Costs Reduction	Defect Rate Reduction	Direct Labour Saved
Output Increase				
Manufacturing Costs Reduction	1.28			
Defect Rate Reduction	1.20	−0.08		
Direct Labour Saved	1.05	−0.23	−0.15	

production, we plan to establish a linear regression model for linking the amount of automation investment and production performance. But two problems must be addressed first:

(a) The improvement of production performance may not be wholly attributable to the instalment of automation equipment or technology.

(b) Some of the enterprises admit that they have enjoyed improvement from the use of automation equipment, but they fail to offer any information about the improvement.

For the first problem, we will centre on the degree of influence, and dilute the improvement information provided. Then the Tobit model can be used for the diluted data to solve the second problem. Table 11.14 shows the analysed results.

Table 11.14 reveals that automation equipment or technology has great influence upon output increase. On average, every NT$ million of investment increases output by 17.7%. The improvement among the enterprises has a difference of 3.66 times. The second significant influence-aspect is direct labour saved; every NT$ million of investment saved 13.1% of one worker. The difference among firms could be up to 8.28 persons. There are no obvious influences upon the reduction of manufacturing costs and the defect rates. However, the reduction of the defect rates among firms could have a significant difference of up to 11.65%. Also, owing to deficient data on manufacturing costs saved by firms, estimation is relatively imprecise compared to other indicators of production performance.

Table 11.14 Relationship between Automation Equipment and Production Performance

Item Performance Indicators Amount	Coefficient Estimation of Automation Investment	Coefficient Estimation of Disturbance Term (D)	Coefficient Estimation of Adjustment Term (λ)	Adj-R^2 (N)
Output Increase (100%)	0.177** (8.17)	3.66** (3.66)	–0.92 (–1.67)	0.7567 (29)
Manufacturing Costs Reduction (100%)	0.019 (2.54)	—	0.06 (0.27)	0.6650 (7)
Defect Rate Reduction (%)	0.111 (1.93)	11.65** (10.08)	0.71 (0.43)	0.8667 (24)
Direct Labour Saved (person)	0.131** (4.52)	8.28** (6.07)	3.31** (2.78)	0.8790 (20)

Notes: 1. "Disturbance Term" refers to the difference among firms, such as the difference in management and production methods.
2. ** means the probability of the corresponding t-value (in parentheses) is smaller than 0.01.
3. N indicates the number of firms who offer information.

Improvement of Ability to Adjust to Market Change

Another purpose of enterprises to adopt automation equipment or techno-logy is to adjust to the fluctuations of the market. This section will explore the influence of automation equipment or technology upon the ability of firms to adjust to the market.

By virtue of frequency analysis ($n = 77$), 76.6% of enterprises think that automation equipment or technology has influenced their ability to adjust, and 23.4% of enterprises regard automation as having no influence.

To know whether those who think automation is influential are sig-nificantly more than those who think automation is not influential, the Z-test (single tail) is used; as a consequence, the Z-value is 5.54, and its corresponding probability value is smaller than 0.01. The result reveals that most of the enterprises think that their adjustment ability is influenced by automation equipment or technology.

So far, we have looked from the standpoint of a "yes or no" reaction. Now we would like to explore the possibility of influence to improve ability by means of the binary probit model. The estimation coefficient for posi-tive improvement of adjustment ability is 0.232 ($S = 0.071$, $p < 0.01$) (log-likelihood value $= -30.75$, $p < 0.01$), which shows that the larger the automation investment, the higher (significantly) the possibility of adjust-ment ability improvement.

In sum, investment in automation equipment or technology by electri-cal component enterprises in 1991 has greatly influenced their production performance and market adjustment ability. In the production performance aspect, various influence indicators are listed according to their magnitude (from high to low) as follows: output increase; direct labour saved; the reduction of manufacturing cost; and the reduction of the defect rates. However, the latter two indicators are not significantly influenced. In the adjustment ability aspect, most of the enterprises feel that the influences exist. Additionally, the more investment in automation, the better the ability to adjust to the market.

Problems and Difficulties of the Electrical Component Firms Undertaking Automation Investment

To learn the problems and difficulties of firms in the process of automat-ion may offer helpful information to the Government which, in turn, can revise policy. In general, a firm would consider the sufficiency of capital, information, technology and technicians, in addition to promotions, in making their automation investment decision. Table 11.15 summarizes the problems and degrees of difficulty faced by the firm.

Table 11.15 indicates that firms feel that deficiencies in automation technology and technicians are two primary difficulties, while deficiencies in information and capital are relatively minor difficulties.

Table 11.15 Problems and Difficulties Encountered by Firms

N = 117

Problems	Percentage (%)	Degrees of Difficulty in Points (Standard Error)
Capital Deficiency	87 (74.36)	2.77 (1.41)
Information Deficiency	70 (59.83)	2.71 (1.16)
Technicians Deficiency	90 (76.92)	3.39 (1.21)
Technology Deficiency	90 (76.92)	3.47 (1.21)
Others	30 (25.64)	3.53 (1.33)

Notes: 1. This is a multiple-choice question.
2. In measuring the degree of difficulty, "1" means least difficult, "5" means extremely difficult.
3. Please see Note 13 (p. 196) for the contents of others.

By means of the Scheffe multiple comparison, one can further identify the degrees of difficulty in order. Table 11.16 shows the results: the biggest problems confronting firms are deficiencies in technology and technicians. In other words, most enterprises face severe deficiencies in technicians and technology; deficiencies in capital and information are relatively less serious.

IV. CONCLUSION AND POLICY SUGGESTIONS

Conclusion of This Study

Using the 124 surveyed firms' data, the primary purposes of this essay are to achieve the following objectives. Firstly, to explore the induced effects of various government automation promotion schemes such as investment tax credit, accelerated depreciation, exemption from tariffs and low-rate loans for the purchase of automation equipment and technology in Taiwan's electrical component industry in 1991. Secondly, to examine how much the relevant firms improved in production performance and

Table 11.16 Differential Comparison of Degree of Difficulties

Problems	Capital Deficiency	Information Deficiency	Technicians Deficiency	Technology Deficiency
Capital Deficiency				
Information Deficiency	−0.06			
Technicians Deficiency	0.61**	0.68**		
Technology Deficiency	0.70**	0.70**	0.08	

Note: This Table is a symmetrical matrix, ** means corresponding probability is smaller than 0.01.

ability to adjust to market change after they implemented automation processes. Thirdly, to collect the opinions of the relevant firms concerning their difficulties in implementing automation and to provide some policy suggestions for enhancing the effectiveness of government promotion schemes.

The major conclusions include:

(a) Concerning the influencing magnitude of the four government promotion schemes on the intention of automation, investment tax credit is the most powerful, exemption from tariffs is next, the low-rate loan programme is third, and accelerated depreciation is last. Moreover, the larger the firm is (in terms of asset value), the larger the magnitude of "willingness" for automation is.

(b) The existence of government promotion schemes is significant, but is less important than practical needs for the firms in the electrical component industry to implement automation. Additionally, since the encouragement to purchase domestic equipment is larger than that for foreign equipment, most firms buy domestically, yet the average expenditure between the two sources is not significantly different. The major reasons why electrical component firms purchase foreign equipment are that "no such equipment is available domestically" and that "foreign equipment has a better quality." Furthermore, the larger the firm and the (pre-tax) profit ratio are, the larger the investment in automation is, though the firm size does not have a significant impact.

(c) In 1991, the investment in automation by electrical component firms had a positive influence on their production performance and ability to adjust to market change. Specifically, production increased 17.7%, where absolute difference among firms ranged up to 3.66 times; the number of workers saved was 0.131 persons per NT$ million investment, and the largest difference in the number of workers saved among firms was 8.28 persons. Though automation had no significant effect on lowering manufacturing costs and product defect rates in 1991, declining defect rates among firms were different for up to 11.65%. It also should be mentioned that the manufacturing cost data provided by the firms were not sufficient, hence the estimation accuracy of that variable is relatively lower than that of other variables.

(d) As for the difficulties encountered by the electrical component firms in the process of automation, insufficient technology and technicians were relatively important, while insufficient funding capital and information were relatively unimportant. Thus, the Government may improve effectiveness of promotion in automation by helping the firms to obtain technology and technicians. Of course, the Government should select those means that are consistent with social cost-benefit principles to achieve the above-mentioned goals.

Limitations of the Study

The above conclusions are influenced by some limitations in the study, which include the scope of the study, sampling, the measurement methods and analysis techniques.

Owing to the limitations of time, cost and precision, the study chose the electrical component industry as the study object. Therefore, the result of this study cannot be applied to other manufacturing industries without reservation. Moreover, investment in automaton equipment or technology in 1991 is the function of the four promotion schemes; hence there is no way to evaluate exactly how much a firm would invest if a certain promotion is cancelled. This study tries, with an experimental idea, to estimate the probability of reducing a certain percentage of investment when an individual promotion is cancelled. This is a prediction rather than a reality. Furthermore, because of the deficiency in information, we can not evaluate the four promotions with cost-benefit analysis, so precise suggestions for policy adjustment cannot be offered.

In the sampling, most of the retrieved samples are from bigger enterprises, and the conclusion may not applied without reservation to small and medium firms in the electrical component industry.

In the design of the survey and measuring method, because a higher degree of measurement was desired (interval and ratio scales), some firms felt upset, and therefore refused to answer. This is especially evident in the production performance indicators, and some firms thought the questions were too sensitive to answer, hence they refused to offer information, which may have led to measurement errors in the analysis.

As to the analysis techniques, due to the deficiency in information, some relatively more precise statistical techniques could not be used. For example, the data for production performance could not be processed by a heterogeneous multivariate multiple regression model (MMRM), so a Tobit model was employed instead. The results may thus be less precise.

Directions of Future Study

This essay only studies the effects of automation promotion schemes, and their influences upon a firm's investment intentions, action, production performance and market adjustment ability in 1991. A future study may broaden the scope of each aspect. In addition, comparing the profits created by means of improved production performance and adjustment ability of firms with increased government revenue net of the decreased revenue due to government promotion schemes is a subject worth exploring.

Moreover, the Tobit model applied to the analysis of production performance is not precise enough. If the related information is sufficient, the MMRM should be employed so that a more precise result would be acquired. Finally, different kinds of enterprises, due to reasons such as extended of machine lifetime, stability of profit, tax restrictions upon definition of costs, ways of managements, and production structure, may be suited to different kinds of promotion. A more precise study would be meaningful for policy implications.

REFERENCES

Asian Productivity Organization (1987). *Productivity Analysis and Projections in Selected Key Areas in Asian Countries*. Tokyo: APO.

Automation Execution Group of the Ministry of Economic Affairs (1989). *Fourth Automation Survey Report of the R.O.C*. Taipei: MEA.

Bates, Constance (1985). "Does Automation Spell the End of Foreign Direct Investment in Low-wage Labour Markets?" Paper presented at the International Conference on Multinational Business, Taipei, R.O.C.

Bureau of Labour Statistics, U.S. Department of Labour (1976). *BLS Handbook of Methods*. Washington, D.C.: U.S. Government Printing Office.

Cochran, W. G. (1977). *Sampling Techniques*, 3rd edition. New York: John Wiley & Sons.

Denison, Edward F. (1974). *Accounting for the United States Economic Growth*. Washington, D.C.: Brookings Institution.

Dillon, W. R. and M. Goldstein (1984). *Multivariate Analysis — Methods and Applications*. New York: John Wiley & Sons.

Haberman, S. J. (1978). *Analysis of Qualitative Data*. New York: Academic Press.

Judge, G. G., *et al.* (1985). *The Theory and Practice of Econometrics*, 2nd edition. New York: John Wiley & Sons.

Kendrick, J. W. (1973). *Post-war Productivity Trends in the United States, 1948–1969*. New York: National Bureau of Economic Research.

Lan, Ke-Jeng, and Tsai Kuen-Hung (1992). "A Generalized Estimation and Application of the Multivariate Multiple Regression Model." *Monthly Journal of Taipei City Bank*, 23(1), pp. 28–38.

Ministry of Economic Affairs (1991). *Statute of Industrial Upgrading and Promotion*. Taipei: MEA.

Modern Business Report (1977). *How to Increase Productivity — A Practical Guide to Improve the Performance of Your Company's Human Resource*. New York: Alexander Hamilton Institute.

OECD (1986). *Productivity in Industry*. Paris: Organization for Economic Co-operation and Development.

Productivity Survey of Singapore (1985). *Productivity Performance of the Manufacturing Sector*. Singapore: NPB Publication.

Richard, A. J. and W. W. Dean (1984). *Applied Multivariate Statistical Analysis*, 2nd edition. Englewood Cliffs: Prentice Hall.

SAS Institute Inc. (1988). *SAS/IML Guide*, Version 6.03.

——— (1988). *SAS/STAT User's Guide*, Release 6.03 Edition.

Silver, M. S. (1986). *Productivity Indices — Methods and Application*. Broodfield, Vermont: Gower Publishing Company.

Smith, A. D., D. M. W. N. Hitchens and S. W. Davies (1982). *International Industrial Productivity — A Comparison of Britain, America and Germany.* Bath, U.K.: Pitman Press.

Index